CITY OF FLOWS

CITY OF FLOWS

MODERNITY, NATURE, AND THE CITY

MARIA KAIKA

Routledge
New York • London

Published in 2005 by
Routledge
Taylor & Francis Group
270 Madison Avenue
New York, NY 10016
www.routledge-ny.com

Published in Great Britain by
Routledge
2 Park Square
Milton Park, Abingdon,
Oxon OX14 4RN U.K.
www.routledge.co.uk

Routledge is an imprint of the Taylor and Francis Group.
Printed in the United Stated of America on acid-free paper.

10   9   8   7   6   5   4   3   2   1

Library of Congress Cataloging-in-Publishing data
    Kaika Maria.
        City of flows: modernity, nature, and the city/Maria Kaika.
            p.cm.
        Includes bibliographical references and index.
        ISBN 0-415-94715-4 (hb : alk. paper) – ISBN 0-415-94716-2 (pb : alk. paper)
        1. Urbanization. 2. Nature and civilization. 3. Municipal water supply. I. Title.

HT361.K35 2004
307.76–dc22

                                                                                          2004011022

Contents

Acknowledgments

The School of Geography and the Environment at Oxford University as well as St. Edmund Hall, St. Peter's College, and Linacre College, Oxford provided a stimulating niche within which the ideas in this book developed. Among the many scholars whom I wish to thank, Erik Swyngedouw must be the first. His contribution to this endeavor is invaluable. He inspired and encouraged me, while being acutely critical through long discussions and animated arguments. He also helped me keep the research plan realistic each time the project threatened to veer off the rails. I am also most thankful to Gordon Clark for guiding, supporting and encouraging me, and for providing the space for this project to develop. I am grateful to Esteban Castro, whose meticulous research on London gave me a great insight. Much of the analysis in Part II draws upon his publications. Many thanks also to Grigoris Kafkalas for his encouragement and for helping me sharpen the intellectual task, but most of all for the lasting friendship which developed alongside this project. I am also grateful to my colleagues at the School of Geography and the Environment and St. Edmund Hall, Oxford. Particular thanks are owed to Robert Whittaker, without whose moral support I would not have been able to produce the final manuscript. Mike Mingos, Principal of St. Edmund Hall, provided valuable guidance on how to juggle teaching duties and research activities. Kay Anderson, on her visiting year at Oxford was there for me at moments of doubt, stimulating my interest in the subject, and showing me how to reconcile being a woman with being an academic. I also owe a big thank you to Tim Marshall, Gavin Williams, Renee Hirshon, Ben Page, Hartmut Mayer, and John Baron for their interest in the topic and for their support, and to Panos Getimis, Harry Coccossis, Giorgos Kallis and Kostas Bithas for their encouragement. My graduate students, Federico Caprotti and Cindy Warwick provided buzz and stimulus, and David Dodman took good care of my undergraduate students while I was on leave. George Taylor's editorial help with the first draft was invaluable. David McBride of Routledge provided encouragement and fine editorship.

The library and support staff of the School of Geography and the Environment were, as ever, extremely helpful. Special thanks to Linda Atkinson, Sue Bird, Ann Lewsey, and Juliet Blackburn for keeping me up-to-date with publications. The assistance of Ruth Saxton, Jan Burke, Ailsa Allen, Jennie McKenzie, Jerry Lee, and Eric Anderson was also priceless. Special thanks to Martin Barfoot for helping me with the photographic work. Sylvia Boyce and Anne Heath of the Transport Studies Unit also deserve a special mention. They hosted me, lent me their ears, and fed me with chocolate and love when the going got tough.

I owe many thanks to a great number of individuals and institutions "in the field" for allowing me access to valuable material: the Water Company of Athens (E.YΔ.A.Π) and in particular Mr Giannis Stevis; the Greek Ministry of Development (GMD); the Division of Water Resources Management within the GMD; the European Commission, DG Environment in particular; the European Environmental Bureau (EEB), Stefan Scheuer in particular; Thames Water; Anglian Water; the Environment Agency, UK. I would also like to acknowledge the support of the staff at the National Library of Greece; the Greek National Archives; the Lambrakis Foundation; the Parliamentary Archives in Athens; the library of the National Technical University of Athens; the library of DG Environment, Brussels; and UNESCO'S International Hydrological Programme, Paris.

I wish to thank my family and friends who sustained me during all the stages of this project. Thanks to my parents Athanassios and Androniki Kaika (Αθανάσιος and Ανδρονίκη Καΐκα) and my brother Dimitrios Kaikas (Δημήτριος Καΐκας) for their love and support. Thanks to George Shoterioo (Γιώργος Σωτηρίου) for his wit and sustaining love, and for allowing me to use his excellent photographs in this volume. Thanks to Georgia Basdani (Γεωργία Μπασδάνη) for her love and encouragement. Lionel Mason and Alison Etheridge hosted me during periods of "homelessness" and Charis Christodoulou's (Χαρις Χριστοδούλου) warmth and engagement added spark to the final few months of this endeavor.

It would be a great omission if I did not acknowledge here the people who laid the foundations for my intellectual development in the beautiful and intellectually stimulating environment of the School of Architecture at the National Technical University of Athens. My studies there provided me with an invaluable background of knowledge and perception, which opened my eyes to different ways of seeing the world. I owe a lot to Nicholas Th. Cholevas (*Νικόλαος Θ. Χολέβας*) for being a wonderful and inspirational teacher and for being the first to encourage me to do research. Eliza Panagiotatou (*Ελίζα Παναγιωτάτου*) put me on the research route and prompted me to trust my intellect. Tassos Mpiris (*Τάσος Μπίρης*) taught me how to imagine space. Sofia Augerinou (*Σοφία Αυγερινού*) and Sofia Antonopoulou (*Σοφία Αντωνοπούλου*) were inspiring teachers.

The Oxford University Division of Life and Environmental Sciences with the approval of St. Edmund Hall financed the release from my teaching duties for one term. Without this, the completion of the final manuscript would have been impossible. The initial research for this project was funded through two major scholarships: one from the National Technical University of Athens, together with the Evgenideion Foundation; and one from the Greek Scholarships' Foundation (*Ίδρυμα Κρατικών Υπο τροφιών*, IKY). Funding for the consolidation of the project was obtained from the European Commission's Fifth Framework programme; the Bossanyi fund for Environmental Studies at St. Peter's College, Oxford; and the Leventis Foundation in Paris.

The empirical material in this book is derived from independent research, conducted in Athens and London between 1994 and 2003. The research on Athens was funded by the Greek State's Scholarships Foundation (IKY) and the research on London was funded by the European Commission's Framework V Research Programme, under the METRON research project, coordinated by Prof. Harry Coccossis. I am grateful to Dr. Esteban Castro for his excellent research conduct and invaluable input on the London case study, under the METRON research project. Much of the analysis in Chapters 6 and 7 draws upon his research findings. The analysis of Athens early water supply history (19th–early 20th century, Chapters 5 and 6) is based on archival research conducted by the author at the National Library of Greece and at the Library of the Greek Parliament, but also draws on earlier, purely historical, secondary sources, and in particular: G. Paraskevopoulos, *The Mayors of Athens 1835–1907* (Athens, 1907); D. Gerontas, and D. Skouzes, *The Chronicle of Watering Athens* (Athens, 1963); S. G. Koumparelis, *The History of the Water/Sewerage Works of the Capital* (Athens, The Sewerage Company of Athens and The Water Company of Athens, 1989); A. Kordellas, *Athens Examined from an Hydraulic Perspective* (Athens, 1979). Many thanks to Blackwell Publishing for granting copyright for material used in Chapters 2, 3, 4, and 7.

Maria Kaika
Oxford

In memory of my grandfather, Γεώργιος Ψωμάς.

Part I

CHAPTER 1
Preface: Visions of Modernization

> Ultimately, the dam had a deep consciousness of its place in the world! It was well aware of the fact that it was a fatal entity, a dividing presence. That's why it showed itself off the way it did that night in front of the engineer's eyes.
>
> *S. Plaskovitis, The Dam (1961)*[1]

When I was a child, the factory where my father worked organized an excursion for the employees and their families. I was promised we would go on a trip out of the city, into nature and the countryside. On arrival—and much to my surprise—I found that, instead of the beauties of nature, it was in fact a big dam and reservoir construction that we were taken to see. We spent the whole day by the dam, marvelling at the power of technology and the ability of humankind to control the flow of nature's water. These trips to the dams were very popular in the 1970s. They were pilgrimages to the revered shrines of technology that displayed humankind's power to transform nature through progress and technology. By visiting the modern shrines *en masse*, people became witnesses to the successful outcome of modernity's Promethean project to tame nature. The remarkable domination of nature and of the landscape to which these technological shrines testified remained inscribed in my memory. In their strange, assertive kind of beauty, they did not seem to belong to either nature or the city. To me, there seemed to be no connection between these proud deities and my everyday life, my home, my city; no connection between the tamed still waters resting at the foot of the dam and water swirling wild at my command through the hose in our back yard. The dam was an elaborate human construction, out there in the wilderness, commanding water to stop flowing, while the flow of water in my home was a natural and simple thing: I simply had to turn a tap or press a switch to satisfy my needs. Similarly, the lights of my city—which gave me a sense of the familiar and homely as soon as I saw them flickering on our way back from the long dam trips—were part of the glamour of the city, and of the coziness of my home, and had nothing to do with nature, which remained dark, silent, and wild.

However, I started reflecting on the connection between the dam and my home when, due to a drought in the early 1990s, our home tap refused to provide its services as expected. We were told that this was the outcome of unprecedented low water levels in the city's main reservoir, which had dropped to the point of revealing the village that had been inundated by the dam. I was suddenly forced to realize that the flow of water into our kitchen and bathroom was not natural at all; that water reached our home after having traveled for miles, through an intricate set of technological networks that transformed it from a natural element into purified, commodified, drinking water. The specter of the drought made me reconsider what I had been taking for granted: namely, the naturalness of the delivery of goods into the domestic bliss of my home, and the clear-cut conceptual separation between my home, my city, and nature. The drought revealed (by disrupting it) the continuous flow of natural elements (water, electricity, gas, etc.) from the countryside into the city and finally into the modern home. What I used to perceive as a compartmentalized world, consisting of neatly and tightly sealed, autonomous "space envelopes" (the home, the city, and nature) was, in fact, a messy socio-spatial continuum.

This book is an attempt to unfold this continuum.

First, I attempt to decipher the historical geographical process through which modernity discursively constructed the modern city and the modern home as autonomous "space envelopes" independent from natural and social processes. Modernity here is understood as a programmatic vision for social change and progress, linked to industrialization and capitalist expansion, and in effect as an ideology for human emancipation. Although the origin and periodization of Modernity and modernization are a source of great dispute in academic literature,[2] for the purposes of this book modernization is understood as the ongoing process that originated with the Enlightenment, but which was realized in the economic, political, and everyday spheres only after industrialization and the expansion of the capitalist world market. The analysis in the book unravels the

"Promethean Project"[3]of modernity, i.e., the historical geographical process that started with industrialization and urbanization and aimed at taming and controlling nature through technology, human labor, and capital investment. The same process aspired to rendering modern cities autonomous and independent from nature's whims. This project transformed socio-natural landscapes across the world and disrupted the preexisting ontological categories of "nature" and "the city".

Second, the analysis juxtaposes *Modernity*, as a meticulous planning and programmatic vision, with *Modernization* as a transient process of "creative destruction" whereby any planned change is mutated inevitably at the moment of its realization, via its interaction with material, cultural, social, economic, and political processes in place. I use this dialectic between clear programmatic visions and complex historical geographical processes to analyze the materialization of modernity's Promethean project. I argue that, although the programming vision was to render cities independent from nature's processes, the materialization of this vision was predicated upon establishing intricate networks and flows of natural elements, social power relations and capital investment cycles, which, in fact, not only did not separate nature from the city, but instead wove them together more closely into a socio-spatial continuum. The modern city and the modern home appear only to function autonomously and independently from natural and social processes, because the flow of natural elements, social relations, and money that support their function remain fetishised (in the case of social relations) or visually severed (in the case of technology networks).

Finally, the book brings to the foreground the fetishised social relations of production and the hidden material networks and flows that urbanize nature. By doing so, it asserts the material, social and historical continuity between nature, the modern city, and the modern home. To this end, it embarks on a historical geographical analysis of the urbanization of water in Western metropolises, drawing mainly on material from London and Athens. Using water as a vehicle, the book follows its flow from nature to the modern city and into the modern home, and explores the margins, outside (dams, reservoirs, etc.) and underneath (networks, pipelines, etc.) the visible and familiar spaces of the modern city and the modern home. The fluid character of water, and its primary importance in the creation of modern cities, permits us to visualize and literally *trace* the dynamic process of the transformation of nature as it moves to the modern metropolis and into the modern home. Baring the flow of water between the natural, the urban, and the domestic sphere reveals that nature and the city are not separate entities or autonomous "space envelopes," but hybrids, neither purely human-made nor purely natural; outcomes of the same socio-spatial process of the urbanization of nature. Water itself is also recounted as a hybrid. As it flows from spaces of production to spaces of consumption, it undergoes changes in its physical, socio-political and cultural character. When it reaches our faucet in the form of potable water it is neither purely natural nor purely a human construction.

The periodization of the analysis in the book follows three main phases in modernity's Promethean project, which go hand in glove with industrial growth, capital expansion, and the production of modern cities:[4]

Modernity's Nascent Promethean Project (early 19th century): The industrial city experiences deteriorating social and environmental conditions, and becomes "the city of dreadful death". Urban rivers become a source of disease and death, the Thames becomes the "Great Stink" of London. Nature seems to be uncontrolled and undisciplined, an impediment to further urban development. Yet, this is also the moment when ambitious plans for controlling nature's water flows are laid and projects for the provision of urban water supply and sewerage networks are in the making.

The Heroic Moment of modernity's Promethean project (late 19th century to the first three-quarters of the 20th century): This period is typified by large-scale urban sanitation projects (water supply and sewerage) as well as the construction of impressive transport and communication networks. The new technology is admired and fetishised, promoting the myth of progress and modernization as an automatic means of producing a better society. Technology, capital investment, labor power, and institutional changes transform nature's material and ideological role in the process of urbanization. From awesome and undisciplined, a source of fear and anxiety, an impediment to urban growth, nature becomes tamed and controlled, the prerequisite for urban and industrial development.

Modernity's Promethean Project Discredited (late 20th century to 21st century): The increasing demand for resources in Western societies, coupled with a crisis in public funding after the 1970s, impedes further improvement of urban infrastructure. A great number of environmental disasters around the world discredit modernity's Promethean project and question the logic and practice of continuous development. From tamed and controlled (the prerequisite for development), nature is now cast as a potential source of crisis, a potential impediment to further development.

The book is organized in two parts. Part I (Chapters 2, 3, and 4) traces the flow of water from the natural to the urban and to the domestic sphere, in order to establish the material social and cultural continuity between these spaces.

Chapter 2 sets the theoretical agenda.[5] It first examines how the nature/society dualism emerged historically as part and parcel of modernity's Promethean project. The analysis imparts the nature/city divide as a spatial expression of the nature/society dualism, and explores how this dualism affected decisions, visions and practices for the production of modern cities. Drawing on examples from architecture and urbanism (Ledoux, Howard, Olmsted, Moses, F. L. Wright, Le Corbusier), art (art nouveau, futurism, surrealism) and literature (Dickens, Huxley), the chapter analyses modernity's dual scripting of both nature (as inherently good/uncivilized) and of the city (inherently evil/the hotbed of civilization). In order to get away from this dualism and its innate contradictions, the chapter offers a reconceptualization of nature and the city as "hybrids", neither purely human nor purely natural. The analysis asserts the dialectical relation between the production of cities and the production of nature, as part and parcel of the same process: the "urbanization of nature".

Chapter 3 follows the flow of water from the places of its production (dams, reservoirs, water towers, pumping stations, purification plants) into the urban domain, focusing in particular on the intricate set of urban technology networks that carry this flow.[6] Using water networks as an emblematic example, the chapter studies the process whereby an input of nature, technology, capital and human labour gives an output in the form of commodities (clean water in this case, and, by the same token, gas, electricity, etc.) or services (sewerage, metropolitan subways, etc.) which are central to the production and metabolism of urban space. The analysis depicts technology networks as the material expressions of the continuous and interdependent relationship between nature and the city, as the mediators through which the ongoing process of the production of space occurs and through which the flow and consumption of goods and services materializes. The shifts in the significance and symbolism of urban technology networks are chronicled: from urban landmarks of modernization, to banal and derelict monuments of an era and a social project that no longer is.

Chapter 4 continues the journey from the urban into the domestic sphere and examines the historical geographical process through which both nature and society became scripted as "the other" to the modern home.[7] It argues that the social construction of the Western (bourgeois) home as an autonomous, independent, private space is predicated upon a process of visual and discursive exclusion of undesired social (anomie, homelessness, social conflict, etc.) and natural (cold, dirt, pollution, etc.) elements. It notes that, while the familiarity of the bourgeois home is dependent upon the visual exclusion of social and natural processes, the very creation of the safety and familiarity of the modern private home is nevertheless predicated upon the domestication of natural elements (water, air, gas, etc.) through a socio-economic production process. The exposure of this contradiction allows for a reconceptualization of the domestic sphere not as an autonomous realm, but rather as a sphere carved out of the dialectics between visible and invisible, clean and dirty, just and injust, a space whose existence depends on the continuous flow of goods, people, and capital outside and underneath its premises.

Part II (Chapters 5, 6, and 7) is a detailed historical geographical analysis of the urbanization of water in Athens and London from the 19th century onwards. The efforts to render modern metropolises autonomous and independent from nature's whims by supplying them with abundant water was predicated upon establishing a complex system of networks that constantly support this flow of water and secure the metabolism of modern cities. The fact that Athens was "a city in ruins" in 1834, when it became the capital of the modern Greek state, makes it an exemplary case for the study of the production of a modern city from scratch through the urbanization of nature.

Chapter 5 depicts early 19th century efforts to sanitize Western cities and render them independent from nature's processes. Securing a constant flow of water, food, heating, etc. would allow for urbanization, industrialization, and capital investment to expand further. Creating the mechanisms, institutions, culture, and material networks that eventually would permit nature's water to run abundantly through the city rested at the epicenter of great cultural, political, and social debates. During this period, channeling water into the growing Western cities was far from an easy task. Lack of public funding, warfare, scientific debates and disputes over technological solutions, kept nature untamed and undisciplined. In the case of Athens, most efforts and funds were channeled toward restoring the city's ancient aqueduct, thus turning modernization into an "archaeological project". In London, more funding opportunities, stemming from capitalist expansion, promoted decidedly modern technological solutions (sewage and sanitation works, pumping stations, etc.). Still, even these were encased in neoclassical forms, as a means of making technology and progress more palatable to the public.

Chapter 6 examines the shift from an "archaeological" to an "engineering" era in the efforts to modernize Western cities by urbanizing nature. This period runs from the end of the 19th century through to the first three-quarters of the 20th century. It is the apotheosis of modernity's Promethean project which succeeds in conquering nature and casting it in the role of the prerequisite for progress and development. This period is typified by large-scale infrastructure projects, which tame nature, harness resources from long distances, and even produce new urban nature. Rivers are reengineered and drawn from miles away into the city to feed the increasing urban thirst for water and the growing needs of industrialization (the Hoover Dam on the Arizona–Nevada border, the Marathon Dam in Athens). At the same time, rivers in cities disappear underground (the Ilissos River in Athens, the Seine in Brussels, several tributaries of the Thames in London), giving way to grand avenues and middle-class quarters (the urban embourgeoisement); man-made parks and lakes (Central Park in New York, the Royal Garden in Athens) make their debut as new urban landmarks, whose production and maintenance is made possible only by making water flow abundantly through the city's underground veins. These projects heralded a new relationship with nature: from "fearful and threatening", nature became "the prerequisite for development".

Chapter 7 examines the most recent phase in modernity's Promethean project.[8] After the 1970s, a decline in funding for public projects led to the deterioration of urban infrastructure. This, combined with the ever increasing need of cities for resources and a number of major socio-environmental crises across the world, generated a systematic critique of modernity and cast modernity's tamed nature in the role of a potential source of crisis. This affected decisions concerning both nature and the city. The inevitability of natural phenomena (e.g., drought), translated into a self-explanatory inevitability of socially constructed phenomena (e.g., water scarcity), led to significant changes in the institutions, politics, and culture of urban water supply in both Athens and London after the 1980s. Despite the discourse on environmental protection, the answers provided to today's discourse of "nature as crisis" are strikingly similar to those that the 19th century provided, i.e., continuous development. However, the discourse of the vision attached to modernity's Promethean project has now changed significantly. From a continuation of the Enlightenment's ideals of progress and human emancipation, at least at the discursive level, this project is today, both in practice and discourse, more than ever a blunt means for expanding the capital base of Western economies. The promotion of water as a commodity and the privatization of the water sector, as well as the subsequent socio-environmental implications of this process, testify to this change.

By looking at the production of modern cities through the lens of the production of nature, by looking underneath and outside the modern city, and the modern home, by excavating the opaque flows and networks that weave together the natural, the urban, and the domestic, we can reconsider the perceived distinction between these spaces. Unfolding the constant material flows of commodified nature, labor power, technology, capital investment, and social relations—all of which had been discursively compartmentalized into distinct spaces in the modern era—opens up the possibility of conceiving nature and the city not as separate entities, but as dialectically related to each other, as the outcome of a unified process—the production of space.

CHAPTER 2

The Urbanization of Nature

> Nature underlies crucial modes of political arguments: justice, chance, freedom, limits of human action, source and possibility of knowledge.
>
> *S. Phelan, Intimate Distance (1993)*[1]

Modernity's Promethean Project

According to the ancient Greek myth of Prometheus, when Zeus withheld the gift of fire from humankind in one of his customary moments of rage, Prometheus (literally meaning the one who foresees) stole a branch of the holy fire and brought it back to Men, thus contributing greatly towards making nature work for the benefit of humankind against all odds — even against the gods' will. Prometheus' act, however, was the embodiment of *hubris*, and the outraged Zeus ordered $K\rho\acute{\alpha}\tau o\varsigma$ (the State) and $B\acute{\iota}\alpha$ (Violence) to seize and bind Prometheus on Mt. Caucasus where an eagle fed daily upon his liver, which would regenerate itself in the evening, thus making the torture last for ever. Despite the torture, Prometheus would never cease to despise Zeus and after thirty thousand years of suffering he was finally released and took his honorary place among the immortals.[2]

The ancient Greek world recognized in Prometheus the benefactor of humankind and the father of all the arts and sciences. Some twenty centuries later, the "enlightened" Western world found in the same mythological figure the cultural icon of the Modern Hero. Although the origin of the term "Modernity" and its chronological boundaries remain a source of academic debate,[3] I hereby subscribe to an apprehension of modernity as a period that began in the 17th century—characterized by a new, forward looking world view and a new set of social expectations. The taming of nature became a major project within modernity's broader aims, a project that scholars came to term "Promethean".[4] Within this context, the modern scientist or engineer would be the new Prometheus, who fights for human emancipation through the domination of nature. The modern hero would employ creativity, ingenuity, romantic heroic attitude, and a touch of hubris against the given order of the world.[5] "Modernity's Promethean project" would defy the power of nature, reject divine order, and launch on a quest to free Man (sic!) from his premodern fears, serve human needs and deliver social equity and material goods to everybody through progress, truth, reason, and rationality.[6]

As part of this project, according to Latour,[7] Western societies set out to "purify" the world in order to study it better. Nature became separated from society in order to be scientifically studied, and ultimately tamed, and the world was separated into things natural (the objects of study of natural sciences) and things social (the objects of study of social sciences).[8] Although not always explicitly addressed, the nature/society relation lay at the heart of numerous early scientific, political, and social writings: Malthus' *An Essay on the Principle of Population* (1798), Engels' *Condition of the Working Class in England* (1844), and Darwin's *On the Origin of Species* (1859) addressed this duality in one way or another. Numerous social-political movements also treated the nature/society relation as central to the question of social organization: social darwinism; the anarchism of Peter Kropotkin (whose *Mutual Aid* (1902)[9] retaliated against social darwinism by advocating a remaking of man and nature through cooperation, rather than competition); environmental determinism; early 20th century neo–lamarckianism; social biology; human ecology; and Nazi eugenics. The list of ideas driven by the desire to emancipate human beings (or social classes, or nations) by resolving the nature/society relationship in a scientific manner, while maintaining the dualism and the devotion in modernity's Promethean project is long.

However, it soon became evident that science, reason, technology, and planning could not work as an *automatic* means for human emancipation (see also Chapters 3 and 7), and that the positive outcome of progress would not be spread evenly throughout society. As Herbert Marcuse[10] argued, the human creativity so celebrated by Enlightenment's thinkers was soon transformed into a sternly productivist instrumental rationality that came to permeate all facets of modern life. As Marx and Engels had pointed out as early as 1859, the project for mastering nature expanded under capitalism to include the mastering and domination of human beings:

> [A]ll progress in capitalist agriculture is a progress in the art, not only of robbing the labourer, but of robbing the soil.... Capitalist production therefore, develops technology, and the combining together of various processes into a social whole, only by sapping the original sources of all wealth—the soil and the labourer.[11]

Recently, the emergence of environmentalism and the ecological movement has fueled a strong critique of modernity's Promethean project,[12] impaired its credibility,[13] and forced the nature/society relation to return to the top of the political and academic agenda.[14] However, the nature/society dualism has not been produced and reproduced only at a theoretical and conceptual/ideological level. Since this separation inevitably permeated social and spatial practices, these ideas often became politicized and were translated into spatial practices: from the production of nature in cities in the form of parks that would help produce better societies, to Nazi eugenics that would manipulate nature in order to produce the perfect human being. Lefebvre[15] touches upon this issue when he points out that the separation between spaces of extraction, production, and reproduction (what he calls "the social building blocks of space" or "space envelopes") is related to the nature/society dualism, and notes that this is also accompanied by the fragmentation of everyday experience, and by an increasing commodification of everyday life. However, Katz[16] as well as Braun and Castree[17] note that, despite the intense study of the nature/society separation in recent academic literature, a systematic analysis of the *spatial* implications of this separation is yet to be undertaken.

In this chapter, I discuss the nature/city dualism as one of the spatial expressions of the nature/society dualism. I examine modernity's contradictory scriptings of nature and the city and investigate how the production of modern cities has historically been infused by particular visions and ideologies about the "nature" of nature and the "nature" of the city. Finally, I argue that urbanization is a process of perpetual socio-ecological change, and consider ways of reconceptualizing both nature and the city, not as static things categorized as either good or evil, but as processes and flows that embody a dialectics between good and evil.

Spatializing the Nature/Society Dualism

> To combat nature or to "enter into" it to the point of penetration; to grasp its dialectical aspects with respect to concentration; to order it geometrically, or to make of it, in cultivating one's garden, ideal nature, a chosen cosmological precinct (earthly paradise, nature propitious) to human living as against wild nature; or pedagogically to invoke it as mirror of truth and goodness of man—these are attitudes to which have corresponded, each in turn, precise and differentiated architectural responses.[18]

Much of modern urban planning has been infused and inspired by particular scriptings of the "nature" of nature and of the "nature" of the city. In the above quote, Gregotti's enquiry into the relationship between nature and the built environment captures the multiplicity of meanings, and imaginings of nature[19]: nature as something that must be "penetrated," conquered, tamed; or, nature as something sacred, as ideal order and pedagogical inspiration. Figure 2.a is a representation of the almost schizophrenic attitude towards both nature and the city found in modernist architectural visions and planning practices. On the one hand, nature stands for the "uncivilized", the dark and untamed wilderness that requires control and whose frontier has to be pushed outwards as "progress" accelerates. On the other hand, nature is also perceived as inherently "good", as the embodiment of some innate superior moral code that has been subverted and perverted through "civilization" and "urbanization" and needs to be restored.

The city also falls into this dual scripting. It is often branded as "evil", harboring the underbelly of modern society, while at the same time, it is heralded as the pinnacle of civilization, as man's triumph over the barbarism of uncivilized earlier times and as a hallmark of the success of the project for pushing forwards the frontier of a wild and untamed "nature" (Figure 2.b). This double coding of both nature and the city as, on the one hand ecologically and morally superior and on the other hand barbaric and uncivilized, has prompted (and still prompts) many debates as well as conflicting spatial and social practices. This quintessentially schizophrenic attitude towards both nature and the city permeates the history of both environmental and urban theories.[20] Many urban planners, thinkers, and architects of the past (Howard, Olmsted, Proudhon, Unwin, or Geddes to name but a few) have invoked a romanticized imagery of an inherently good pristine "nature" as an inspiration and a practice for sanitizing the city, both literally (in terms of, for example, combating pollution) but also symbolically (in terms of, for example, providing "social sanitation" from urban crime, "deviance" and "undesirable" marginal

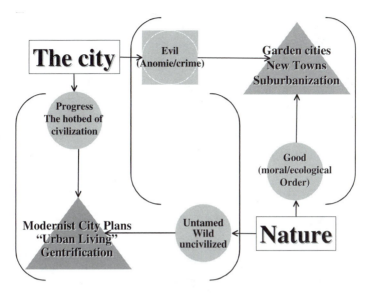

Fig. 2.a Modernity's double scripting of City and Nature.

urban groups). Simultaneously, however, the antipode of a "good" nature—the imagery of an evil, wild, and dangerous nature—is also employed as the counter-example to what a well ordered rational modern city should be. Expressions such as "the urban wilderness" and "the concrete jungle" invoke images of an out-of-control urbanization process and an uncivilized "nature", both of which need control and mastering.

In modernity's Promethean project, the nature/society dialectics has always been at the center of efforts to create a better society by creating a better urban environment. From the attempts of the 18th and the 19th century to create a "sanitized city", to the early 20th century's strive for a "rational city", to the contemporary quest for a "sustainable city", inspiration is sought for in ideas about the "greening" of the city and reducing pollutants[21] of all kinds emanating from urban life. It is, however, the "nature" of the perceived pollutants changed with time. In the 18th century it was miasmata and putrid air, in the 19th century rats and manure, in the 20th century bacteria, and today it is carbon dioxide. Despite the historically and geographically specific nature of what constitutes "threat" and "pollution" for urban environments, the above conceptualizations of an ideal city all share an understanding of nature and the city as two distinct, yet interrelated, domains. In the next section I will examine how changes in the understanding of what "nature" is, inspired views about what the city ought to be during the 19th and 20th centuries.

Fig. 2.b Pushing the frontier of nature; modernity's creative destruction is visualized in this 1910 painting by Robert Delaunay. Trees bow as progress pushes forward. Robert Delaunay, Eiffel Tower with Trees, Oil on Canvas, 1910 from the series "Visions of Paris". Solomon R. Guggenheim Museum, New York.

The Nature/City Dialectics in Modernist Planning

Nature and the "environment" have been central to urban change and urban politics since the birth of planning. The horrid environmental conditions in early industrial cities inspired generations of writers, social engineers, philanthropists, philosophers, and planners. Charles Dickens, for example, gripped by a nostalgia that creeps up whenever the modernist process of "creative destruction" erases the imprint of the past, chronicled the life of London's underclass and lamented the loss of an allegedly superior, organic, non-urban social order. Visionaries of all sorts bemoaned the loss and change and proposed solutions and plans that would remedy the antinomies of urban life and produce a healthy "wholesome" urban living. In many of these accounts, the city figures as the antithesis of the assumed harmonious and equitable dynamics of "nature", while the "urban question" necessitates (so they argue) a decidedly anti-urban development trajectory. The founding fathers of modern sociology, Tönnies and Durkheim, were also captivated by the rapid modernization process and the accompanying rise of an urban order, which each of them put in contradistinction to an idealized and disappearing rural, environmentally equitable, harmonious, and inherently humane social order.[22]

The 19th century socio-environmental urban blight threatened not only the well-being of the elites; it began to challenge the very bedrock of capitalist society as the marginalized and the oppressed began to demand access to better environmental conditions (in terms of shelter, food, hygiene, medicine, and consumer commodities). However, prioritizing the recapture of "nature" conveniently swept the class character that underpinned socio-environmental injustices under the carpet. With only a few dissenting voices — such as that of Friedrich Engels, who linked up the horrid living conditions of the working class in 19th century Manchester with labor-bourgeoisie relations under capitalism — most theorists and planners argued that it was the nature of the city and not that of society that needed to change. Buckingham's 1849 utopian urban vision, for example, declared that the quest for a better city and a better society should rest on the principle of restoring natural order and sanitation:

> [T]o unite the greatest degree of order, symmetry, space, and healthfulness, in the largest supply of air and light.... And, in addition.... a large intermixture of grass lawn, garden ground, and flowers, and an abundant supply of water...[23]

According to this vision, by producing a city more in tune with the rhythms and rhymes of nature itself, a better society would "naturally" follow. It is not surprising then that visionary elites began to experiment with new forms of urban living that would change spatial organization and possibly alleviate social conflict while leaving social organization intact. Lord Leverhulme's Port Sunlight, the paternalistically designed proletarian utopia at the rural side of the Mersey was an early attempt to sanitize the industrial city and combine nature with "healthy" living as a means to stem the rising tide of social unrest and to safeguard the aesthetic and moral order of the elite. In Great Britain, Sir Titus Salt, inspired by similar anti-urban theories and plans, decided to relocate his business outside of Bradford (in northern England). In 1870 he built Saltaire,[24] a new factory surrounded by a small town to house all his workers, thus pioneering Victorian industrial paternalism. The new environment for his workers was not only well organized and closer to "nature"; it was also away from the social unrest in which Bradford was embroiled at the time. Shortly later, Ebenezer Howard's *Garden Cities of Tomorrow* (1898) would codify the "imagineered" urban utopia in a systematic, rational, and "scientific" planning practice for an inclusive, orderly, and friction-less quasi-urban form of spatial organization, based on a harmonious coexistence of urban and rural conditions:

> [N]either the town magnet nor the country magnet represents the full plan and purpose of nature. Human society and the beauty of nature are meant to be enjoyed together. The two magnets must be made one. As man and woman…supplement each other, so should town and country. The town is the symbol…town and country must be married.[25]

Inspired by Howard's ideas, British New Towns, a postwar development (1946), breathed the same anti-urban spirit, while Prince Charles's crusade for urban villages is one of the most recent large-scale applications of similar anti-urban principles. While Howard's ideas greatly influenced Great Britain, on the other side of the Atlantic, another great figure, Frederick Law Olmsted, had already (since the 1870s) advocated a more symbiotic relation between nature and the city as a means to eliminate evil and promote "the pursuit of commerce."[26] The sanitizing and purifying delights of "air and foliage", he argued, would turn parks and green havens into the new and true centers of the city.

In the 20th century, the nature/city debate (and divide) remained at the heart of ideas and plans for the modern metropolis. During the 1930s, the avant-garde movement of Futurism renounced anything to do with nature and the natural world as a thing of the past with its only remaining appeal an aesthetic one. The movement rejected all inspiration drawn from nature as "architectonic prostitution", and asserted that everything natural should be eliminated from the consciousness of the modern urban dweller. Instead, the new society should draw inspiration from technology, the machine, the mechanical world. Around the same period, however, Le Corbusier and Frank Lloyd Wright, the gurus of 20th century modernism, introduced nature as a means of restoring a healthy vitality to modern urban living, while maintaining the belief in the power of technology to change society. Still, the notion of "nature" would take on very different meanings and interpretations for both of them.[27] In Le Corbusier's 1922 utopian plan for *Ville Contemporaine*,[28] nature took the form of regimented green spaces, which would provide the setting for his "machines for living in"[29] within an orthological, well-ordered spatial symmetry made up of building blocks of very high densities, segregated by class. On the other hand, Frank Lloyd Wright pursued an integration of green spaces and built form in very low density schemes. His *Broadacre City* (1924–1930s) was a utopia advocating the right to land ownership for everybody, but was also a development whose function depended heavily on the automobile, a scheme close to that of what would become the standard American suburb.[30] In both cases, the ideal living environment, which would guarantee social harmony and ease the tensions and class conflicts that characterized capitalist cities, was advocated at an ideological level by the idea of bringing human beings closer to nature, as LeGates and Stout[31] argue. However, at the material level, the successful "cleansing" and "sanitizing" of urban environments was almost invariably translated in spatially explicit social segregation right from the start, from the planning phase. Le Corbusier's *Ville Contemporaine* was conveniently already segregated by class in its very plans, while the function of *Broadacre City* was based on the assumption of universal car ownership. Moreover, it made car ownership a necessity for anybody who wanted to participate in the new green utopian world.

The idealized visions of how nature would sanitize the city—both materially and spiritually—celebrated a particular imagining of a manufactured "nature" as a healing force while condemning the "nature" of the capitalist city as dehumanizing. While both Wright and Le Corbusier intended to take further the 19th century ideas of marrying nature with the city as a means of restoring social harmony, their scripting of the city/nature relation and their recipe for stopping socio-environmental urban degradation was different: bringing nature back into the city, in the case of Le Corbusier; and bringing the city into nature, in the case of Wright.

While urban reformers reveled in the utopian idea of creating a wholesome urbanism by injecting the idealized virtues of a life closer to a form of balanced and harmonious "nature", a new generation of city-lovers came to the defense of the urban. Lewis Mumford, for example, reveled in the contradictory nature of modern urbanization.[32] To him, the delight of the urban dwells exactly in its ability to create opportunities for social disharmony and conflict, on the breath of the new, the cracks and meshes that enable new encounters, and where the unexpected can turn up just around the corner. In contrast to the vibrant character of the city center, nothing ever happened in the landscaped gardens of the newly developing suburbs. Marking the staleness of artificially green urban/suburban environments, Christopher Alexander distinguishes between "natural" cities and "artificial" cities, the former arising "spontaneously, over many, many years", the latter being "cities and parts of cities which have been deliberately created by designers and planners."[33] He identifies the soft disorder—the gentle frictions associated with mixing, heterogeneity, difference, and the playful ease of everyday life—with "natural" cities, and argues that they are the social equivalent to the benevolent disorder of nature itself. Subsequent urbanists, from Jane Jacobs to Henri Lefebvre to Richard Sennett, made similar claims about the necessity of "disorder" for urban vitality.

However, it is also this same dialectic of order/chaos, opportunity/fear that perpetuates the conservative imagery of cities as places of social and environmental disintegration and moral decay.[34] The denial to acknowledge this dialectic lies at the heart of failed attempts to plan for a totally rational urban space during modernity. Notwithstanding the heroic attitude in the efforts of these great urban thinkers and planners to humanize (and "ecologize") the city by means of restoring a presumably lost natural order, most of their attempts to produce a "natural" fix for the ills and pains of modern urbanization failed dismally to achieve the harmonious urban order its advocates had hoped for. With the arrogance of a spatial fetishist (believing a better urban environment would automatically produce a better society) and the hubris of a modern hero, they were acting the same way as the planner in Italo Calvino's *Invisible Cities* who attempts to put forth a perfect plan for making Fedora the perfect city. Somehow, though, the city keeps escaping the fate he had designed for her and keeps transforming on her own accord, perpetually in front of his eyes, before he ever managed to complete his plans:

> [L]ooking at Fedora as it was, he imagined a way of making it the ideal city, but while he constructed his miniature model, Fedora was already no longer the same as before, and what had until yesterday a possible future, became only a toy in a glass globe.[35]

Failing to acknowledge the complexity of the urban, the rationalization process of modernist planning produced unpredictable urban environments. Green spaces quickly became dark, crime-ridden areas, avoided by women or children unless permanent supervision could be guaranteed. As the deserts bloomed into suburbs drowned in greenery, ecological and social disaster hit: water scarcity, pollution, congestion, and lack of sewage disposal combined with mounting economic and racial tension.[36]

The urban basis of environmental problems—and the dialectics between nature and the city—could no longer be ignored at a material level. The production of space encompasses both social categories of nature and the city. While on a world scale we are rapidly approaching a situation in which more than half of the world's population lives in urban settings, urban-natural formations correspond, more than ever before, to landscapes of power within a dominant neoliberal agenda, where islands of extreme wealth are interspersed with places of deprivation, exclusion, and decline. While Davis depicts the environments of the underbelly of the city as "dangerous ecological war zones",[37] many of the subtropical gardens in permanently irrigated gated communities display a level of biodiversity that is matched only by that of the Amazonian rainforest.[38] Unhealthy high ozone concentrations in city centers, the proliferation of asthmatic and other respiratory diseases (tuberculosis is now again endemic in the rat infested poor Bengali neighborhoods of East London), and spreading homelessness are reshaping urban landscapes and may claim more casualties than even the most pessimistic accounts of the impact of global warming predict. Today, it is clear that even if an environmental "fix" for urban problems could "restore" some form of nature in one place, it would accelerate socio-ecological disintegration elsewhere.

The fact that environmental problems are inseparable from the function of the urban environment and society was fully acknowledged by the environmental movement that blossomed in the 1960s and early 1970s. Echoing the voices of this movement, McHarg's seminal book *Design with Nature* (1969) drafted the first guidelines for "ecologizing" the city, no longer by bringing nature in the form of green spaces inside the city, but by bringing nature squarely into the multiple relations that structure the urbanization process and by treating nature and the city as interacting processes rather than inert things.[39] In these first seeds for political ecological thinking, nature and the city appear as a single interacting system. Changes to any of the parts will affect the operation of the whole.

The Urbanization of Nature…or…the Environment of the City

Following upon the environmental movement, over the past few years a new *rapprochement* has begun to assert itself between ecological thinking, political-economy, urban studies, critical social theory, and cultural studies of science. William Cronon,[40] for example, in *Nature's Metropolis*, tells the story of Chicago from the vantage point of the socio-natural processes that transformed both city and countryside and which produced the particular political-ecology that shaped the transformation of the Midwest as a distinct American urbanized socio-nature. Mike Davis, for his part in *City of Quartz* and in more recent publications,[41] documents how nature and society became materially constructed through Los Angeles' urbanization process, and documents the multiple social struggles that have infused and shaped this process in deeply uneven, exclusive, and empowering/disempowering ways. Erik Swyngedouw, Roger Keil, Gene Desfor, and Matthew Gandy[42] have pioneered the integration of the nature debate into the urban debate, balancing the advancement in theorizing the city/nature relationship with rigorous empirical analysis. The rapprochement of social ecological and urban thinking culminates in David Harvey's *Justice, Nature and the Geography of Difference*[43] where he insists that, as a matter of fact, there is nothing particularly "unnatural" about New York City! Cities are dense networks of interwoven socio-spatial processes that are simultaneously human, material, natural, discursive, cultural, and organic. The myriad of transformations and metabolisms that support and maintain urban life, such as water, food, computers, or movies always combine environmental *and* social processes as infinitely interconnected.[44] Imagine, for example, standing at the corner of Piccadilly Circus and consider the socio-environmental metabolic relations that come together and emanate from this global-local place: smells, tastes, and bodies from all nooks and crannies of the world are floating by, consumed, displayed, narrated, visualized, and transformed. The Rainforest shop and restaurant play to the tune of eco-sensitive shopping and the multibillion pound eco-industry while competing with McDonald's and Dunkin' Donuts; the sounds of world music vibrate from Tower Records and people, spices, clothes, foodstuffs, and materials from all over the world whirl by. The neon lights are fed by energy coming from nuclear power plants and from coal or gas burning electricity generators. The cars burning fuels from oil-deposits and pumping CO_2 into the air, affecting forests and climates around the globe, further complete the global geographic mappings and traces that flow through the city, and produce London as a palimpsest of densely layered bodily, local, national, and global—but geographically uneven—socio-ecological processes. This intermingling of things material and symbolic combines to produce a particular socio-environmental *milieu* that welds nature, society and the city together in a deeply heterogeneous, conflicting and often disturbing whole.[45]

Perpetual change and an ever-shifting mosaic of environmentally and socio-culturally distinct urban ecologies—varying from the manufactured landscaped gardens of gated communities and high-technology campuses to the ecological war-zones of depressed neighborhoods with lead-painted walls and asbestos covered ceilings, waste dumps, and pollutant-infested areas—shape the process of a capitalist urbanization. The environment of the city is deeply caught up in this dialectical process as are environmental ideologies, practices, and projects. The idea of some sort of pristine nature that needs to be saved (First Nature) or of a city as an entity separate to socio-environmental processes, becomes increasingly problematic as historical geographical processes continuously produce new "socio-natural" environments over space and time.[46] In sum, the world is a historical geographical process of perpetual metabolism in which "social" and "natural" processes combine in a historical geographical "production process of socio-nature" whose outcome (historical nature) embodies chemical, physical, social, economic, political, and cultural processes in highly contradictory but inseparable manners.

This constructionist perspective considers the process of urbanization to be integral to the production of new environments and new natures. It also sees nature and society as fundamentally combined historical-geographical production processes.[47] Consider, for example, the socio-ecological transformations of entire ecological systems, sand and clay metabolized into concrete buildings. Similarly, the contested production of new "genotypes" such as Oncomouse™ on which Haraway elaborates,[48] or Dolly the cloned sheep[49] support the impossibility of an *ontological* basis for a separation between human beings and nature, between nature and culture. Anthony Giddens[50] suggests that in this context we have reached "The End of Nature". Of course, he does not imply that nature has disappeared, but rather that nothing is out there anymore that has not been transformed, tainted, metabolized by society/culture. Latour contends that

> "nature" is merely the uncoded category that modernists oppose to "culture", in the same way that, prior to feminism, "man" was the uncoded category opposed to "woman". By coding the category of "natural object", anthropological science loses the former nature/culture dichotomy.[51]

As Lewontin suggests, modernity's nature is no longer fearful or strange. It is instead more open to fulfilling promises and desires, yet remains full of conflict and tension:

> A rational environmental movement cannot be built on the demand to save the environment, which, in any case, does not exist. Rather, we must decide what kind of world we want to live in and then try to manage the process of change as best we can approximate it.[52]

A City of Flows

The question that now begins to gnaw at your mind is more anguished: outside Penthesilea does an outside exist? Or, no matter how far you go from the city, will you only pass from one limbo to another, never managing to leave it?

I. Calvino, Invisible Cities (1974)[53]

Cultural studies of science, more than any other discipline, contest the idea that our knowledge about entities perceived as "natural" can be fixed, or that scientific knowledge provides "the truth" about a nature that is "out there" to be discovered. The analysis of the proliferation of modernity's "hybrids" in the work of Haraway and Latour illuminated the nature/society debate since it enabled everyone (including scientists) to see the impossibility of an *ontological* basis for a separation between human beings and nature, between nature and culture.[54] The irony, of course, is that these "impure" objects emerged out of the laboratories where the fundamental purpose had been to purify the world by separating it into distinct categories. Hence, Latour argues, the emergence of these objects was a hubris against modernity's project to purify the world. Their name, "hybrids", originates from the Greek ὕβρις, which means insult or violation but also signifies: "an impious disregard of the limits governing men's actions in an orderly universe...the sin to which the great and gifted are most susceptible."[55] Indeed, the proliferation of hybrids can be seen as an insult to the constructed order of a modern world that neatly separated things into "natural" and "cultural", as a hubris that reveals (most of the times unwittingly) the flaw in modernity's armor—it simply cannot deliver on the promise of a neatly separated and elegantly ordered world.

The proliferation of entities of ambiguous nature that are neither purely "natural" nor purely "non-natural" becomes more and more the "normal" outcome of modernity's production processes. Swyngedouw and Kaika[56] take Latour's and Haraway's analyses into the urban debate, arguing that the existence of modernity's quasi-objects and hybrids can be extended to include spatial categories such as the modern city. Examined as one of modernity's socio-natural hybrids, the city is full of contradictions, tensions, and conflicts. Viewing the city as a process of continuous—but contested—socio-ecological change, which can be understood through the analysis of the circulation of socially and physically metabolized "nature", unlocks new arenas for thinking and acting on the city: society and nature. Representation and being are inseparable, integral to each other, infinitely bound up. The city becomes the palimpsest landscape that captures those proliferating objects that Haraway calls "Cyborgs" or "Tricksters"[57] and to which Latour refers as "Quasi-Objects". They are intermediaries that embody and mediate nature and society and weave networks of infinite transgressions and liminal spaces.

In this sense, there is no such thing as an unsustainable city in general, but rather there is a perpetual process of urbanization of nature, a series of urban and environmental processes that negatively affect some social groups while benefiting others. As Raymond Williams points out in *The Country and the City*,[58] the transformation of nature and the social relations inscribed therein are inextricably connected to the process of urbanization. The dialectic of the environment and urbanization consolidates a particular set of social relations through what Harvey calls "an ecological transformation which requires the reproduction of those relations in order to sustain it."[59] This process takes place today at a global scale, and the socio-ecological footprint of the city has become global. As in Calvino's *Penthesilea*, there is no longer an outside or a limit to the city. The urban harbors social and ecological processes that have a myriad of local, regional, national, and global connections, and occur in the realms of power in which actors strive to defend and create their own environments in a context of class, ethnic, racial, and/or gender conflicts and power struggles. Of course, under capitalism, the commodity relation veils the multiple socio-ecological processes of domination/subordination and exploitation/repression that feed the urbanization process and turns the city into a metabolic socio-environmental process that stretches from the immediate environment to the remotest corners of the globe. The apparently self-evident commodification of nature that fundamentally underpins a market-based society not only obscures the social relations of power inscribed therein, but also permits the disconnection of the perpetual flows of transformed and commodified nature from its inevitable foundation, i.e., the production of nature. In sum, the environment of the city (both social and physical) is the result of a historical geographical process of the urbanization of nature. Excavating the flows that constitute the urban would produce a political-ecology of the urbanization of nature.

If we were to capture some of the metabolized flows that weave together the urban fabric and excavate the networks that brought them there, we would "pass with continuity from the local to the global, from the human to the non-human."[60] These flows would narrate many interrelated tales of the city: of its people and the powerful socio-ecological processes that produce the urban (complete with its spaces of privilege and exclusion, of participation and marginality); of rats and bankers; of diseases and pork belly speculation; of chemical, physical, and biological transformations; of global warming and acid rain; of capital flows and the strategies of city builders; of plans implemented by engineers, scientists and economists. They would make up the (hi)story of a city of flows.

In the next chapter, we shall follow the flow of one of these elements, water, into the city and tell the story of the networks underneath and outside the city that contribute to the continuous transgressing of the boundaries between the natural, the urban, and the domestic, and point at the continuity and the dialectics of the production of space.

CHAPTER 3

The Phantasmagoria of the Modernist Dream

"O, Texaco, Motor Oil, Esso, Shell, great inscriptions of human potentiality, soon shall we cross ourselves before your fountains and the youngest among us will perish for having contemplated their nymphs in naphtha…"

L. Aragon, The Paris Peasant (1926)[1]

In Chapter 2, the city was exemplified as the metabolic and social transformation of nature through human labor, a "hybrid" of the natural and the cultural, the environmental and the social. Entering the city posits the city as flow, flux, and movement, and suggests social, material, and symbolic transformations and permutations. Yes, the city is a material entity, a "thing", but this thing exists in a perpetual state of transformation and change; it is a perpetual passing through deterritorialized materials. Harvey, Sennet, Castells, and Merrifield,[2] to name but a few, have depicted the city as a circulatory conduit, a flux that is always material (in all possible senses, including symbolic and discursive flows), but never fixed. Deleuze and Guattari capture this dialectic of process and thing in their definition of the city:

> The town is the correlate of the road. The town exists only as a function of circulation and of circuits; it is a singular point on the circuits which create it and which it creates. It is defined by entries

and exits: something must enter and exit from it. It imposes a frequency. It effects a polarization of matter, inert, living or human; it causes the phylum, the flow, to pass through specific places, along horizontal lines. It is a phenomenon of transconsistency, a network, because it is fundamentally in contact with other towns. It represents a threshold of deterritorialization because whatever the material involved, it must be deterritorialized enough to enter the network, to submit to polarization, to follow the circuit of urban and road recoding. The maximum deterritorialization appears in the tendency … to separate from the backcountry, from the countryside.[3]

The material mediators, the carriers of the flows that constitute the urban are technological networks: water, gas, electricity, information, etc. Given their central role in the production of modern cities, technology networks are integral parts of the urban fabric and of the process of transformation of nature into the city and vice versa.[4] These networks were part of modernism's quest to sanitize and rationalize urban space and indeed, to construct it as a node, a point of reference. Endowed with modernity's technological networks, the urban fabric became a nexus of entry-exit points for a myriad of interconnected circuits and conduits.

Although academic literature has addressed the importance of the operational, economic, and social role of technology networks in the function of the modern city[5] it can be argued that their cultural, ideological, and aesthetic role has been largely overlooked or neglected. This is not particularly surprising given their visual absence from contemporary cities. For it is true that—despite their importance for the function of the contemporary city—technology networks are today largely hidden, opaque, invisible; disappearing underground, locked into pipes, cables, conduits, tubes, passages, and electronic waves. However, urban networks have not *always* been opaque. Along with their "urban dowry" (water towers, dams, pumping stations, power plants, gas stations, etc.), they have undergone important historical changes in their visual role and their material importance in the cityscape. Indeed, as the following sections will investigate, throughout the 19th century (when the urban niche as agglomerated use values—a theater of accumulation and economic growth—was still under construction) urban networks and their connecting iconic landmarks were prominently visual and present in the urban landscape. They were the iconic embodiments of, and shrines to, a technologically scripted image and practice of "progress".

However, once completed, the networks became buried underground, invisible, banalized, and relegated to a marginal, subterranean urban underworld. Their contemporary hidden form contributed to severing the process of the social transformation of nature from the process of urbanization, blurring the tense relationship between nature and the city further. Perhaps more importantly, the hidden flows and their technological framing occlude the social relations and power mechanisms that are scripted in and enacted through these flows; that is, they contribute to the process of commodity fetishism.

Using water and water networks as the emblematic example, this chapter addresses the dialectics between the economic/functional role of urban networks on the one hand, and their aesthetic/ideological and cultural position and representation on the other. An analysis of this dialectic permits an understanding of the shift from celebrating urban technological networks in the beginning of modernity to their subsequent underground burial during high-modernity. This, in turn, elucidates the dialectic of visibility/opacity of networks.

Commodity fetishism—a Marxist concept that brings together economics, politics, and culture—will be the entry point into the excavation of the dialectics between the economic/political and the cultural/ideological role of networks and their often hidden material existence. I will first examine how urban networks became "urban fetishes" during early modernity. They were compulsively admired while they were materially and culturally supporting and enacting an ideology of progress. Their subsequent underground disappearance and the ruination of their urban dowry during high-modernity showed that this ideology of progress failed.

On Commodities as Fetishes and as Wish Images

There it is a definite social relation between men, that assumes, in their eyes, the fantastic [phantasmagoric] form of a relation between things. In order therefore, to find an analogy, we must have recourse to the mist-enveloped regions of the religious world. In that world the productions of the human brain appear as independent beings endowed with life and entering into relation both with one another and the human race. So it is in the world of commodities with the products of men's hands. This I call the Fetishism, which attaches itself to the products of labor so soon as they are produced as commodities, and which is therefore inseparable from the production of commodities. This Fetishism of commodities has its origin...in the peculiar social character of the labor that produces them.

K. Marx, (1859: 165)[6]

All goods necessary to sustain human lives are produced. Water, food, clothing, housing, even air, undergo a production process involving the extraction of raw materials and their subsequent transformation through human labor. Under market exchange conditions and capitalist relations of production, these goods enter the social and urban fabric as commodities. The particular use values of goods that satisfy the wants and desires of individuals and social groups become combined with the distinct, universal, and homogenized characteristic of their exchange value. The exchange value acquired by commodities is based precisely on the fact that they are *produced* through a process that presupposes the transformation of nature through human labor, under specific social relations of production. Although the natural foundation of this socio-environmental metabolism that we call the labor process is an essential mechanism in the creation of exchange value, the link between nature and the final product (commodities) is severed and the socio-economic conditions of their production are obscured. Commodities begin to appear as mere embodiments or containers of exchange value. In this way commodities become naturalized, and the qualitative relations involved in their production process become quantified.

Blurring the socio-environmental process of their production by grounding their character as universally exchangeable for anything else is an amazingly powerful ideological mechanism. Severing materially and symbolically the connection between producing exchange and use values contributes to masking the qualitative social and environmental relations of production. Acquiring exchange value, without revealing at the same time the social power relations of their production, permits commodities to be presented as exceptional, as *outside* and *over* the thing that really makes them exceptional, i.e., the social metabolism of nature.[7]

According to Marx,[8] commodities become fetishes when the quantification of qualitative relations abstracts and "obscures the nature of social reality." From obscuring social reality there is only a small step towards Eagleton's aphorism that "commodities supply their own ideology in the market."[9] Hence, commodity fetishism provides a cunning answer to the contradictions stemming from the need to sustain and increase the exchange value of commodities without revealing the socio-environmental relations of their production. It is a kind of perverse "exchange," producing "material relations between persons and social relations between things."[10]

Indeed, the autonomy of the commodity as a fetish, and the desire to acquire the commodity often does not even depend on its use value, or on the buying capacity of the consumer. According to Benjamin,[11] one can perfectly well desire a commodity which one cannot afford. The young (and the not-so-young) man's (and woman's?) dream to acquire a Lotus car exists irrespective of their economic status and ability to actually acquire this wish image (of themselves driving in a Lotus). And the more the socio-environmental relations embodied in the production of commodities are rendered opaque, the more the uniqueness of the commodity and its phantom-like character can be celebrated. In the advertisement for another car, named after Picasso, the production process is presented as being totally automated, performed by robots, anthropomorphic and witty, but also clean and shiny. The elimination of the image of human labor involved in the production process (i.e., the reification of social relations of production) assists the promotion of the commodity as a wish image. The price the consumer is prepared to pay depends heavily on the ability of the market to present the commodity as severed from its production process. It is, Benjamin argues,[12] the "estrangement of commodities"—their ability to become more distant and difficult to acquire—that makes them capable of becoming "wish images". Commodities do not only carry their materiality; they also carry the promise and the dream of a better society and a happier life. The delights and the desires of the fetish, something we are continuously reminded of through the spectacular commodified displays of shopping centers and the promises of advertisements, permit exactly to recast and re-imagine the world in a delightful manner. Of course, fetishization invariably fails to deliver on its promises as the perpetual nourishment of the old with the new, and the phantasmagoric character of the commodity subverts the possibility of actually experiencing and living the desires promised by the commodity.

In what follows, we will examine the role of modernity's urban technological networks as fetishes and wish images; as the embodiments of modernity's Promethean project for human emancipation through technology and reason. We will trace how these characteristics transformed alongside social and historical changes.

The "Urban Dowry" That Modernity Produced

Like other commodities in a market economy, the urban environment (roads, parks, buildings, networks) is also produced and commodified through the transformation of nature by human labor and capital investment.[13] However, although the urban is part and parcel of our everyday experience, the human labor and social power relations involved in the production of cities are reified. A new housing development scheme is hardly ever advertised and promoted in the market by publicizing the amount of sweat and labor expended in its production, the negotiations between employers and employees over their payment, the difference (or not) the payment made to the lives of the builders, or the social power relations that were enacted between the developers and the local community.[14] Rather, the production of the urban remains fetishized, since the social relations of its production remain unspoken. The urban environment becomes naturalized, as if it were created smoothly and miraculously, as if it had always been there, distinct and separate from natural and social processes.

Technological networks for their part, being a constitutive part of the urban, play a very special role in the process of commodification. Being part of what Castells termed "the collective means of consumption,"[15] their use value dwells in their faculty for *facilitating* the process of socio-environmental transformation and commodification of goods. Networks are the prerequisite for delivering the final product of the process of transformation of nature to the city and to the market. First of all, they are essential in the transportation of utilities: water, gas, electricity, and their transformation into use and exchange value. Water supply networks, for example, are the means of transforming H_2O (a natural element) into potable, clean, translucent water (a socially produced commodity embodying powerful cultural and social meanings).[16] Water enters one end of the network as H_2O and subsequently undergoes a chemical and social transformation to end up at the other end (the tap) as potable water, as a commodity properly priced and treated. As water becomes urbanized, commodified and domesticated, it becomes severed from its role as mere use value and vests new roles and coding: aesthetic, in spas and fountains; moral and cultural, in practices of bodily hygiene and cleanliness, etc. As water travels through urban networks acquiring symbolic, cultural and exchange value, it further facilitates the commodification (and subsequent fetishization) of a number of goods and services "external" to it, yet directly linked to the existence of water's networks: swimming pools, spas, entertainment grounds, indeed everything that makes up city life, could not have existed without the support of technology networks. Think of the bright lights of Las Vegas; they could not have existed in the middle of the desert, and the consumption associated with the entertainment industry would not have been possible to flourish, had it not been for a set of (invisible) networks that carry water and electricity in a long strip of land in the middle of nowhere. In short, the process of commodification and subsequent fetishization of all urban goods is facilitated by the existence of urban technology networks. Networks express through their material existence the socio/economic *processes* and the material *flows* of the transformation of nature into commodities. They represent, as they cut their way through and underneath the urban, the production process.

Despite them being essential in the process of commodification and consumption, until recently (when they started becoming privatized), there was no distinct price tag attached to networks (unlike other commodities). The fact that most utility privatizations around the world avoided asset privatization (the UK water industry makes a great exception to this, and thus a very interesting case to study)[17] demonstrates the difficulty with commodifying utility networks, and the collective means of consumption in general. The difficulty of directly commodifying networks, however, does not mean that they do not have an exchange value; their exchange value is embodied in the exchange value of the commodities they deliver. When one pays for one's water, one pays also for being connected to the water network; when one pays for a swim in a spa, the price includes connection and labor charges for the production and maintenance of the water supply network; when one pays for a meal in a restaurant, this also includes charges for electricity, gas, and water networks.

In short, technology networks are the carriers of goods and services that promise to deliver the modernist dream for a happier, better society, with supply of water, electricity, health, food for all. This is exactly where the fetishization of urban technology networks dwells: in being carriers of the modernist promise of participating in the phantasmagoric new world of technological advancement and progress; a world in which human freedom and emancipation resides in connecting to technology. It is this belief that lay at the heart of the fetishization of networks during early modernity. Indeed, throughout the 19th century, networks of technology fitted perfectly to Marx's definition of the fetish as a "bewildering thing full of metaphysical subtleties and theological capers"[18] but also to Benjamin's definition of fetishized objects as "wish images," abstractions which "cease to be a product controlled by human beings" and take a "phantom like objectivity and lead their own lives."[19] The opening quote of this chapter by Louis Aragon pays tribute exactly to this role of networks. As we will explore in the next section, they became autonomous embodiments of progress and material evidence for the ideology that a better society was under construction.

Early Modernity (Mid-19th Century to 1914)

Work continues. The grunt into hard clay. The wet slap. Men burning rock and shattering it wherever they come across it. In the east end of the city a tunnel is being built out under a lake in order to lay intake pipes for the new waterworks. During the eight-hour shift no one speaks. All morning they slip in the wet clay unable to stand properly, pissing where they work, eating where someone else shit.... Above ground.... the excavations and constructions were also being orchestrated. The giant centrifugal pumps, more valuable than life, were trolleyed into place with their shell-shaped impellers that in Commissioner Harris' dream would fan the water up towards the settling basins.... "The form of the city changes faster than the heart of a mortal," Harris liked to remind his critics, quoting Baudelaire.... Harris imagined a palace for it. He wanted the best ornamental iron. He wanted a brass elevator to lead from the service building to the filter building where you could step out across rose-coloured marble.... He was a man who understood the continuity of the city.... This was choreography in 1930.

M. Ondaatje, In the Skin of a Lion (1988: 108–111)[20]

The Industrial Revolution was accompanied by the secularization of society and a growing belief in reason as the means of solving social problems. The work of, for example, Henri Saint-Simon and Auguste Comte tried to reconcile progress with order by developing a "science of society".[21] Rousseau's idea of "Man being good by nature but ruined by civilization" became linked to the belief that human reason was the means for achieving "the good" in human nature. During early modernity, the amelioration of city and society became part and parcel of a quest for equality and freedom through reason and progress, of the Promethean promise that science and technological innovation would pave the way for breaking the chains of slavery to nature and to other human beings (see also Chapter 2). Technology *in itself,* it was believed, would improve living standards and social environments, and would *automatically* lead to a better world. As long as there was progress, there would be no fear of going backwards, no question or doubt about the positive trajectory towards fulfilling Mankind's mission. The disempowered were bound finally to enter the paradise of technological freedom if only they would be patient and hardworking enough to serve the god of technology for an undefined and undefinable length of time. Freedom was promised at each turn of the corner, to be relentlessly frustrated again by the next promise.

With the rise of the "Age of Reason"[22] and the secularization of society, the built environment also underwent important changes. A canonical example of these changes was Claude Nicolas Ledoux's 1780s design for the surveyor's house on the river Loue. The architectural design was the embodiment of the idea of mastering nature—in this case, a river. With the aid of technology, the river would fit into man's desired course, and enter the service of humankind, while at the same time, it would make the built environment around it functional. The future was open and everything seemed possible. However, the new "revolutionary architecture", to which Ledoux subscribed, co-existed with a deeply entrenched and conservative spirit, which was expressed in the morphology of its buildings. They embodied the enduring aesthetic appeal of historical forms (Chapters 5 and 6 give detailed empirical analysis of this phenomenon). As Gympel puts it, despite the inevitable fascination with the new and the unknown, "people were torn between a sense of euphoria at the progress and a romantic blurring of the past".[23] From the very beginning, modernity reveled in the complexity and co-existence of progressive and reactionary forces in the shaping of the urban form and of an intermingling of fear and fascination that accompanied the introduction of technological innovations, so well described in McLuhan's *Mechanical Bride* and Leo Marx's *Machine in the Garden*.[24]

Despite the mixture of public fear and fascination that met the expansion of technology and its networks, from the mid-19th century onwards, the expansion and consolidation of free trade, as well as the establishment of a global monetary system and mass movements of goods and people dictated the need to connect the world via the expansion of all kinds of networks. Railways, steamships, and the telegraph were slowly becoming part of daily life. Being "connected" to networks (domesticated water, railways, telegraph, etc.) became identified with being connected to the future, to progress, and ultimately to the possibility of a better society. Technological networks and constructions became the most prominent *material* expressions of progress in the urban sphere, the very embodiment of modernity. The more the urban environment would be filled with networks, the closer humankind would appear to approach the final goal of emancipation and freedom from the tyranny of nature (see Chapter 5). Being connected to technology meant *in itself* emancipation, was *in itself a way of* participating in the new society. Being excluded from the networks of technology, on the contrary, symbolized exclusion from the spheres of the powerful. Hence, the connection to the electricity or water networks of the city, or, similarly, the connection of one's home to a network of highways became a symbol of prestige and authority on the one hand and a battlefield of controversies and power struggles on the other.

These new technological marvels were staged in a series of world exhibitions in order to demonstrate the promise of progress to the public. The new technological temples were disguised with old and familiar forms and morphologies, and draped in imperial grandeur (Figure 3.a; see Chapters 5 and 6). This tempered the fear of the new and created an image of continuity, while their spectacular adornment suggested a triumphant future.

Asserting Technology's Power and Aesthetics

By the late 19th century, social reformers worked hand in hand with engineers to construct a better, more sanitized world.[25] The early threat imposed by the introduction of technology gradually began to give way to a "new deal" between man and technology, a deal based on the assumption that technology would improve the conditions of life. People not only accepted new technology and materials, but began to aestheticize them in new ways: they were no longer imitating historical forms, but were instead making a statement about the power of engineering science and reason. The Eiffel Tower, constructed for the 1889 Paris World Fair and "assembled out of steel girders, illuminated with electric lights, powered with dynamos and petrol engines, linked by copper wires,"[26] became the iconic statement of technology's duty to impose its own aesthetics. For Eiffel himself, the tower expressed "its own unique beauty"[27] and, despite the original decision to tear it down after the exhibition, it remained there, dominating the Parisian landscape as a triumph of engineering and

Fig. 3.a Water cathedrals: Abbey Mills Pumping Station, London. A Classic example of Gothic industrial architecture, built by Joseph Bazalgette between 1865 and 1868. Reproduced by kind permission of the Guildhall Library, Corporation of London.

technology finally asserting its own special aesthetics. Similarly, the factory Peter Behrens designed and built in Berlin in 1908 for the AEG company marked the beginning of a period when the urban technological dowry marked its own aesthetics in the urban landscape.

Central to the late 19th century public's technology frenzy and fascination with technological myths and urban utopias was the state's role as a facilitator of growth and a promoter of technological change and innovation.[28] Technological innovation was expected to assist not only with capital expansion, but also with improving the rapidly deteriorating living conditions of the working class, which were causing social unrest. The horrid living conditions in 19th century industrial cities, in combination with poor sanitary conditions, culminated in serious social upheavals such as the Paris Commune in 1871 and the 1889 London Dock Strike. In addition to the social unrest, the growth of epidemic diseases such as cholera and typhus (two cholera epidemics hit London, in 1831 and again in 1848–49)[29] made the quest for urban sanitation and rationalization inevitable. Out of this emerged the sanitation movement in the 1840s. Chadwick embarked on his mission to link cleanliness with water supply with the full support of the state and urban elites. Coley[30] reports that the Medical Officer of the Public Health authorities in London recognized that the importance of engineers was on a par with that of the medical profession. Urban water supply and sewerage networks began to penetrate the city (along with rail and telegraph) while dam, water tower, and reservoir constructions (the urban dowry) accompanied that development.

The urban sanitation conquest brought water squarely into the sphere of money, cultural capital, and power relations, as detailed in Chapter 4. The commodified domestication of water also redefined representations of the body and bodily relations along class and gender lines. It announced the withdrawal of the bodily hygiene of the urban elite from the public or semi-public sphere and its retreat into the privacy and intimacy of the bathroom and the toilet, while it allowed for an extra mark of distinction of class and gender: the deodorized body of the new urban elites was distinguished from the smelly peasant and sweaty proletariat, and, as Swyngedouw notes, the perfumed body of women was distinguished from that of men.[31]

At the same time that the "back to nature" movement, with its garden city utopias, was proposing an anti-urban solution to urban problems, the urban environment was saturated with networks that would make the city at least as healthy as the countryside. Early modernity's technological faith in a universal justice under the equalizing and totalizing powers of technology was widely held. Urban networks and connections not only sustained this faith but also *visualized* the ideology of emancipation through progress

in everyday urban experience. Urban space became saturated with pipelines, cables, tubes, and ducts of various sizes and colors; things that celebrated the mythic images of early modernity, literally carrying the idea of
progress into the urban domain and providing the confirmation that the
road to a better society was under construction and paved with networks.
They soon became personifications of progress and were marveled at. In
short, they became fetishized, making Louis Aragon note in 1926:

> Painted brightly with English or invented names, possessing just
> one long, supple arm, a luminous faceless head, a single foot and a
> numbered wheel in the belly, the petrol pumps sometimes take on
> the appearance of the divinities of Egypt.[32]

Not only were networks of technology fetishized as the material expressions of the ideology of progress. Along with the networks, the elements
of the built environment that supported their functional role (water
towers, power stations, reservoirs, pumping stations, etc.)—what we have
called the urban dowry of networks—were also fetishized. As Portaliou
argues: "[t]he proliferation of phantasmagorical forms in public spaces
encloses the aura of art and the content of fantasy and senses within
the commodity's pitiless power, hidden behind the phantasmagoria".[33]
Michael Ondaatje's historical novel *In the Skin of a Lion* tried to retro-
spectively capture the process as it occurred at modernity's height. He tells
of Commissioner Harris' dream of an aestheticized "palace of purification" (a water pump), which amounts to a shrine to progress in all its
fetishistic beauty:

> From across the province the subcontractors brought in their
> products and talents to build a palace for water.... Harris has
> dreamed the marble walls, the copper-banded roofs. He pulled
> down Victoria Park Forest and the essential temple swept up in its
> place.... The architect Pomphrey modelled its entrance on a Byzan-
> tine city gate, and the inside of the building would be an image of
> an ideal city.[34]

The urban dowry became conspicuous in cities during late modernity.
These concrete shrines embodying the networks stuck out of the city
landscape; they provided the best form of landmarks in the image of the
city and became the "stuff" of artistic renditions of the cityscape, such as
Becher and Becher's photographic projects of water towers.[35] Their beauty
and fascinating character was no longer achieved through ornamental
display; it lay instead, in the promise they were carrying for a better future

and a more equal society. As Plaskovitis notes, the urban dowry of technology networks gained a life of its own, became a thing in itself and for itself:

> Oh yes! Ultimately, the dam had a deep consciousness of its purpose! It must have been so well aware of the fact that it was a dam, a fatal existence, dividing existence, in order to be able to show itself off the way it did that night—for the first time, that night—in front of the engineer's eyes.[36]

For those marvels of technological innovation and urban progress that were part of the networks but situated outside the urban area (e.g., dams, hydroelectric stations, etc.), guided tours and spectacles were organized to visit and admire them, to pay homage to the constructions that would transform people's lives. Visiting dams was a very popular activity in the early 20th century and remained popular until the late 1960s. It was indeed a quasi-religious experience, with people traveling hundreds of miles away to bow in front of dams in the middle of nowhere. Equally, boat trips through the sewerage system of Paris used to be a prestigious middle class activity during late 19th and early 20th centuries.[37]

Fetish vs. Wish Image or…the Commodity in the Market vs. the Commodity on Display

The phantasmagoria of and fascination with technological networks suggests that they became fetishized in a double sense.

First, in a Marxist sense, these networks were instrumental in reifying social relations. The fascination with technology and technological constructions in and of themselves made progress appear to be merely a matter of construction, of technological innovation and of connection. The fetish role of networks and the emphasis put on the new and the innovative masked the underlying relations of production and social power relations, which remained symptomatically the same.

Second, in the way Walter Benjamin would define the fetish, they became wish images, objects of delight and desire in themselves, signs of a better society that was yet to arrive. Where Marx used "phantasmagoria" to describe the fetish character of commodities in the market, Benjamin was interested in the commodity *on display,* in its representational value. "Everything desirable from sex to social status could be transformed into commodities as fetishes-on-display that held the crowd enthralled even when personal possession was far beyond reach. Indeed, an unattainably high price tag only enhanced a commodity's symbolic value".[38] In their fetish role, networks and their nodal infrastructures were not just carrying water, electricity, etc. into the city, but also embodied the promise and the dream of a good society. The cathedrals of progress represented, displayed, and celebrated the aestheticized dreams of tomorrow's utopia.

The desire to connect to them went beyond the desire to acquire the utility; it was a desire to connect to progress, to a better society, to human emancipation. Their display kept the dream alive, kept their phantasmagoric character vibrant; the city itself was the shop window for their display. It is the *materiality* of the fetish object, infused with a utopian dream, that permits the visualization of the dream itself. Despite their failure to deliver the promised better society, technology and networks became wish images for a better society that could be anticipated.[39] Technology as the *means* to achieve a better society was mistaken for the *actualization* of that better society. Urban technologies and technology networks were among the most prominent material expressions of the process whereby "[c]ommodity fetishes and dream fetishes become indistinguishable".[40]

But it is precisely this second element of fetishized desire that would eventually erode and subvert the fetish character associated with their commodified reification. This subversion was expressed in material and visual terms within cities, and transformed the very experience of urbanity in profound ways. The fetishized objects of desire—embodied in networks and enshrined in their urban dowry—became *eidola*, idols adored in and of themselves. Marveling at networks, dams, or water towers as embodiments of urban emancipation obscured the exploitation of living labor and the socio-ecological transformation involved in the process of their production. Stripping those objects of their social meaning left them as just idols, phantom-like material expressions of a myth of progress and an ideology of automatic emancipation that never came. However, as Benjamin argued, "once the initial hollowing out of meaning has occurred this meaning can at any time be removed in favour of any other".[41] Indeed, as we shall see in the section that follows, the subversion of technology networks' social meaning, the reification of the social relations of their production, and the inscription within them of an ideology of progress were products of the tumultuous reordering of modernity in the 20th century.

Modernity Recast (1918–1960)

The Paris International Exhibition of 1900 not only familiarized the world with technology; it also familiarized European engineers with the wonders of Taylor's experimentation in "scientific management" in the United States. After WWI, the economies of European countries, badly affected by wars, turned to the principles of scientific management.[42] The "Americanization" of European industries continued until the dawn of WWII. However, for a short period of time during the interwar period, hope revived as the modernist dream extended from rationalizing public (urban) space to also planning and building private happiness. The quest for technology moved from the sphere of public works and city networks to the factory system and to the home, introducing new relationships between man and machine.[43] The "key characteristics of the machine" (such as functionality, efficiency) were translated into the urban and domestic sphere, where through design and architecture, emerged a new way of living[44] (see Chapters 4 and 7). Le Corbusier's *Citrohan House* (1922) was named and designed after the car Citröen, and became the iconic example of the house as "a machine for living in". Schutte-Lihotzky's *Frankfurt Kitchen* also translated the factory's functionality into the domestic space.

At the same time (as we will see in the Chapter 4) the process of rationalizing, sanitizing and cleansing the city with the aid of technology also expanded from the sphere of the public to the private and domestic sphere. With the aid of technology, buildings and people alike would become individualized, sanitized, and disconnected from each other and from social and natural processes. It was no longer in the urban (public) sphere where emancipation potentially resided and could be enacted, but rather in the utopia of the private home, the island of internal connections where everything arrived, and from where everything left. The domestic sphere took over the ideologies of the urban and reinterpreted them, creating a new ideology (and a new promise) which evolved around the belief that the myth, the desire, and the wonder should be searched for in the domestic, the individual, the disconnected, the isolated, the suburban. The promise of emancipation and freedom resided in the intimacy of the detached house. The perfect house would be clear, pure, functional, safe, the perfect "machine for living in", protected from the anomie of the outside, the urban. It became, as Davis called it, the "prison house".[45] The separation between production and reproduction, between thing and social relations, and between commodity and nature was perfecting its cultural and aesthetic shape. The realm of reproduction was where fulfillment resided and happiness was constructed. The 19th century idea of the sanitized, piped, wired, plumbed city was to be extended to the idea of the sanitized, piped, wired, plumbed house—the classic icon of 1950s and 1960s advertisements for home durables and home style—which promised, once again, the final delirious satisfaction of our dreams and desires.

The Subversion of the Old Fetish

While the factory assembly line—as practice and metaphor—permeated every aspect of peoples' lives (from the city itself, which was designed and planned after the machine; to their place of work; to their "mechanized homes" back to the mechanized recreation and shopping spaces), there was a flipside to the intimate relationship between Man and Technology: The futurist movement represented the machine as erotic, but also, as violent and domineering. Once put into the hands of the employer, technology came to determine the movements and timing of workers. An industrial worker reported in 1937:

> I suddenly realize in one senzation that there is no escape. It is all unavoidably real and painful. How much energy I must expend today has been predetermined by my employer.[46]

The introduction of assembly line production techniques was followed by strikes and the demand for the 8-hour working day.[47] This marked the beginning of the realization that the technological fix might not actually realize the dream of freedom and progress. Both Fritz Lang's *Metropolis* and Chaplin's *Modern Times* became cultural expressions of this creeping doubt that the realization of the materiality of technology might not necessarily bring with it the mythic images and imagineered utopias that surrounded it. The familiarization with technology and technological forms started revealing its fetish character:

> [t]he shop is beautiful. Machines, blue steel, huge piles of stock. Interesting patterns of windows are darkened by the early hour. This is the impression one gets before he becomes a part of the thing. The beauty is perceivable then. The unbiased observer cannot relate it to the subjective outlook he later acquires.[48]

As modernity progressed, shattering conventional understandings of space and time,[49] the emancipatory powers allegedly inhered in urban technology began to fade away. The contradictions and tensions of capitalist modernization increasingly revealed that at the end of the day, technological innovation and progress were profiting only those who had control over the means of production. At the same time, labor was turned into an appendage to the idea and practice of progress. It became abundantly clear that, although technology networks *did* deliver the promised material in the form of commodified goods, they somehow failed to deliver in their wake a better society.

Along with the modernist dream, the fetish character of networks and technological artifacts collapsed under the weight of unfulfilled promises. The once prominently visual statements of technology's emancipatory powers could no longer feed the urban dream and function as an urban fetish either in terms of reifying social relations or in terms of echoing desire and fascination. Jules Verne[50] in his 1863 futuristic account of 1960s Paris still sees giant water works and mesmerizing pumping stations along the banks of the Seine, and parallels them with the beating heart that satisfies the thirst of the city. In Verne's early modern projection of a late modern city, the marvellous technology of water supply is there for all to gaze at and contemplate. Dams, water towers, sewage systems, and the like are celebrated as glorious icons, carefully designed, ornamented, and prominently located in the city, testifying to the modern promise of progress.

However, by the 20th century, the symbolic and material shrines of progress had lost their mobilizing powers and began to disappear from the cityscape. Stripped from their ideological meaning, water towers, dams and plants became mere engineering constructs, often abandoned and dilapidated, while water flows also disappeared from the cityscape and from the eyes and imagination of the urban dweller. Of course, networks remained inevitably etched into the city fabric. While the ideology of the power of technology faded, urban networks and constructions were left behind in the cityscape, still prominently visible, but now sad material reminders of a promise that was never to be fulfilled (Figure 3.b). The ruins of a now outlived urban dream revealed, more clearly than ever before, the phantasmagoric nature of the artifact and the hidden scripting of their making. Once their initial social meaning and their symbolic representation was hollowed out, they became re-inscribed with a different meaning: that of the material embodiments of the failure of the emancipating project of modernity.

After World War II, the ambiguity and multiplicity of technological systems was accentuated. The link between technological progress and nazism took the material forms of Speer's buildings and autobahns and the Fordist logic of Hitler's extermination camps. The nuclear quagmire revealed that the revered technology harboured a decidedly destructive underbelly. Technology and progress remained inscribed in people's lives after World War II as a necessity rather than a desire or wish.

By the middle of the 20th century, cities in the industrialized world were left with the uncomfortable situation of being filled with material statements of an unfulfilled (and unfulfillable) promise, accentuated by two world wars and a period of economic depression. Urban technology networks and constructions became material embodiments of disillusionment.

Fig. 3.b Past glory and banalized presence. Once dominating the skyline, water towers today are dwarfed and suffocated by the city growing around them. Photograph: George Shoterioo.

With the patina of time added over them, urban technological cathedrals turned from landmarks into scrap heaps (Figure 3.b), rusting like the modern urban dream of emancipation and equality. Dams ceased being popular destinations for weekend excursions, and the once visually prominent technology networks started gradually disappearing underground or fell into ruin (Figure 3.b). It is only recently that 19th century urban technological cathedrals, the urban dowry of modernity (pumping stations, purification plants, reservoirs) were re-discovered and mummified as they became transformed into shopping centers, cultural destinations, or theme parks (Figure 3.c) with no reference to their previous history: the

Fig. 3.c Athens gas works plant, now turned into a cultural center. Photograph: George Shoterioo.

Tate Modern (previously a power station and currently a contemporary art museum) and the gas works in the centre of Athens (Gazi; it is now a culture center) are but a couple of examples of this trend.

Not only the urban dowry, but also networks themselves in all their forms and shapes (cables, pipes, aerials, etc.) were swept away as part of modernism's quest to rationalize urban space, giving way to a pure, clean, and transparent new urban form.[51] In New York City's skyline or in Northern European cities, one can no longer see any connection cables, aerials, or pipes. Conversely, in less developed countries, where modernity is still pretty much under construction, even in some parts of the European south, we can see, skylines filled with cables and aerials (Figures 3.d and 3.e).

By contrast, in the advanced capitalist world, the supply of water, electricity, gas, and information now appears to enter miraculously the domestic sphere, coming from nowhere in particular and from everywhere. Even garbage disposal has become a matter of throwing things in a hole in the wall, where both trash and smell miraculously disappear. For the urban dweller, the end of the process of garbage disposal is the moment when the bag is thrown into the hole. The underbelly of the city, the locus of the "uncanny"[52] (see also Chapter 4) remains a latent memory relayed to the unconscious presence of a dark underworld. The backyards with the garbage bins, and the underground sewerage pipes faded from view. People stopped traveling to see the glorious dam constructions erected during modernity's Zenith.

The rationalization of urban space and the eclipsing of the networks of production and distribution further severed the link between product and production process. It also contributed to a masking of the social relations through which the metabolic urbanization of water takes place. The veiled subterranean networking of water, electricity, and gas facilitated the severing of the intimate bond between use value, exchange value, and social power. The end of visible flows into the domestic sphere became

Fig. 3.d "Networked" skyline, Athens. Photograph: George Shoterioo.

Fig. 3.e Clear skyline, London. Photograph: Maria Kaika.

naturalized and inevitable, yet severed from any apparent connection to anywhere else (see Chapter 4).

Re-Scripting the Urban Dream

While 19th century technological cathedrals became banalized, and slowly turned into urban ruins, a new form of urban networked spatiality emerged. Urban and regional highways become the new phantasmagoric networked constructions, fitting into modernism's quest for speed and efficiency and linking privatized suburban spaces to the core of the city, but also to the countryside and to nature. Le Corbusier's planning visions brought forth a new world of sanitized urban mobility; the futurists loved speed and free movement; Robert Moses created New York City as a city of movement and provided direct links between the modern, networked, private home and places of consumption, leisure, and work, often literally by passing or overriding spaces of marginality and anomie, more often than not in the name of providing public access to nature (the beach, the rivers, parks, forests, etc.).[53]

The emergence of the private sphere as a space of freedom and emancipation; the new urban networks that supported access to and from the newly created private suburban paradises; and the newly created (commodified) "countryside" and places of mass consumption further eroded any visible connections between the urban and the domestic and eliminated clues to the production process connecting them. Regardless, high modernity with its crusade towards rationalization and clarity created a city of rhizomatic underground networks, which ceaselessly transform nature into city. The burial of networks was so successful that many of them are today undecipherable.[54] The ideal city, the new utopia, was clean and sanitized, both in visual and literary terms. Water, for example, as Latour and Le Bourhis[55] note, has become truly invisible, or has been turned systematically into something self-evident, an apparent triviality, located simply at the mouth of the tap. This "silencing" of water and other networked relations rendered it into what it is not— H_2O. The new urban fetish, then, lay, amongst others, in the apparent aesthetic disconnection from all the old, dirty, unsafe, and ugly networks.

The disconnection between the private and the socio-ecological was taken to its extreme form in the disconnection of dwelling from the city itself through suburbanization. The production of a clean, harmonious, natural environment that would have no reference (aesthetic or functional) whatsoever to the production relations underneath this clarity, completed the severing of the ties between surface appearance and the underground flows and networks. All this mess that necessarily accompanies the production of any kind of clarity was literally swept underneath the carpet, relegated to the underworld. Of course, as Boyer notes, "[t]he real city, never actually displayed, gradually disappears from view: its chaos, its class distinctions, its snares and vices, all of these lay outside the circular frame beyond the spectator's gaze".[56] The mess, the dirt, the underbelly of the city became invisible both socially and environmentally, banned from everyday consciousness. The myth of progress, which had produced mesmerizing urban technological cathedrals whose aesthetics belied the social realities of the industrial city, was no longer required. The city had by now turned into a space of consumption and spectacle—a place where there is nothing else but the spectacle of the market.[57] The city as a flow of goods and services and a process became increasingly invisible, while the image of the city of speed, a flow of people and vehicles came to dominate the urban landscape.

Making the Visible Invisible

No matter how rational, sanitized, and clean (both in symbolic and literary terms) our cities have become, the "urban trash" in the form of networks, dirt, sewerage, pipes, and homeless people lurks underneath the city, in the corners, at the outskirts, bursting out on occasion in the form of rats, disease, homelessness, garbage piles, polluted waters, floods, and bursting pipes. They remain stubborn reminders of the materiality of the networked city and undermine its smooth facade. Despite the quest for clarity, purity, and sanity that was prominent throughout high modernity (or, rather, precisely because of this quest), the underlying contradictions of urban life, the ones that actually make it possible for clarity to exist, i.e., the urban "trash" and underlying invisible networks—both inorganic (sewerage, water pipes) and organic (homeless people)—remain markedly present. The dystopian underbelly of the city that at times springs up in the form of accumulated waste, dirty water, pollution, or social disintegration produces a sharp contrast when set against the increasingly managed clarity of the urban environment. The contradictions cannot be successfully contained or displaced.

Environmental problems are the acute expressions of this. They are directly linked to urbanization and to the function of cities.[58] Whether we consider water, energy, food or clean air, socio-environmental issues are city-centric, and their unpredictability exemplifies the fallacy of the myth of the perfectly managed city. As Raymond Williams[59] pointed out in *The Country and the City*, the transformation of nature and the social relations inscribed therein are inextricably connected to the process of urbanization. As Harvey puts it, the dialectic of the environment and urbanization consolidates a particular set of social relations through "an ecological transformation which requires the reproduction of those relations in order to sustain it".[60] The commodity relation veils and hides the multiple socio-ecological processes of domination/subordination and exploitation/repression that feed the capitalist urbanization process and turn the city into a polymorphous metabolic socio-environmental process that stretches from the immediate environment to the remotest corners of the globe. Indeed, the apparently self-evident commodification of nature that fundamentally underpins a market-based society not only obscures the social relations of power inscribed therein, but also permits the disconnection of the perpetual flows of transformed and commodified nature from its inevitable foundation, i.e., the transformation of nature.[61] If we take

London, for example, there is a great story to be told about the unmapped and untraceable water supply and sewerage networks that dwell underneath the city, hidden most of the time, but revealing their existence in unpredictable ways and moments (recently in the form of problematic water quality in some areas, high leakage rates, bursting pipes, internationalization of water companies, and "fat cat" water company directors).

Walter Benjamin[62] identified the urban underworld with the urban hell that exists underneath the urban splendor. For him, everything about urban life was hell disguised as heaven. However, we should perhaps search instead for a dialectics whereby heaven *requires* its hell in order to exist.[63] Despite efforts to manage and control the city, it remains a realm carved out of the dialectics between clean and dirty, justice and injustice, high society and underworld, lofts and basements, heaven and hell. In fact, heaven can establish itself as such only by contradistinction to a certain hell. The urban paradise needs to exploit organic and inorganic, human and nonhuman urban trash in order to sustain itself. It is this dialectics that not only makes the city disaster-prone,[64] but also produces these dazzling spaces that are always up for grabs, open to continuous struggles and renegotiations, permitting change and new lifestyles; a space where heaven and hell coexist, and where it is up to human beings to choose between struggling for emancipation and freedom, or falling under the spell of heavenly dreams.

The dialectics between heaven and hell that produces urban space is what I will turn to next. I will follow water as it enters the "space envelope" of the domestic sphere and see how the invisible networks that exist outside and underneath the modern house contribute to the production of the detached, self-contained, heavenly space of the home, while at the same time—and precisely because of their opaque character—they constitute the domestic uncanny, which surfaces at moments of crisis, threatening the costly and laboriously obtained domestic bliss.

CHAPTER **4**

Nature as the Urban Uncanny

This is the true nature of home—it is the place of peace: the shelter not only from all injury, but from all terror, doubt and division. In so far as it is not this, it is not home; so far as the anxieties of the outer life penetrate into it, and the inconsistently—minded, unloved, or hostile society of the outer world is allowed by either husband or wife to cross the threshold, it ceases to be a home; it is then only a part of the outer world, which you have roofed over and lighted fire in.

J. Ruskin, Sesame and Lilies (1891: 136-37, cited in R. Sennett,
The Conscience of the Eye, 1990: 20)[1]

The Dwelling Spaces of Individual Freedom

The idea of the house as a means of separating the inside from the outside, nature from human beings, the public from the private sphere, has existed since antiquity. For Heidegger, the house is understood "as the most primitive drawing of a line that produces an inside opposed to an outside".[2] The debate as to whether this line is (or should be) rigid and unsurpassable, or indeed, as to whether it should exist at all, also goes back to the antiquity. In Plato's *Republic*, the *polis,* the public sphere, is defined as the opposite of the private sphere. Again, in *Statesman,* Plato juxtaposed critically the public sphere of the *agora* to the private sphere of the house-hold (*oikos*) and argued that both realms are eligible for political praxis. It was only from the Enlightenment onwards, that the construction of the private space of the modern (bourgeois) house as isolated, apolitical, and

51

separate from the public sphere was understood as a particularly positive development in the Western world. As the opening quote by Ruskin demonstrates, the right to a private space became closely linked to the idea of individual freedom (of the white Western male subject) that constituted the core of Enlightenment thinking, and access to an isolated private sphere became part of a broader social project of emancipation.[3] Individual freedom became the sacred *principle* of the modernizing Western world, and the individualized space of the private house became its sacred *space.* Through this social process, the *house* (a material construction, an edifice) was turned into *the home* (a place imbued with cultural and ideological meaning). The dwelling space of the modern (bourgeois) individual became constructed not only as a line separating the inside from the outside (a house), but also as the epitome, the spatial inscription of the idea of individual freedom, a place liberated from fear and anxiety, a place supposedly untouched by social, political, and natural processes, a place enjoying an autonomous and independent existence: a home. In the opening quote of this chapter, Ruskin offers a definition of the "true nature of home," by singling out two basic qualities that a house should possess in order to become a home. Both qualities have to do with the capacity of the edifice to keep outside: (1) social processes and social relations (crime, socially excluded groups, homelessness, undesired others, etc.), but also (2) natural processes and natural elements (dust, cold or polluted air, rain, dirt, sewage, smog, etc.)

Thus, according to Ruskin, the modern house becomes the modern home (an autonomous protected utopia) through a dual practice of exclusion: through ostracizing the undesired social as well as the undesired natural elements and processes. The social and spatial implications of the first of these preconditions for the construction of the autonomous modern Western home (the exclusion of social processes) have been analyzed and detailed in numerous studies in geography, architecture, anthropology and sociology.[4] However, the socio-spatial implications of the second precondition (i.e., the exclusion of nature and of socio-natural processes) have not been adequately researched or documented.[5] This is exactly the focus of this chapter. Following up on the analysis of the separation between nature and society in Chapter 2, and the investigation of the spatial implications of this separation in the city/nature relationship in Chapter 3, I investigate further the materiality versus ideological boundaries between the natural, the urban, and the domestic by using, again, one natural element—water—as a vehicle.

I will first examine the historical geographical process through which nature became scripted as "the other" to the private space of the bourgeois home in Western societies and how this particular form of alienation contributed to the conceptual construction of the home as a space autonomous and independent both from natural processes and from the urban domain and became constructed as a distinct and autonomous "space envelope."[6]

Scripting Natural Processes as "The Other"

Modernity emerges from the belief that man is fundamentally a clean body.

N. Lahiji and D. S. Friedman, Plumbing (1997)[7]

Water, like other natural elements (gas, oil, etc.), is produced, purified, standardized, and commodified. As water is abstracted, dammed, channelled, stored, distilled, and chlorinated, its physical and social qualities change as it inevitably becomes subject to social relations of production. In short, water becomes a modern "hybrid" (see Chapter 2): neither purely natural nor purely a human product; something that is *materially* produced as a commodity (and thus subject to social relations of production), but *socially* constructed as part of nature (and thus supposedly alien to social processes).

In the Western world, water was traditionally searched for outside the house, often outside the settlement area, and brought into the house through painstaking efforts, predominantly carried out on the part of women, a practice that can still be found in non–Western societies.[8] However, through a historically and geographically specific process of domestication and commodification (part and parcel of Western industrialization and urbanization), access to water in the Western world has been made as easy and simple as turning a tap inside the private space of one's home. The domestication of water changed the traditional places where this element can be found. As water travels through a myriad of intricate physical socio-spatial networks (channels, reservoirs, pipes, taps) from spaces of production (dams, wells, reservoirs, pumping stations, purifying stations) to spaces of consumption/reproduction (city, home), it is not only its physical and social qualities that change, but also its relationship to space. Water's dwelling space shifts geographically from the countryside (rivers, lakes, boreholes) to the city (public ornamental and drinking fountains) and finally to the house (taps, baths, private swimming pools, private ornamental fountains, ponds).

Although the incorporation of urban water into the economic mode of production had been taking place since medieval times, the most far-reaching changes in the character, treatment and spaces of water took place during the 19th and early 20th century. During that period, the increasing incorporation of water into the economic and social life of expanding urban areas, combined with the discovery of the link between water and epidemics, generated a science, economy, and practice of treating and purifying water. This practice led to the material production of purified drinking water as a new modern hybrid; and to the discursive construction of two distinct types of water: "good water" (clean, processed, controlled, commodified) and "bad water" (dirty, grey, metabolized, nonprocessed, noncommodified). The first category includes water for drinking, bathing, swimming, baptizing, etc. while the second comprises untreated metabolized water, to be found in city rivers, lakes, rainwater, sewerage, etc. It was therefore established that before water is allowed to make contact with the human body, it has to be controlled and mastered, processed and produced, like almost every other form of nature. While contact with bad water was considered to be deleterious, if not harmful, to the human body, good water became the cleansing, purifying, healthy element (Figures 4.a and 4.b).

The material and discursive production of two distinct kinds of water meant that access to water became mediated by increasingly complex social and material relations umpired by the market. The changes in the physical and social character of water went hand in glove with the creation and allocation of specific spaces for the use of "good" and "bad" water. A set of new spaces (such as swimming pools, spas, and private bathrooms) were created and specially allocated to the interaction between the human body and "good" water. In a way, these new spaces were a post-Enlightenment Western reinterpretation of the concept of the Arabic or the Roman bath, within a capitalist context: privatized and/or commodified. Getting in touch with water in the form of bathing in a bathtub, swimming in the newly devised and constructed temples for swimming, or purifying mind and body in the middle class's favorite spas was considered to be a safe and sanitizing activity. In contrast, getting in touch with water in an uncontrolled and unregulated manner (swimming in rivers and lakes, getting wet in the rain, or drinking untreated water) became a negative and potentially harmful activity.

Thus, while water in the city became a source of threat, something to be controlled or eradicated from the cityscape, water in the house became exactly the opposite: the purifying, cleansing element, proudly displayed by the middle classes who could afford to have it running inside their home. The *hydrophobia* developed towards the uncontrolled waters of the public (urban) domain, was paralleled by a *hydrophilia* towards the controlled

Fig. 4.a "Good" water. Photograph from an Orthodox Baptism. Photograph: George Shoterioo.

waters of the private space of one's home, which by the late 19th century included its designated wet rooms (bathroom and kitchen) as indicators of social status.[9] In Britain, middle class houses began to feature private bathrooms from the 1880s, and by the 1930s, they had become a common feature of working class houses too, while the water closet became a requirement in 1936.[10] In Paris, the bourgeoisie started installing private bathrooms in the first decades of the 19th century, and after 1850 new "bathing institutions" appeared in the popular quarters of the city. By the mid-20th century the distribution of water in private houses had become a

Fig. 4.b "Salus populi suprema lex"; the polluted river Thames with John Edwards, owner of Southwark Water Works, sitting on a metal hemisphere in the middle of the river while Southwark residents shout complaints. Etching by George Cruikshank, 1832. Reproduction by kind permission of the Guildhall Library, Corporation of London, Satirical Print collection, London Archive, record number 20319.

common feature.[11] In Athens, by 1928 all new apartment buildings were being built with a fitted bathroom, offering the delights and pleasures of domestic water supply to the emerging middle classes.[12] In the United States, 93.5% of urban dwellings had running water by 1940.[13]

As availability of and access to commodified water increased in the domestic sphere, availability of "good" (that is, drinking) water in the public sphere became confined to the past in the Western world. Public fountains, for example, slowly disappeared from the urban domain in the Western world, corresponding to the reconceptualization of water as a commodity, while they still remain an integral part of urban life in the Islamic world, corresponding to the Islamic law defining water as the undeniable right of people and animals alike.[14] Indeed, in Western metropolises publicly available, free-of-charge, clean drinking water is a rare species. The simple ethnographic test of walking into any coffee/sandwich bar in London asking for a free glass of (tap) water, invariably results in a frown and a perplexed look followed by: "We only sell bottled water." Until recently, on some European flights one could not get a glass of water unless one were prepared to pay for it; and nightclub owners would block the cold taps in the bathrooms to prevent patrons from drinking free water. This latter practice has only been made illegal in the light of people dying from dehydration after taking ecstasy tablets. In January 2003, free water availability was made a legal requirement by the US Department of Gaming and Racing.[15] Before that, selling drinking water had become a major source of profit, as an interview with a nightclub owner for the *Columbusalive* magazine indicates: "These days the club sells as much water as beer, at $2.75 a bottle…. they drink a hell of a lot of water, and I charge as much for water as I do with beer."[16]

Along with publicly available "good" drinking water, uncontrolled, dirty "bad" water was also slowly but steadily eradicated from the visible urban domain. In London during the 19th century,[17] for example, over a dozen rivers were covered by streets in an effort to rationalize urban space and to eliminate the threat of epidemics. All European and most North American cities experienced a similar process. Roger Keil, in his excellent book on the urbanization of Los Angeles documents the loss and rediscovery of the LA river, while Latour and Hermant record the existence of an invisible Paris.[18] In sum, the bourgeois home became the natural space to look for freely flowing good water and a conceptual distinction, if not separation, was generated between the urban as the place where "bad" water dwells (together with other urban anomies) and the protected space of the home where "good" water emerges in its commodified form. "Good" nature (purified water, air conditioning, electricity, etc.) became part of (and a basic precondition for the construction of) the protected inside of the modern home. At the same time, the domestically metabolized "bad" nature (dirty water, polluted air, sewage) became part of the outside, "the other", the antipode to the comfortable, protected inside of the home. Thus, while modernity produced nature as a commodity and made it an intrinsic part of modern life, it simultaneously conceptually constructed nature as an externalized "other" for which "socially constructed places" were created. This double process of casting processed nature outside the modern home, while allowing controlled commodified nature inside, reinforced the ideological construction of the private sphere as the utopia of the autonomous and the protected, and of the modern private individual as clean, pure, and free of fear and anxiety.

The conceptual distinction between good and bad water also perpetuated (and in many ways accentuated) the gender distinction related to its handling. Using water in the household had traditionally been the task of women, whereas handling and taming water outside the house (from field irrigation to dam construction and the conquest of the sea) was traditionally the task of men. Illich chronicles how, from washing the floor to cleaning the dead, women's perceived "deep connection to nature" had given them jurisdiction over handling water in the domestic sphere.[19] Women's traditional task of collecting water for domestic use from wells or springs constituted (and still does in many parts of the world) an extra burden on their already heavy daily schedule[20] but it simultaneously produced a predominantly female domain around the well, the public fountain or the river, and, in many cases, provided one of the few opportunities for women to socialize freely. However, when water was domesticated in the Western world, the traditional gender distinction around handling water did not change: it was again the wet rooms of the bourgeois home that became the place of women in the domestic spatial arrangements that accompanied the social division of labor, thus endorsing the confinement of women to the domestic sphere.[21] Indeed, kitchens and bathrooms are often depicted in modern (Western) art and literature as the "kingdom" of women, as the ritual of handling water and cleaning the home remains one of the few domains where women's judgment and expertise remains unquestioned.

> Never before had a woman worshiped her home the way I worshiped mine. My grandmother used to say: "I like cleaning my home by myself".... Like my grandmother used to do, I too, threw away the mop pole and fell down on my knees to mop the floor with my own palms, with devotion. And while mopping I

was caressing it [the floor]…the way a mother would caress her ill child.[22]

The above passage comes from *The Twirling of the Circle*, a semi-autobiographical late 20th-century novel written by Maria Iordanidou and set in postwar Athens. The narrator, a woman who works hard to support her family, takes both pride and pleasure in making time to clean her home. In an almost perverse manner, cleaning her home becomes an act of worship as it becomes identified with caring for her family. What Rose termed the "elevated status of housekeeping"[23] is expressed here in the identification of an act of worship with that of cleaning one's home and has even permeated the language. In the original Greek text, the word λατρεύω signifies both "to worship" and "to clean." Thus, the first sentence can be translated as either: "[n]ever before had a woman *worshiped* her home the way I *worshiped* mine"; or: "[n]ever before had a woman *cleaned* her home the way I *cleaned* mine." Thus, the act of worshiping one's home (and family) collapses linguistically with that of cleaning one's home, indicating the extent to which the role of women as home cleaners and water handlers is socially and culturally embedded.

However, it is always "good" water alone that becomes women's, and it does so only after it enters the protected "space envelope" of the domestic sphere (Figure 4.c). In contrast, the process of taming "bad" water as well as that of producing "good" water (the construction of dams, wells, aqueducts, the irrigation of fields, etc.) remains predominantly the task of men. In short, the gender division between places and activities of production and reproduction was itself reproduced through the process of domestication of water in the Western world.[24]

The control of nature's water also contributed to the production of the new set of marks of social distinction that could be embodied by the modern individual. As Swyngedouw contends,[25] the olfactorial segregation between class and gender (rich smelling clean/poor smelling foul, women smelling of roses/men smelling of tobacco) was made easier with the domestication of water. As Sibley argues,[26] the social imperative to distinguish between good and bad, pure and impure became carried by the body itself, by the skin, the *epidermis*. If, however, we were to elaborate further on Sibley's analysis, we could argue that this epidermalization first has to be materially produced. In order for the skin, the *epidermis*, to be able to carry the socially constructed marker of pure/impure, perfumed/malodorous, a whole set of material connections have to be laid in place and maintained. The body remains the carrier of the symbolic marks of social distinction, but space (such as underground urban space) is the carrier of the material constructions and connections that make this symbolic distinction possible. Thus, the separation of the city and the home as two

Fig. 4.c Developing an intimate relationship between women and domesticated water. Illustration from a 1892 French calendar. Buisson, 1991, Périscope, *L'Usage domestique de l'eau*, p.29. ©PEMF, France.

of modernity's distinct "spatial envelopes", is not just an expression of epidermalized distinctions of social status; it is one of the very mechanisms that enables these distinctions to exist. This makes space more than just a parameter in the social construction of the body, as this is documented in Pile's excellent analysis *The Body and the City*.[27] The dwelling places of modernity embody the material connections that make the social construction of bodies possible, by first materially constructing "others", in the form of natural or social processes, and then keeping them outside.

Keeping "The Other" Outside

> The "elements" lose their natural determinations, including their sitting and situation, as they are incorporated into the "space envelopes" which are fast becoming the social building-blocks of space.
>
> *H. Lefebvre, The Production of Space (1974/1994: 329)*[28]

The previous section examined the socio-spatial processes through which water and the social relations involved in its production became "the other" to the private space of home. This section examines how the exclusion of this "other" (in the form of natural or social processes) is in fact central to creating the sense of familiarity, safety, and isolation inside the modern home. In other words, how this act of exclusion becomes an act of creating space—the private, isolated space of the home[29]—and how it contributes to the conceptual construction of nature and the home as distinct and autonomous "space envelopes," as Lefebvre put it.

In the opening quote of this chapter, Ruskin defines the "true nature of home" as "a shelter from anomie and division." Dirt, fear, and anxiety stemming from social and natural processes are supposed to have been exiled from the isolated private space of the home and instead confined (if not relegated) to the urban space or to nature. Thus, excluding socionatural processes as "the other" becomes a prerequisite for the construction of the familiar space of the home. The inside becomes safe, familiar, and independent not only by excluding rain, cold, and pollution, but also through keeping fear, anxiety, social upheaval, and inequality outside.

Of course, the practice of keeping natural elements outside the home is not particularly new; but rather goes hand in glove with the whole history and *raison d' être* of architecture. The purpose of building a home through human history has been precisely that: to create a familiar environment by establishing a high level of control over the interaction between the edifice and its environment; to construct an inside in opposition to an existing outside. The ancient Greek word for household *οικος (oékos)* has the same root as the word for the familiar *οικειος (oekéos)*. However, what distinguishes the modern home from earlier forms of "dwellings" is that never before had the level of control over the outside been so high or achieved so fully as in modern buildings.

Producing a spatial outlet for Enlightenment ideas, modernist planning and building launched a crusade to impose clarity between functions, to distinguish between private and public space, and to separate nature from the built environment. It did so by establishing practices of control and networks of distribution of both produced nature and social relations. Epitomizing this attitude, the famous *Charter of Athens* that came out of the *IV Congrés International d' Architecture Modèrne* (CIAM, 1933), Le Corbusier and Jean Giraudoux depicted home, work, recreation, and traffic as distinct components of modern living, while asserting the need to engage with technological innovation. To this end, the laying down of a sophisticated set of networks for the flow of socio-natural processes (water, sewage, electricity, gas, etc.), was complemented by the laying down of a set of rules for the flow of socio-economic processes (zoning of urban functions and land use, movement of pedestrians and vehicles, distinction between places of production, reproduction and recreation, etc.). Technological advancement (plumbing, central heating, air conditioning, etc.) made the exclusion and control of natural elements more efficient and sophisticated than ever before, ensuring that the modern home would function safely, securely, and autonomously. Unwelcome social and natural elements (from sewage to homelessness) were exiled underneath or outside the modern home, below the streets and inside the walls, eliminated into underground passages, sent to a domain separate to that of the dwelling places of the modern individual. To do justice to modernist planning, it should be noted that its original aims were linked to social struggles for creating spaces that would act as a shelter away from the alienation of waged labor. Nevertheless, practices of modernist planning failed to open up space for everybody through the creation of safe private *and* public spaces. Instead, they succeeded in rendering the line that separates the inside from the outside, the public from the private, more solid than ever before, virtually impenetrable, at least at a discursive and representational level. A sublime visualization of this contradiction within modernity's creative destruction is Giovanni Battista Piranesi's (1720–1778) *Carceri* drawings. They are an early harbinger and a gothic representation of a modern world which opens up space and potentials for emancipation, only to reclose it and alienate its dwellers/inmates. According to Tafuri, Piranesi's drawings are expressions of "the new existential condition of human collectivity, liberated and condemned at the same time by its own reason."[30]

However, when we move from the discursive/representational level to the material/spatial foundations of the separation between public/private, nature/home, it can be argued that this same act of exclusion that separates and demarcates the inside from the outside in fact puts these two supposed opposites in a dialectical relationship of interdependence to each other, within which they are both sustained and continue to function. While the inside (the familiar) needs the outside (the unfamiliar) to construct and define itself as a distinct space, the excluded outside in turn functions by following the logic of the inside. In doing so, the outside always remains inside in a certain way, subject to the rules and the logic dictated by the inside: there can be no homelessness without an economic, political, and social process that produces the home as a commodity; no refugees without practices of exile from a country of origin; no margin without a center; no periphery without a core. As Wigley put it: "By being placed outside, the other is placed, domesticated, kept inside. To be excluded is to be subjected to a certain domestic violence."[31]

The Selective Porosity of the Modern Home

Social Processes

The exclusion of social processes is, according to Ruskin, the first basic precondition for the production of the modern home. However, this section will explore how the very act of trying to keep social processes outside inevitably puts this space (the home) into a dialectical relationship of *dependence on/autonomy from* the very processes that it tries to exclude. To start with, the material creation of an isolated private space, almost by definition puts significant claims on social (that is, public) space. The creation of protected, privately policed, and guarded domestic spaces depends upon the appropriation (and, in effect, destruction) of public (social) space, which becomes privatized. Davis presents the city as a continuous alternation between utopias of private policed green areas and dystopias of public areas or areas housing the socially excluded, while Deutsche[32] dwells on the same dialectic between private/public, exclusion/ inclusion and records how homelessness is cast out of practices of exclusion; the marginal places claimed by the homeless are what is leftover from the process of carving out places for the private sphere. Spatial claims made by the private sphere (domestic or other) are always translated into the deprivation of the public sphere from these same spaces and the reduction of spaces of the margin. Anderson and Jacobs[33] offer an excellent account of a social movement against private claims over public spaces in Australia, concluding that both public and private space should be understood as sociospatial constructions, rather than natural categories.

Thus, contrary to the first of Ruskin's claims, the creation of the private space of the home fails to offer shelter from division, since its very social and material production is predicated precisely upon practices of division. As for providing shelter from anomie (the second of Ruskin's claims), the modern home falls short of offering this as well: not only did it fail to exclude social anomie from its interior, it also ended up reproducing fragmentation and inequality inside it.[34] Through the process of division of labor and the allocation of different spaces to different users (stratified by gender, age, status, etc.) the social and gender inequalities, power relations and violence that were meant to be kept outside became reproduced within the "ideological prison" of the private space of the modern home.[35]

Natural Processes

The previous section examined the first precondition that Ruskin demarcated as necessary for the construction of the modern home (the exclusion of social processes) and exposed its contradictions. This section will turn to the second precondition (the exclusion of natural processes), in order to suggest that similar contradictions are in place with respect to the ideology of excluding natural processes as a prerequisite for constructing the private space of home.

To start with, it should be noted that natural elements are not in fact kept altogether outside the modern home; but rather are selectively allowed to enter after having undergone significant material and social transformations, through being produced, purified, and commodified. Polluted air and recycled water, for example, have to undergo a complex chemical and social process of purification before they are allowed to enter the domestic sphere of consumption. In fact, the more human activities transform nature, the more the intervention of technology (water purifiers, air conditioning, ionizers, etc.) becomes necessary in order to cancel the effects of this transformation and to render nature "good" again before it is allowed to enter the private home in the form of a commodity. Thus, although excluded ideologically, natural processes (just like social processes) remain connected materially to the inside of the home, constituting an integral part of its material production and its smooth function.

Yet, as we have seen, the function of the modern home as safe and autonomous is predicated not only upon the entry of "good" nature, but also upon the ideological and visual exclusion of "bad" nature. However, this ostracized "bad" nature is largely the byproduct of the metabolism of the "good" nature that is allowed inside: sewage is the byproduct of domestic water consumption; urban smog is the result of the need to produce warmth inside one's home and to commute for miles in order to inhabit suburban domestic paradises. In fact, both the "good" nature that enters inside and the bad nature that is kept outside the modern home are socio-natural hybrids, transformed through human economic and social activity, and thus neither purely natural nor purely a human construct (see Chapter 2). Viewed in this light, the socially constructed categories of "good" and "bad" nature become blurred. The purified water that flows into the modern home is as much the product of the interaction between the physical environment and human beings as the water that flows out of the modern home in the form of sewage. The production and flow of both hybrid forms of water depend upon the existence of a complex set of material and social networks.

However, these material and social networks are visually excluded. The pipes and cables involved in the production of nature are kept away from the eyes of the home dweller, buried inside the walls of the modern home or underneath the modern city. Even the once iconic landmarks of modernist planning, the urban dowry of modernity (water towers, dams, pumping stations, power plants, gas stations, etc.) became invisible or banalized in the form of urban ruins (see Chapter 3). Thus, the function of the modern home as safe and autonomous is predicated not only upon the exclusion of "bad" nature from its premises, but also upon the visual exclusion of the networks and social relations that produce and transport "good" nature into the domestic and pump "bad" nature back into the urban domain. In short, the material and social networks involved in the production of "good" nature and in the metabolism of "bad" nature exist and operate in a way that serves the logic of the inside, yet remain invisible, hidden outside and underneath the modern home. In this way, the networks of production of the socio-natural hybrids that enter into and are expelled from the modern home, also constitute the "other," the "outside" to this modern institution. Although visually excluded and ideologically denied, these networks of socio-natural transformation that lie at the core of the production of the modern city also lie at the core of the production of the safety and familiarity of the modern home.

If, again, the case of domesticated water is used as an example, the above contradiction can be explored further. The presence of good water inside the house is based on the existence of a set of networks of, and connections to, both things (dams, reservoirs, pipes) and social power relations (struggles over the allocation of water, over policies of pricing and privatization) that exist outside the domestic sphere. All of the above elements are visually excluded from the sphere of everyday domestic life, yet they are organized in such a way that allows this inside to function supposedly autonomously. While the dweller experiences the familiarity and comfort of his/her domestic tap, bathtub, or swimming pool, the intricate set of networks that produce this bliss remains invisible to him/her, hidden underneath and outside the house. It is precisely this visual exclusion of production networks, of metabolized nature and of social power relations, that contributes greatly to the production of a sense of the familiar inside one's home. In a deceitful way, remaining unfamiliar with the above socio-natural networks is a prerequisite for feeling familiar within one's own home.

Hence, we can detect an interesting parallel between the ideological exclusion of social processes and the ideological exclusion of natural processes from the domestic sphere. In both cases, the sense of familiarity within the modern home is predicated upon its material connection to the very elements and processes which are excluded ideologically. The "other" in the form of natural processes or social relations of production is simultaneously inside yet outside, domestic yet unfamiliar, homely yet unhomely. Thus, although the modern home is ideologically constructed as independent and *disconnected* from natural processes, its function is heavily dependent upon its material *connections* to these very processes, which are mediated through a series of networks and social power relations.

In the light of the above argumentation, Heidegger's metaphorical description of the divide between the inside and the outside of the home as a "line" becomes rather too rigid to express the complex dialectical relation that exists between these two spaces and to capture the ever shifting boundaries between the inside and the outside of the domestic sphere.[36] Perhaps a more pertinent way to describe this line would be to compare it to a porous membrane, a membrane which separates the two spaces yet still allows significant but controlled interaction between them. This membrane works as a filter that allows certain elements in, while excluding others. Walter Benjamin refers to porosity as "the lack of clear boundaries between phenomena, a permeation of one thing by another, a merger of, for example old and new, public and private, sacred and profane".[37] By keeping out the undesired (most of the times non-commodified) natural and social things and processes, and by welcoming the desirable ones (filtered, produced, and commodified), the modern home has acquired a selective porosity by maintaining a set of invisible connections that enable it to function in its supposedly autonomous manner.

In conclusion, it could be argued that relegating social and natural processes outside the dwelling spaces of modernity—the two cornerstones for producing a home according to Ruskin's vision—are conditions that have been met only at an ideological (representational-visual and discursive-perceptive) level. In fact, both social and natural processes have been hidden rather than ostracized altogether outside the modern home. Representative of modernity's inherent contradictions, the modern home, in a simultaneous act of need and denial, hosts in its guts everything it tries to keep outside. It is its connection to everything it tries to disconnect from, to the invisible material and social relations that lie underneath its visible counterparts, that makes the modern home appear to be functioning in an autonomous way. In a subversive manner, remaining unfamiliar with the socio-natural networks that produce and maintain it, is a prerequisite for feeling familiar within one's own home.

The Threatening Geographies of the Familiar

The construction of the familiarity of the domestic sphere as the place of peace, free from division and anomie, but also as the epitome of the familiar, a place free from anxiety and terror, is predicated upon keeping the social and material elements that constitute "the other" invisible and outside. Nevertheless, we have seen that this invisible excluded "other" is simultaneously needed as an essential part of the construction of the familiarity of the inside.

Yet at times of crisis, hidden elements can surface unexpectedly, and familiar objects can behave in unusual ways. For example, at times of water shortage, taps fail to provide water, and during blackouts the flick of a switch no longer results in instant light. Such moments reveal the presence of the excluded "outside" as a constitutive part of the "inside". A leakage or burst pipe (Figure 4.d) reveals a hidden and intricate system of pipes and water mains; a dry tap due to water shortages or maintenance works refers to the complex network of production and distribution of water; and the accumulation of garbage as a consequence of municipal strikes forces the

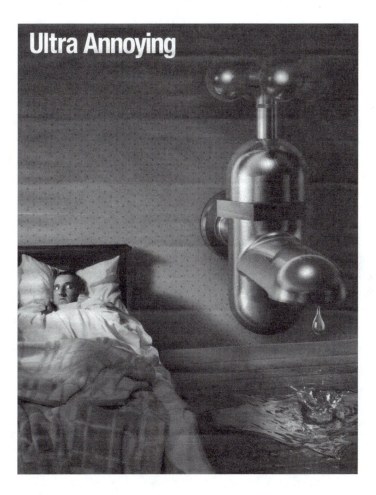

Fig. 4.d A tap which behaves unexpectedly is "ultra annoying". The "unhomely" within the comfort of the "homely". Cigarette advertisement campaign, October 1999. Photographer: Erwin Olaf. Reproduction courtesy of Erwin Olaf and M&C Saatchi.

public to consider the complex process of waste collection and disposal (see Figure 4.e).

Such incidents produce a feeling of uneasiness, discomfort, and anxiety, which threatens to tear down the laboriously built and elaborately maintained security and safety of familiar spaces. These occurrences put the normalized character of the control and commodification of nature into question, and threaten the smooth functioning of the domestic sphere. Such an exposure of the limits of domestic bliss and a revelation of its dependency on social relations of production generates a feeling of "not being at home in one's own home".[38] This *unhomely* feeling within the *homely* was termed by Sigmund Freud as "the Uncanny" [*das Unheimliche*]. In his essay with the same title Freud notes that the German word *heimlich* signifies the homely, the familiar.[39] However, *heimlich* can also mean "the concealed, what is kept from sight, withheld from others".[40] The linguistic opposite of *heimlich*, the word *unheimlich* signifies the thing that "ought to have remained secret and hidden but has come to light."[41] Thus, Freud makes the significant remark that *"heimlich* is a word whose meaning develops in the direction of ambivalence, until it finally coincides with its opposite, *unheimlich. Unheimlich* is in some way or other a subspecies of *heimlich".[42] It is precisely this familiar character of the *heimlich*, which produces the *unheimlich* effect when the former behaves in ways outside

Fig. 4.e Piled up refuse during a three-day strike of municipal workers in Thessaloniki, Greece, Autumn 2003. Photograph: Maria Kaika.

the ordinary, or when things that ought to have remained hidden come to light. Freud investigated cases where the *heimlich* becomes *unheimlich*, such as epileptic fits or manifestations of insanity, and argued that the "uncanny" effect that such situations produce is due to the fact that these manifestations hint at processes that work and lie beyond what is the "ordinary appearance of things".[43] It is when the predictable nature of the familiar acts in unpredictable ways that the uncanny effect is produced.

The haunted house is the most obvious and most cited spatial expression of the uncanny, a case of the manifestation of the unfamiliar within what is the most familiar environment. However, a building showing its "guts", the networks that support its function, can produce a similar uncanny effect, a feeling of discomfort. Renzo Piano and Richard Rogers' *Centre Pompidou* in Paris (1972–1976) is a good example of the uncanny effect produced by turning a building inside-out. The pipes, lines, and cables of this building seemed to be out of place when they unexpectedly appeared on its façade in 1976. This appearance of typically hidden elements, although widely praised by "informed" scholars and architects, was not originally equally appreciated by the Parisian public that remained perplexed for a while at the bold revelation of the building's guts.[44] A more recent example is Rachel Whiteread's *House* (1993–1994) a much cited installation in London's East End, comprising a full-scale cast of the interior of a three storey terrace Victorian home scheduled for demolition. The installation unsettles the boundaries between inside/outside, open/closed, and private/public space, thus producing an uncanny feeling to the viewer. Despite it being announced as temporary, the installation raised high levels of controversy, including the Bow Neighbourhood Committee demanding its demolition (*The Herald Magazine*, May 26, 2003).

Closer to the experience of the everyday is the example of the Dyson vacuum cleaner, in which the usual opaque bag is replaced by a transparent cylinder, thus revealing rather than hiding away the amount of dirt and grime that has been removed from the home. Since it reveals unwanted elements that ought to remain hidden, it is a typical example of the uncanny. Now a big market success, originally no major electronics company would purchase the design (despite the fact that the design world marveled) and it finally had to be marketed by the inventor himself. A similar feeling of discomfort and anxiety in the everyday, whereby "one no longer feels at home in his most familiar environment"[45] can be produced by a tap drying up, a dripping tap, piled up refuse, or a bursting pipe. A disrupted domestic routine threatens to undermine the air of familiarity that a home is supposed to exhale. As Wigley puts it:

> [T]hrough the systematic concealment of the uncanny in everyday life, the familiar is actually a mode of uncanniness. Just as alienation of modern life is not simply produced by the abyss underlying all structures but by the covering over of the abyss, it is equally produced by covering over the uncanniness behind and of the familiar.[46]

One of the reasons why anxiety and discomfort is produced by a domestic network crisis is precisely because it forces us to reflect on the existence of things and social and economic relations to which the home is connected and which, when disrupted, render the normal function of our lives anomalous and reveal that the familiarity based on the supposed autonomy of the private space is itself a form of alienation. It is for this reason that Heidegger urges us to interrogate the familiar, since "the familiar carries an air of harmlessness and ease, which causes us to pass lightly over what really deserves to be questioned."[47] Familiarity can veil the complex fabric of social and spatial relations involved in its own production, thereby assisting in the process of commodity fetishism. The familiarity of the domestic space conceals the violence (in the form of social power relations) dwelling in the institutions, which make the construction and sustenance of any edifice possible. For example, the potential violence of a tap dwells within the hands of the institutions that have the power to turn water supply on or off. By being unaware of this violence, by being trapped in a constructed domestic familiarity, we remain alienated in the very space that is supposed to be the most familiar to us. The bourgeois home operates as a blissful private shelter insofar as it is selectively sealed from the world outside. One can be lost forever inside one's own painstakingly created familiarity, insofar as one is confined inside it. By eliminating (visually, perceptually, and discursively-ideologically) the material connections and social relations that make its existence possible, the modern home acquires the properties that Bachelard assigned to it: of both a refuge and a prison.[48] According to Wigley, the innocence of the familiar, if not interrogated, "alienates by masking a more fundamental alienation: the obviousness and self-assurance of the average ways in which things have been interpreted as such."[49]

This form of alienation not only makes us prisoners of our own fears and needs, but also facilitates practices of exclusion. The supposedly undisputed imperative of maintaining public order and domestic bliss is often used as the main justification for political practices of exclusion: from the emergence of North American gated communities to the South African Apartheid regime, such practices are performed in the name of keeping social processes under control. But, in a stunningly similar manner, practices of social exclusion and political hegemony occur also in the name of keeping natural processes under control. For example, the process of burying urban rivers underground in the name of keeping "bad" nature away has been invariably connected to the clearance of slums along the banks of urban rivers, and was, more often than not, hailed by the authorities as an "inevitable" side effect of the necessary process of sanitizing urban space.[50] This sanitization "opened up" space for the urban embourgeiosement[51] since it provided room for the "free" movement of people, vehicles, goods and capital. This manipulation of patterns of urban social stratification in the name of controlling "nature" is part of the history of most Western metropolises. When the Seine (Zenne) in Brussels was covered during the 19th century, the settlements around its banks were swept away, giving way to what now constitutes the *centre ville*. This process was glorified by the city's patrons, the king, and the political elites, since the slums gave way to an emblematic example of 19th century bourgeois architecture. In the same way, the embankment of the Thames in London was part of the glorification of the British Empire, while also contributing to what Oliver refers to as "cultural amnesia": a process which goes beyond changing the public's ideas of what a natural river should look like to changing perceptions of what the socio-natural urban landscape should look like.[52] In *Concrete and Clay,* Gandy explores analogous practices in New York: the disappearance of New York's black Seneca village in the name of creating "nature" in the city under Olmstead's plans for Central Park, or the practices of social exclusion hidden in the modernist designs of Robert Moses, the city's celebrated master planner.[53] Tournikiotis and Papadakis report on a similar process that took place in Athens in the 1930s, when the sanitation of the Illissos river resulted in the clearance of the illegal settlements along its banks, making room for the creation of one of the city's most expensive middle class areas, all in the name of keeping nature under control.[54]

Although the above examples are drawn from the early period of modernizing and rationalizing space in the Western world, practices of social control and hegemony in the name of nature are not confined to that historical period (high modernism) or to that geographical area (Western world) only. Such practices are still present in the Western and the developing world alike. In his *Flows of Power,* Swyngedouw explores how in present-day Guayaquil, Ecuador, mechanisms of social exclusion ensure that water flows abundantly into private pools and water fountains inside the secluded, policed, private bourgeois homes, while 36% of the city's population lacks access to piped potable water.[55] In the Western world, such practices take place in a somewhat more sophisticated manner. Gandy interprets the recent introduction of environmental management technologies in New

York, as a means of creating new investment opportunities for surplus capital. In a similar vein, Nevarez investigates the case of southern California, whereby public anxiety induced by rhetoric about the possibility of an imminent water crisis became a major political and economic tool for a consent-building exercise in favor of importing additional water supplies to the area.[56] Chapter 7 documents in detail another example of similar practices linked to the history of the drought experienced in Athens during the early 1990s, during which the water company decided to disrupt water supply. Suddenly, and unexpectedly, taps inside people's homes refused to provide their services as expected; they became a form of domestic uncanny: familiar objects that behaved in unfamiliar and disrupting ways. From being invisible and unproblematic, the connections between the house, the city, and nature's water became the number one topic of media coverage and public awareness, a source of public anxiety and a threat to domestic bliss. The experience of pending disaster was accentuated by the water company's media campaign insisting that the specter of drought announced the imminent death of the city from thirst. This threat and its careful nurturing, in turn, facilitated a specific set of policies: the decision to increase the price of water by up to 300% through a stratified price tariff (which affected mostly lower end consumers) and an emergency bill for the creation of a new dam project at Evinos River.

The above examples illustrate how the anxiety produced by the uncanny (interpreted as the manifestation of one's own alienation within one's familiar space) can be used as a political tool for the manipulation of public opinion and as a vehicle to push through specific political-economic agendas. The reason why the manifestation of the alienation within our most familiar environments assists in such political practices is due to the uncanniness experienced as fear of loss of the safe and the sublime. As Sibley contends, anxiety can be deepened by the creation of a false sense of security.[57] If this holds true, then it would appear that the modernist enterprise to create binary distinctions and boundaries in order to do away with fear and anxiety, actually served to deepen the very same problem it tried to eradicate. However, as we will explore in the final section of this chapter, the unexpected surfacing of typically hidden elements that brings to the foreground a recognition of the condition of alienation within the most familiar of environments, rather than being a source of fear and anxiety, has the potential to be a source of knowledge and emancipation.

Interrogating the Familiar

> We are nomads born, haptic creatures, and we spend our lives forgetting it. Architecture is the evidence of this denial.... We pile up

stones feverishly in an attempt to reproduce the container, the vessel, the thing, producing the image at the expense of the voluptuous. We, like Sisyphus, never reach the goal because the impossibility of so doing is programmed into the rules of the game.

J. Bloomer, Architecture and the Text (1993: 32)[58]

Bloomer's assertion of the impossibility of constructing a familiar environment appears to be standing at the antipode of Ruskin's century older declaration of the feasibility of such an enterprise. Insofar as Ruskin's declaration echoes the optimism of the Enlightenment about the possibility to do away with human fear and alienation, Bloomer's quote echoes postmodernist pessimistic denial of the possibility to do so and acceptance of the condition of human alienation as an inevitable way of being. However, these two view points share more in common than it might appear at first glance. For, although Bloomer appears to disagree with Ruskin about the possibility to achieve materially the "voluptuous" in the form of the ideal familiar home, she nevertheless subscribes fully, along with Ruskin, to the sacredness of the platonic ideal-type of the home as "the sublime", "the vessel," "the container," and to the importance of trying to reproduce it. In fact, what Bloomer and Ruskin have in common is that they portray alienation and fear as the result of failing to produce materially this ideal-type, which nevertheless remains sacred to both of them.

Somewhere between Enlightenment's optimism and postmodernist pessimism lies modernity's contradictory efforts to construct a disconnected modern home and a disconnected modern individual within a world that becomes increasingly connected; the contradiction between the ideology of the disconnected home as a sacred principle, and the impossibility to produce it materially. Reflecting this contradiction, the modern home became simultaneously both the *par excellence* cultural sign of sublime modern living and its antipode: the *par excellence* cultural sign of the uncanny, of the alienation of the modern individual within his/her most familiar environment.[59] Indeed, in literature, art, media, film, etc., the home functions as the representation of the celebrated modernist dream of sublime Western living, but it also functions as the paradigmatic cultural sign of its antipode: of fear and anxiety. From Edgar Alan Poe's (1809–1849) short stories, to Kafka's (1883–1924) *Metamorphosis*, to Harold Pinter's (1930–) *Homecoming*, the home moves away from its role as a signifier of familiarity and bliss and becomes instead the emblematic representation of the uncanny. By putting one small detail of the familiar environment out of place—yet still within the familiar domestic sphere—by revealing the contradictions and the uncanny qualities of modern living, nothing remains the same; the sublime, normalized character of modern dwelling is upset. In a similar manner, the unashamedly modernist movements of Dadaïsm and Surrealism also disputed the sacredness and the sublime character of modern living and used the uncanny to replicate the individual's alienation within his/her own private space. Surrealist art, such as Duchamp's "readymade" objects, included urinals rebranded as "fountains" and displayed on pedestals as works of art; Dadaist poetry included "automatic poems" and "sound poems" (Figure 4.f), respectively, a string of coherent words with correct syntax yet with no apparent meaning and a string of letters put together in a way that makes them look like words, yet which are not.[60] Magritte's series of paintings entitled *The Treachery of the Images* (*La Trahison des images*) feature everyday objects in great representational detail, yet the scripture above the objects suggests that they are not what they seem. A painting featuring a photographic representation of a pipe also involves a caption informing us that "*ceci n'est pas une pipe*". Similarly, a photographic representation of an apple should not be taken for granted since, Magritte informs us in the same painting that "*ceci n'est pas une pomme*". These

KARAWANE

jolifanto bambla ô falli bambla
grossiga m'pfa habla horem
égiga goramen
higo bloiko russula huju
hollaka hollala
anlogo bung
blago bung
blago bung
bosso fataka
ü üü ü
schampa wulla wussa ólobo
hej tatta gôrem
eschige zunbada
wulubu ssubudu uluw ssubudu
tumba ba- umf
kusagauma
ba – umf

Hugo Ball (1917)

THE HYPERBOLE OF THE CROCODILE COIFFEUR AND THE WALKING STICK
(Die Hyperbel vom Krokodilcoiffeur und dem Spazier-stock)

St. Elmo's fire races round the beards
of the anabaptists
they pull their davy lamps from out
of their warts
and stick their back sides in puddles
he sang a nail-dumpling on pack-ice
and whistled for her so sweetly round
the corner the slattern
that a casting-grate skidded
4 eugenes on tour in Scandinavia
millovich blue crate
is a smash hit
the tardiest siskin wellingtons the
gruel pole
of a butterbag in pewter plumage
between the hair-cream of the sewer-man
hair-raising journey on the steep cliff
the mother emits a squawk
and falls down, perfectly, dead
as father's tomahawk
sinks into her head
the children dance a round,
off into the sunset,
the father stands, head bowed,
on the gun boat's prow
staggering-dumb jackamandrills
somersault on marmalade belts
off into the tea-set
Viennese rear customs office vowels
full of grizzliness
the circus-hating keel
would hang the profile
in the international canals
sacramental-marshals
quartet-Mephistopheles
scanning-scandals
Tristan Tzara, Walter Serner and Hans Arp

Fig. 4.f The uncanny in the language: (Left) Dadaist "sound poetry" (author's interpretation of the original play with the typescript). (Right) Dadaist "automatic poetry". http://www.bohemia-books.com.au/anit/dada/dada-perfs/simpoet2.

works of art produce an effect of feeling unfamiliar and ill at ease with the most familiar objects, words, concepts, and spaces. The subversive use of the uncanny in these movements aims at bringing the viewer/reader face to face with their alienation experienced within their most familiar environment and with their most familiar objects.

However, the modern home does not function only as a sign or a representation of the uncanny, as Vidler depicts it. Going beyond the contradiction between materiality and representation, between reality and the ideal type, this chapter illustrates that the dwelling places of modernity are hosts of the uncanny in their very structure. Once stripped of their well-constructed clarity and familiarity, or in moments of crisis, they are revealed as being themselves objects of surrealist art, pointing at the alienation of the dweller that inhabits them, subverting the image of the dwelling as the epitome of the familiar. In a simultaneous act of need and denial, they guard in their guts and in their underbelly everything they try to keep outside: sewerage, pipelines, dirt, rats, pests, crime, disease, the homeless.

Thus, questioning the familiarity of our most familiar environments can be an act of subversion in itself. Not only because it reveals the alienation within the familiar, but also because it undermines the belief in the possibility of producing a space that is totally disconnected from both social and natural processes. Questioning this belief becomes particularly important at a time when excess individualism has replaced civil action, and when Giddens' notorious aphorism—"no one any longer has any alternatives to capitalism"[61]—has resonated widely. Exposing the dysfunctionality of the private spaces where blind individualism can be practiced in isolation calls for a reflection on alternative ways of engaging with the world. As Mary Douglas[62] suggested, exploring the margins is important since it opens both destructive and creative possibilities. Exploring the uncanny materiality of "the other" in the form of the invisible metabolized nature or technology networks points at the social construction of the separation between the natural and the social, the private and the public. It reveals the individual, the social, and the natural, as a socio-natural continuum that disrupts the boundaries between the above socially constructed categories. Demonstrating the ideological construction of private spaces as autonomous and disconnected and insisting on their material and social connections calls for an end to individualization, fragmentation, and disconnectedness that are looked for within the bliss of one's home. It calls for engaging in political and social action, which is, almost invariably, decidedly public.

Part II

Part II (Chapters 5, 6, and 7) explores further the theoretical themes studied in Part I. Using Athens and London as case studies, it analyzes the efforts to render modern metropolises autonomous and independent from nature's whims in the 19th and 20th centuries, and studies how supplying modern cities with abundant water was predicated upon expanding the complex system of networks that support the metabolism of the city. The fact that Athens was "a city in ruins" in 1834, when it became the capital of the modern Greek state, makes it an exemplary case for the study of the dialectics between the production of a modern city from scratch and the production of nature. It also makes it an interesting case to contrast to the process of modernizing more developed Western metropolises, such as London.

The analysis in Part II is organized around three distinct periods, which correspond to the changing role of nature[1] in the urbanization process:

1. The 19th century: awesome and fearful nature, nature as an impediment to urban development
2. Early 20th century: tamed and disciplined nature, nature as the prerequisite for progress and development
3. Late 20th and early 21st centuries: nature as a source of crisis, necessitating a reassessment of urban development practices.

These three periods (exact dates inevitably are case specific and vary from city to city and from country to country) correspond to the structure of the three final chapters of the book.

Awesome Nature: Modernizing as an Archaeological Project

Modernization in Europe and North America was inseparably linked with industrialization and capital accumulation. This social and economic process was complemented by a cultural process of constructing a common identity for the industrialized world: the identity of the West. This project was pioneered during the Enlightenment, and derived much of its inspiration from ideas about democracy and freedom originating in Greek philosophy and political thinking. As part of this process, Greece was reinvented as the cradle of Western civilization, while, ironically, it remained under Ottoman rule—and thus still part of the Orient—until 1830. However, despite the celebration of Western culture as promoting democracy, equality and freedom, the inequalities produced by the pursuit of capital accumulation (deteriorating living conditions for the working class and a surge of social upheaval) and the declining environmental conditions in urban centers (recurrent cholera and typhoid epidemics, smog) testified to the opposite. The socio-environmental imbroglio threatened to tear apart Western capitalism and thus quickly became a main preoccupation of the bourgeoisie. The Age of Reform made poverty alleviation and urban sanitation a central part of urban policy, and an essential part of modernization. After the link between dirty drinking water and cholera was established, the provision of clean water became central to the process of urban sanitation. Sanitation was not only a material imperative. It was also a matter of prestige for the urban elites who saw urban-social reform as their responsibility, and realized that this would contribute towards maintaining their established positions of power that were now threatened by social unrest.

This chapter examines the 19th century process of investing some of the profit of the growing capitalist economy into the construction of sewage and water supply systems. The efforts to sanitize cities in Western Europe (in particular London) and North America are juxtaposed with similar efforts in Athens. There, a lack of funding combined with the West's fascination with bringing Greece's classical past back to light (part of constructing a common identity for the West) resulted in subverting the process of watering and sanitizing the city into an archaeological project. First, the project for watering Athens was identified with excavating and restoring the city's ancient aqueduct (Hadrian's Aqueduct), with the belief that this would improve water supply and simultaneously reconnect the city to its ancient veins. This decision was nourished by the mounting interest in archaeology in Western Europe and North America as a means of excavating the origins of Western civilization. Second, the project to sanitize Athens was linked to a process of disconnecting the city from its recent (Ottoman) past. As part of this process, the municipal authorities declared a war against dust, an element connected to the European imagery of the Orient. To this end, a good part of the city's meager water resources was used to eliminate dust by sprinkling the city streets daily. Third, city authorities promoted Athens' image as a beautiful, green, and clean Western city in order to connect it to the West. This included using some of the city's water to create a royal garden in the city center—a petty project of Greece's foreign queen that was in direct conflict with the increasing need for water from the part of the city's growing population.

Constructing the Identity of the West

Industrialization in Europe and North America greatly intensified urbanization in the 19th century. Britain's urban population became larger than its rural population by the middle of the century. The population of London rose from 675,000 in 1750 to 1 million in 1801, which was double the population of Paris.[1] The increased accumulation of industrial capital and the internationalization of trade meant that the urban bourgeoisie was increasing its power and material wealth, some of which was invested in monumentalizing urban space. Cities became the stage on which the bourgeoisie could conspicuously consume luxury goods. A competition between the great Western cities and the international bourgeoisie culminated in the institution of World Exhibitions, which showcased technological achievement, exotic goods and bourgeois grandeur. If one strolled in the "right" parts of town, he or she could think that the industrialized world had realized many of the Enlightenment dreams: scientific progress, technological innovation, beautiful monuments, broad boulevards, shopping arcades displaying luxury goods from around the world, and easier communication and travel. Modernization seemed nearly complete and, like the Enlightenment itself, it was a distinctly Western enterprise. However, the West as a geographical social and cultural entity was in constant flux. The social economic process of industrialization and capitalist formation, a common denominator for the industrialized world, was in need of a complementary cultural denominator, a foundation upon which to construct the West as a coherent geographical, historical, and cultural entity.

This cultural process of producing a common identity for the West had two components. The first was the construction of "the other" in the form of the Orient against which the Western identity could be cast. As Edward Saïd beautifully demonstrated in *Orientalism*, "European culture gained its strength and identity by setting itself off against the Orient as a sort of surrogate and even underground self".[2]

The second component of the construction of the identity of the West was the assertion of the existence of a distinct Western culture to include common political and social ideals as well as a common origin. Following the Enlightenment's legacy, this vision was largely inspired by ancient Greek culture, philosophy and political thinking. While ironically Greece was at the time still under Ottoman rule and thus part of the Orient, its classical past provided the foundation on which to construct the common identity of the Western world. The romance the Enlightenment had with 5th century BC Greece provided the background for the European bourgeoisie's infatuation with everything Greek. Between 1750 and 1850, European and North American cities experienced a revival of classical Greek style in art and architecture in the form of neoclassicism. The neoclassical style was adopted as the "official" style for public buildings and private bourgeois homes alike, since it was considered to be "the noblest" form (that is, the closest to the origins of Western civilization), representing the ideals of Western democracy and freedom. The Ashmolean Museum in Oxford (designed by Charles Robert Cockerell, 1839–1842; Figure 5.a); The British Museum in London (designed by Robert Smirke, 1823–1847); La Bibliotheque Nationale in Paris (designed by Henri Labrouste, 1862–1868); La Galleria Vittorio Emanuele in Milan (Giuseppe Mengoni, designed 1861, built 1865–1877); United States Capitol in Washington, DC (Thornton–Latrobe–Bulfinch, 1793–1830; dome by Thomas Ustick Walter, 1851–1863); and even the Statue of Liberty and

Fig. 5.a The Ashmolean Museum in Oxford is the first public museum in Britain. Designed by Charles Robert Cockerell (1839–1842), it is an eclectic interpretation of Greek and Roman classical architecture. Photograph: Martin Barfoot. © School of Geography and the Environment, University of Oxford.

Observation Tower (Frederic Bartholdi, 1884–1886) are all examples of neoclassical buildings designed and built within that time frame.

In 1866, the Danish architect Theophil Hansen proposed "the nobler Greek style, where the aesthetic whole symbolized the hoped-for parliamentary integration of peers and people"[3] for Vienna's Parliament building. This same architect was commissioned to build a number of neoclassical public buildings in Athens after Greece gained independence from the

Ottoman Empire in 1830. In a way, Hansen's creations (the National Library of Greece, 1834; the Academy of Athens, 1862) re-imported an increasingly international Europeanized Greek style into Greece.[4]

The same quest for discovering and establishing the cultural history and identity of the West also manifested itself in a crusade for archaeological excavations.[5] Williams[6] argues that the thriving of "humanistic" archaeology during that period aimed—among other things—at "gratifying the self-esteem of the Westerner" and helped to anchor Western identity on steadier ground. A fierce yet "noble" competition was established amongst Western European archaeological institutions toward excavating the origins of Western civilization. The discovery and subsequent excavations at Pompeii (1763–) helped ignite this interest, which was expanded to Greece with great enthusiasm after 1830. A number of archaeological institutes "branched out" in Athens after independence, and subsequently competed against each other in excavating the origins of European civilization: the German Archaeological Institute (1875), the American School of Classical Studies (1881), and the British School at Athens (1886).

Apart from its strong ideological connotations and its link to the construction of the identity of the West, many art historians[7] argue that the emergence of the neoclassical style was a practical way of dealing with the bafflement caused by the need to build monumental nonreligious buildings for a secularized world. Until that moment in history, the majority of monumental buildings had been religious in function and thus their style and form had religious connotations to the public imagery. As Schorske[8] put it, because of the lack of historical tradition in building monumental secular buildings, "historical erudition had…to fill the void."

Dignifying Progress

The "Greek revival" did not only vest secular public buildings. New types of buildings such as railway stations, subway stations, factories, pumping stations, and power plants were constructed to host new technologies, and they too required a new architectural language—a challenge to architects and engineers alike. As a way out of this riddle, the neoclassical style was chosen for many of these buildings as a means of making new technologies and their urban landmarks more "noble" and more in tune with the tastes of the bourgeoisie, who, at the end of the day, were the ones funding them (see Chapter 3). The Fairmount Waterworks in Philadelphia (early 19th century), the Abbey Mills Pumping Station in London (mid-19th century), and the Pennsylvania Railroad Station in New York (built 1910, demolished 1964) were all expressions of technological innovations which were draped with neoclassical ornament, in an effort to "dignify" progress by dressing it up in the ways of the past.[9] As Schorske notes, while: "science and law are modern truth,…beauty came from history."[10] Even buildings and constructions outside or underneath the city (such as dams, pipes, and other networks) were adorned with neoclassical trimmings despite the fact that this decoration was invisible and, as such, superfluous. It was quite ironic that an historical style became the first aesthetic representation of the innovations of an era (modernity) which despised the past and declared its determination to break irrevocably with history.

This irony becomes easier to interpret if we note that the choice of the forms of the classical past was also part of a broader ideology trying to provide a link between technology and democracy at a symbolic level. The need to assert this link became stronger as increasing inequality and uneven development attested to the failure of technology to deliver automatically the promise for a better and more democratic society for all, contrary to the Enlightenment ideology. The neoclassical style, which was unearthed from a humanistic tradition, was used as an aesthetic antidote to the dehumanizing aspects of industrialization and modernization, as a means to make technology and innovation more palatable to the general public (see Chapter 3).

Modernization as Sanitation

The 19th century was not only a period of "beautification" of Western urban centers; it was also a period of intense political and social debates as well as social upheaval. The deteriorating social and environmental conditions in urban centers bruised the bourgeoisie's pride in being modern and Western. Cities were growing increasingly different from the healthy and orderly entities that Enlightenment thinkers had envisioned them becoming. The accumulation of capital and luxury goods and the monumentalization of urban space went hand in glove with an increase in inequality, uneven development, and the accumulation of environmental and social problems: poverty, dire living conditions, and an undisciplined urban nature that took its toll on urban populations in the form of disease and recurring epidemics. In 1832 a cholera epidemic in Britain killed around 20,000 people, while in 1849 another cholera outbreak killed over 2,000 people in London in just one week.[11] If one walked through the "wrong" parts of the town, one would encounter "the city of dreadful night" described with the bleakest colors in poems, novels, and journal reports of the time, but shielded from the eyes of the bourgeoisie. The impoverishment of the working classes and the deterioration of living and environmental conditions in urban centers led to social upheaval and strikes, which threatened capitalist growth and the established power of the bourgeoisie. The monumentalization of urban space and the presentation of technology as "noble" through neoclassical veneering proved inadequate to counteract the dehumanizing effects of industrialization and to convince the public of the benefits that technology would eventually bring to their daily lives.

Soon, the fetishism with technology as an automatic means for human emancipation (see Chapter 3) found its antipode in the act of *sabotage*. The word most likely originates at the moment when a French weaver on strike "cast his woden[sic] shoe—called a *sabot*—into the delicate mechanism of the loom upon leaving the mill".[12] This was a kind of reverse fetishism, which attributed to technology the dreadful living and working conditions of the working class. Sabotage was "officially" promoted by the Industrial Workers of the World against the dehumanizing aspects of technology and, according to Emile Pouget's[13] guidelines, a good act of sabotage should aim at: "[letting] the capitalists...know that the worker will not respect the machine until it has become his friend that will reduce his physical labor instead of being, as it is today, the enemy that steals his bread and shortens his life."

The birth of ideas of social reform in the ranks of enlightened middle class intellectuals accompanied the revolutionary spirit of the working class. Armed with good will and a substantial dose of idealism, most reformists fought for a better society, mainly by fighting against urbanization—against cities themselves—rather than against the root cause of inequality that was producing urban problems. In Britain, Ebenezer Howard's utopian visions of garden cities provided an anti-urban solution to urban problems. In France, the pioneering British reformer Robert Owen, together with Charles Fourier, promoted the spirit of small scale cooperative social organizations over large-scale capitalist expansion. North American Progressivism also advocated pre-industrial community-type settlements with emphasis on education. Mary Parker Follett's community centers and Jane Adams' Hull House settlement in Chicago operated within this tradition. To be sure, these movements were important in promoting social reform and were instrumental in the later development of a more interventionist state. However, their well-meaning utopianism kept their founders from addressing immediate practical solutions for real problems in real (existing) cities.

To be fair, however, there were many enlightened reformers, including medical and engineering professionals, who fought with great fervor to improve public heath and sanitation in existing cities. The confirmation of the suspected link between cholera and dirty drinking water in 1854 by John Snow turned the development of networks for clean water supply and sewage into an imperative for promoting the health of urban populations, regardless of their class or social status. For their part, the urban bourgeoisie not only acted as "benefactors"—partially funding public engineering works—but also managed these new institutions. Thus, while linking their name to the improvement of public health, they were also securing their decision-making power over land and natural resources allocation.

During the 19th century, sanitation projects became a matter of prestige and national pride in Western cities. The pollution of the Thames, the heart of the capital of the British Empire, was considered to be "a national—and an imperial—humiliation"[14] since, according to Halliday's[15] remarkable study, the "great stink" of the Thames made no social distinctions: it was foul for the London's slums and for the Houses of Parliament alike. The elimination of the "great stink" became a national project of the first order and was pursued through grand scale engineering works. The construction of the London sewers by the Metropolitan Board of Sewers (established in 1848) extinguished this odor along with cholera epidemics; the embankment of the Thames[16] tamed the river bank and controlled the flow of water; famous health reforms were introduced; and the City of London appointed John Simon as the first sanitary inspector (1848–1856). Paris did not fall behind in its pursuit of sanitation. Baron Haussmann transformed not only the city above ground with his grand boulevards, but also the underground city. During his service as Prefect of the Seine (1853–1870), while sweeping away many parts of medieval Paris to open up space for grand boulevards, he also built sewers and water mains for parts of the expanding city center.

Although the importance of sanitizing Western metropolises was undisputed, the means by which this would be achieved became a source of great contestation and conflict. Competing positions over resource allocation often led to legendary battles, which were fought at the material as well as at the symbolic levels. Halliday[17] reports how in 1865 Sir Joseph Bazalgette, the embodiment of the modern heroic engineer, had to fight hard for many years, against all odds, to gain approval and funding to complete his vision for building the London sewers. The debate between John Simon and John Snow over the best practice to sanitize the city of London was another sanitation war, fought over allocation of public funding, but also over scientific prestige. John Simon was a strong supporter of the "miasmatic" theory, which advocated that disease (including cholera) is contracted through foul air. This doctrine had strong supporters, including Florence Nightingale and the powerful Edwin Chadwick. The theory called for the air of London to be regularly purified, and advocated the expenditure of money and effort on removing foul smell from dwellings rather than improving water supply or building sewers. John Snow's theory, on the other hand, maintained that cholera is a water-borne disease, contracted through polluted water, a position that demanded that water supply and the construction of a sewage network be made the top priority for allocation of public funding.[18]

In the following sections I will examine how similar conflicting interests over water supply and sanitation were played out in the allocation of funds and water in Athens. I will focus in particular on how the promotion of Greece as the cradle of Western civilization, combined with the lack of funding for the newly liberated state, affected the ways in which modern-ization and sanitation projects were pursued in that corner of Europe. What is particularly interesting in the case of Athens is the fact that it aspired to become a peer to the industrialized Western cities, while itself being still in ruins, and with no funds (private or public) available to finance modernizing projects. Eager to Westernize, yet unable to initiate a process of industrialization, Greece was inspired by Europe's fascination with its classical past and turned its modernization—including the sanita-tion of Athens—into an archaeological project during the 19th century.

The Material Production of Geographical Imaginations

As we have seen in the previous section, the legacy of the Enlightenment hailed Greece as the origin of Western democracy and civilization. In this spirit, liberating Greece from Ottoman rule became a collective project of the West. The philhellenic society, *Philike Hetairia*, formed in 1814 in Odessa and instrumental in sparking the Greek War of Independence (1821–1830), counted numerous friends amongst the Western European bourgeoisie and intelligentsia. The Greek War of Independence was even partly funded through Western European capital, starting with an initial loan of £800,000 from Britain in 1824, followed a year later by a further £2 million (also from Britain).[19]

The celebration of Greece as the cradle of Western civilization had profound effects on the way emerging Greek élites perceived Greece's place in the Western world, and its own modernizing process after liberation from the Ottoman Empire. After independence, the main aspiration of the young Greek state was to enter the constellation of Western European states as soon as possible. However, these high aspirations did not match the humble reality of post-independence Greece. The country was ravaged by warfare and sparsely populated (17 inhabitants per square km in 1839), with an economy based predominantly on peasant agriculture.[20] The rural landed elites, social and economic remnants of the Ottoman semi-feudal regime, opposed both domestic reform and the introduction of capitalist forms of production.

The formation of a domestic bourgeoisie that could initiate a process of industrialization and urbanization was very slow and, according to Tsoukalas, never actually happened.[21] Thus, following the Western model of modernization in the form of industrialization was a very difficult task for 19th century Greece. A domestic bourgeois class was absent and the emerging merchants had fled abroad, forming a Greek diasporic bourgeoisie. Without these groups to assist industrialization, the state assumed a central role in dissolving the semi-feudal mode of production and in establishing an institutional framework that would favor capitalist formation.[22] Vergopoulos remarks that "it was not bourgeois society that constituted the operational axis of social formation in Greece (as liberal theory would have expected it to be), but rather the State".[23] However, the Greek state did not possess financial or other means to initiate a capitalist formation by itself. Unlike most Western European states, it had no colonies from which to extract wealth, and the debt that it had been carrying since the Independence loans continued to increase, thus impeding its role as the main initiator and financier of industrial-economic development. This led to what Karydis[24] characterizes as an "unstable capitalist development," limited to following the development of foreign centers rather than pursuing a trajectory of its own. Attracting capital investment from abroad also proved very difficult for Greece, despite the fact that the state promoted private property rights, freedom of enterprise, free movement of commodities and labor, and even free land allocation for industrial development. The production factor that was in short supply was not land, but capital. Moreover, as Agriantoni[25] notes in her exemplary study, labor power was also in short supply, since the majority of the population were still occupied as farmers and/or part-time craftsmen/women. Many others *chose* to be occupied as only part-time industrial workers on top of their primary jobs in agriculture. A further barrier to the exploitation of the abundantly available undeveloped land was the absence of adequate transport infrastructure since the few existing roads were designed to serve the previous semi-feudal system. For all the reasons stated above, 19th century Greece failed to become a hub for capital investment (domestic or foreign) despite the institutional privileges and incentives generously and enthusiastically provided by the state.

Modernizing Athens

Athens was chosen as the capital of modern Greece in 1834[26] and became the showcase of the young state. Modernizing Athens became a major preoccupation of the country's intellectual and political leadership. However, post-independence Athens was a capital in ruins (Figure 5.b). It had been ravaged twice by the Turkish army during the War of Independence, first in 1822 and again in 1826 when, as Mpiris[27] reports, the remaining population abandoned the city *en masse*.

By the time it became the capital city, it presented an image of *tabula rasa*, with most of its buildings destroyed. Even after its population started returning slowly, it was still less than 25,000 in 1851 (in comparison, London's population was already 1,655,000 in 1831). The new capital constituted more a platonic idea of a city, a settlement aspiring to become a city, rather than an existing urban center; it was only the presence of a marketplace, of main routes, and of entry/exit points that marked the territory as a settlement.[28] In 1830, The French traveller Michaud in his *Correspondance d'Orient* painted a bleak image of the city:

> [W]e are walking within piles of scattered ruins, pathways formed in the middle of wrecks, jumping at each step over piles of stones, parts of walls, pillars, stretched over the dust…. Today, there is not a single street, a single public square, a single garden, a chapel, nor a church.[29]

Clearly, early 19th century Athens possessed no economic, social, or geographical assets that could justify its choice as the capital of the Greek nation. But it had a glorious past and it was chosen as the capital mainly in anticipation of "the benefits that the Greek state would reap if the famous city regenerated itself as its capital."[30] However, in contrast to Western

Fig. 5.b Athens in 1835. A capital in ruins. Mpiris, 1996, p. 9. Reproduction by kind permission of Dr. Manos Mpiris.

economies and Western metropolises, which were growing and thriving, 19th century Greece and its capital lacked the means to materialize any clear development project. No single social group could assume the role of the driving force behind modernization, and the shaping of the urban space of Athens remained up for grabs for the best part of the 19th century, open to competition between a number of actors: a strong diaspora bourgeoisie, Christian land elites, the Royal Palace, the municipality of Athens, and the central state.

The *diaspora bourgeoisie* consisted of merchants and bourgeois of Greek origin who had systematically fled abroad under Ottoman rule in search of more liberal territories. They thrived in Odessa, Constantinople, Trieste, London, and Paris, and became interested in exploring (and exploiting) the newly opened corridors of opportunity in independent Greece,[31] which provided relatively safe territory, cultural links, and great potential for gaining and exercising political control (one thing to which they did not have access in their homes abroad). By 1841, as Moskoph[32] reports, 21 out of the 102 Greeks participating in the highest ranks of the political leadership came from the diaspora circles. However, both Moskoph[33] and Tsoukalas[34] contend that the diaspora bourgeoisie were reluctant to transfer their successful economic operations into Greek territory.[35] To them, Athens became a place of safe residence and a territory for exercising political power, and later on, a place for financial speculation, but it never became a territory for sound economic investment.

The *Christian land elites* sprang from the landed ruling élites of the Ottoman Empire (Figure 5.c) and represented a remnant of a semi-feudal mode of production. With no domestic bourgeois class to antagonize them, they were able to hold on to their social and political power, and opposed the Greek state's attempts to promote institutional reform and modern capitalist enterprise. However, they were very keenly involved in political decisions about the production of the urban space of Athens, mainly through land speculation since many of them were the owners of land in and around the city center. Their names—Sissinis, Zaimis, Lontos, Deligiannis, Notaras, Kallifronas—are still inscribed in the body of Athens in the form of street names.[36]

The *local municipality* rose from the administrative and institutional structures of the Ottoman period. The local and regional systems of governance that emerged immediately after the war of independence were neither democratic nor representative in the modern sense and, as Koliopoulos and Veremis argue,[37] were often very close to the very same powerbrokers that operated under Ottoman rule (Figure 5.c). The conflict between these power centers and the more liberal central government was constant and fierce.

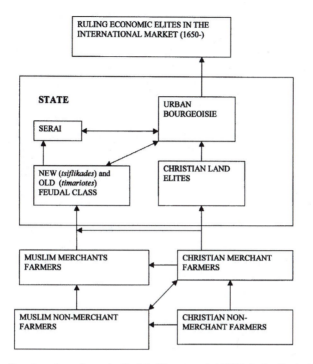

Fig. 5.c The flow of surplus value under the late Ottoman period (1600–) after Moskoph (1974).

The Royal Palace was headed by King Otto and Queen Amalia, who were imported from Bavaria in 1832 (Otto was the son of Ludwig I of Bavaria). There was also a nobility circle surrounding the royal couple, also mainly imported from Bavaria, who were assigned to key public offices.

The *central state* favored transforming Greece into a more dynamic capitalist society. Yet, as we have seen, it had very limited financial means available. Clogg[38] notes that between Independence and the 1870s, the central power had been changing hands between Ioannis Kapodistrias, dedicated to domestic reform and independent development, and Ioannis Kolletis, loyally attached to foreign interests and in favor of colonial relations with the industrialized countries of the West.[39]

All of the above actors held very different, and often contradictory, agendas, accompanied by distinct and conflicting interpretations of what modernization should mean at an ideological/discursive level, and what it should involve at a practical/material level. For the diaspora bourgeoisie, modernizing Athens became synonymous with the process of establishing symbolic power over the city by commissioning the best foreign architects to design impressive public buildings that would embellish the city while at the same time conspicuously display the names of these "national benefactors." For the peasants-turned-manual-labor workers who were slowly moving into Athens in search of a job, the process of modernization signaled the struggles for better wages, housing and living conditions. For the local and national state as well as the land elites, Athens became the arena for competition between traditionally strong local power centers, reminiscent of Ottoman socio-political power structures, and a moderniz- ing central state in pursuit of dismantling Ottoman social and institutional arrangements and favoring the formation of a domestic bourgeoisie that would aid the transition towards capitalism. Still, despite opposing agen- das and conflicting interests between the above actors, there was agreement that the modernization of Athens should be a process of "Westernization".

Modernization as an Archaeological Project

Despite the dismal material conditions, the aspirations of the slowly returning Athenians were very high indeed, and the belief that Greece was going to enter the European world in full glory, wearing Athens as its crown, was deeply rooted. The following excerpt from the 1834 speech by Kleomenis, President of the Committee for the Restoration of Athens, vividly illustrates this optimism:

> A marvellous voice, a voice reassuring the world of a great future is echoing today to the ears of humankind! Athens! Athens! The ancient metropolis of the world, the temple of admiration of centu- ries is being erected; the glorious Athens!!! Prepare, prepare the way of the Lord![40]

However, with no financial means other than occasional benefactions from the diaspora bourgeoisie, Athens could not compete with the achievements of its European counterparts or comply with the rules of beautification, sanitation, and rationalization that were developed and applied in other Western metropolises. What Athens could do, however, was display itself on the pedestal that the West had created for it as the place of origin of Western culture, and connect to the industrialized world at a symbolic/cultural level. Unable to pursue Westernization as a social economic process, the young Greek state instead asserted geographical imaginations and ideologies as real[41] and promoted its cultural image as a Western state. To this end the state promoted an iconography of Athens that connected the city to its ancient past by:

1. reconnecting the city to its past by excavating the traces of its classi- cal history and proudly displaying them in the Athenian landscape

2. disconnecting the city from its more recent (Ottoman) past—which was linked to the Western European imagery of the Orient—by eradicating traces of this past from the city's landscape

3. promoting, where possible, its image as a beautiful, clean, rational, sanitized, Western city

A further extract from Kleomenis' 1834 speech encapsulates the ideology promoting modern Athens as the direct descendant of classical Athens, whose beauty had been perverted through centuries of Ottoman rule, but which could now finally be retrieved and restored:

> We are proceeding [toward modernization], but, where are we to go to? Where are we to step? At every step we encounter piles of both ancient and recent bones! We bump into mud-bricks of both ancient and recent blood…we are walking over layers of ancient laurel!…. Workers! Go deeper! Find again the traces of the demigods, which remain unfading, incised onto the ground of these very streets.[42]

Beautification and past glories aside, as the city's population and territory grew (Table 5.a), Athens was faced with intense socio-environmental problems from which politics and society could not shy away. One of them was recurring cholera epidemics. In June 1835, 235 people died and over 4,000 were taken ill[43] by the epidemic, which reappeared in the summer of 1854. Only a few wealthy households could afford to connect to the city's central water supply network after 1834. For the rest of the population, water was collected (by women) from wells and springs on a daily basis, or sold door to door by water vendors at high prices (see Chapter 4). Water supply and sanitation became a central issue for the growing Athens. Even at the symbolic level, the promotion of an image of a clean, sanitized, Western city was dependent upon ample water supply. Thus, urbanizing adequate amounts of fresh water became one of the most important aspects of the social and political life of the city. This was recognized by the French politician Clemenceau who exclaimed, during his visit in Athens in 1899: "The best politician amongst you shall be the one who will bring water into Athens" (cited in Gerontas and Skouzes, 1963: 111).

However, supplying Athens with adequate piped water required capital investment, human labor, technology, social consensus, political stability and commitment. As we have seen, most of these factors were absent from 19th century Athens. With limited water resources and limited funds, the provision of water and sanitation became an important source of social conflict and political anxiety. The competing visions of modernization

Table 5.a The Population of Athens between the Years 1820 and 1940

Year	Population
1820	10,000
1830	20,000
1851	24,754
1853	31,122
1860	65,000
1879	68,677
1888	133,000
1890	114,355
1898	114,000
1900	200,000
1904	215,000
1910	190.000
1923	800,000
1928	704,247
1940	686,629

Note: The figures after 1910 correspond to the joint population of Athens and Piraeus.
Compiled from: Mpiris (1939; 1996), Gerontas and Skouzes (1963), Kalantzopoulos (1964), Clogg (1984), Leontidou (1989), and data from ΕΥΔΑΠ.

between the different actors noted earlier culminated in competing views on how best to allocate the city's meager water resources:

1. As part of the project of promoting Athens as a sanitized city, but also as a means of disconnecting Athens from the Orient, the municipality (and the entrepreneurs who undertook the relevant task) promoted the daily sprinkling of the streets with water to eliminate dust, an element linked to the Western European imagery of the Orient and absent from the "civilized" Western European cities.

2. As part of the project to model Athens after the image of a Western city, Queen Amalia claimed a good part of the city's limited water resources in order to create a Royal Garden in the city center. The substantial amounts of water needed for this project brought Amalia into direct conflict with the citizens.

3. As part of the idea of reconnecting the city to its ancient veins, and in response to the lack of funding to develop a new water supply system, the idea of restoring Hadrian's Aqueduct, the city's ancient aqueduct, was promoted as the best solution which, it was believed, would improve water supply while at the same time reconnecting the city to its glorious past.

In the sections that follow, I will look more closely at how these three visions of modernization were expressed in battles over the allocation of the city's water. This conflict was often between using water as a means to create use value (as a means of watering the urban population and conforming to basic sanitary requirements) and using water as a means to create symbolic value (the use of water to beautify urban space through introducing green spaces, eliminating dust, etc.).[44] I will examine how this dialectic between nature as use value and nature as symbolic value in the creation of urban space was played out in this process of supplying Athens with water.

The War Against Dust

> In the 1870s most of the streets were not paved. But even those that were covered with gravel were still smothered with a thick layer of fine powder, which tormented the Athenians in the form of dust in the air during the summer, and in the form of thick mud during the winter. In order to deal with the situation, part of the municipal budget was allocated…for the elimination of dust and mud.[45]

During the 19th century the city was perceived as "an evil smelling place"[46] but at the peak of the sanitation movement the "utopia of the odorless city" appears for the first time as a desirable and possible future for industrialized cities.[47] However, as argued in Chapter 4, cleaning and sanitizing the city meant not only purifying it from environmental miasmata (garbage, dust, dirt, etc.), but also from perceived social miasmata (social upheaval, the "immoral" behavior of the working classes, homelessness, and crime). For most Western cities the process of sanitizing urban space was invariably connected to clearing away slums and illegal settlements—an approach that remains popular in contemporary Third World urban policy. In 19th century Athens, sanitation also held this double meaning of both environmental and social/cultural cleansing. However, although the concept of environmental miasma was also identified with disease and foul smell, the notion of social miasma was linked not only to urban crime or to an urban underclass that was yet to be clearly formed, but also to the traces that the city's Ottoman past had left behind. These comprised not only Ottoman architecture and Turkish inscriptions, but also dust and mud, elements connected to the Orient in Western European imagery. Indeed, Western art often portrayed non-Western cities—Constantinople, Cairo, Alexandria—behind a veil of dust which identified them as "oriental" while at the same time draping them in an aura of mystery and exoticism.[48] Although acceptable and even welcomed as an element of exoticism in the context of an oriental city, dust in the Western-to-be Athens was not viewed so charitably. Charles Tackerman, diplomat and U.S. ambassador in Athens (1867–1874) wrote in 1870:

> However pleasant Athens may be during the winter and especially during the spring, it is simply and clearly detestable during the summer.... There is a certain breeze, but it is hot and morbid, filling the empty streets with dust, similar to the one which used to annoy the ancient Athenians. The dust, swirling within clouds of smoke, is blinding to the unfortunate pedestrian.[49]

Since it annoyed Western visitors, dust had to be cleared from the Athenian landscape. However, dust proved much more resilient than the architectural traces of the Ottoman past, which, along with a number of Byzantine churches, were simply demolished. A war was declared against dust by the local authorities, and the weapon of choice was the ever scarce water. And although, according to Illich "purification is by no means a process for which water is always needed",[50] in 19th century Athens purifying the city from the undesired parts of its past and supplying it with ample water became two very closely related processes. The city as "a place that must be constantly washed"[51] was an idea that developed along with miasmatic theory. According to this partially wrong yet powerful doctrine, not only physical but also moral degeneracy could be transmitted through dust and polluted air. Halliday cites a relevant publication by Professor Booth in *The Builder*, who suggested watering the streets so that evaporation "will carry up with it into the atmosphere....the various decomposing and decomposed organic matters floating about and which otherwise allowed to remain would be productive of contagious miasms".[52]

The miasmatic dogma was adopted by the local authorities of Athens, who decided it was essential to sprinkle the streets daily. Eradicating dust became a task as important as eradicating disease and epidemics, and the municipality allocated a good part of the otherwise tight municipal budget as well as a part of the meager water resources to this end. The sprinkling of the streets of Athens started in 1855, a year when water availability was so low that the Ministry of Domestic Affairs intervened by asking the local authorities to take immediate action. Anninos and Paraskevopoulos[53] report that the sprinkling was performed with special carriages owned by the municipality, and soon carriages belonging to private entrepreneurs had joined the army in the battle against dust. In 1879, a temporary increase in the volume of water coming into the city allowed for a more systematic sprinkling. The battle against dust gathered speed. However, as Gerontas and Skouzes[54] assert, the effort to turn Athens into a dust-free heaven was a futile exercise since the city's roads were not paved and the sprinkling carriages often produced more dust than they eliminated. Still, the exercise helped to construct an image of a "caring" and "active" municipality, while it provided a good source of profit for the entrepreneurs who were involved.

In 1894 an unprecedented scarcity of water inhibited the sprinkling of the streets, and the battle against dust appeared to be lost.[55] Dust was then cast in a different light and described as "the golden dust"[56] in an effort to reinterpret the phenomenon by (once again) linking it to the golden era of classical Athens: the dust produced by the once "golden" city could be nothing but "golden" itself. The inevitable comparisons to other Western European metropolises were also made, but optimism prevailed once again and the dust that tormented Athens was considered to be a minor defect compared to the smog that was tormenting London during the same period. Then mayor of Athens Kyriakos declared: "only when the smog disappears from London will the dust disappear from Athens".[57]

The 20th century found Athens gradually turning into an attractive, yet still "dust-tormented" city. The phenomenon receded only when pavement of the roads began in 1905.[58]

Modernizing as Connecting to the West

The conflict between water as use value and water as a means to create symbolic value was exemplified in a striking manner in Queen Amalia's crusade for the construction of a Royal Garden in Athens. The ambition of the newly appointed Queen to create a Royal Garden in an otherwise tree-less and water-less city generated great tension between the need to provide water to an expanding urban population and the spur to use water for feeding the ambition and aesthetic whims of an imported Queen. Amalia considered the creation of the Royal Garden to be a personal project of the first order. Sharing the view of many Western visitors, the royals were not impressed by what they found on their arrival in Athens. They expected to see a glorious capital city, but were faced instead with a city in ruins. Amalia's project for a Royal Garden was one by a queen who had to glorify (and justify) her existence in the city, but also an effort to Westernize a distressingly non-Western city. To this end, as Kairofylas[59] reports, the Royal

Garden was designed along the lines of the garden of Munich, and Schma-rat, a garden expert from Bavaria, was appointed as the royal gardener. Amalia even brought soil from her beloved homeland, Bavaria, a gesture the Greek public considered an insult. The queen carved out and appropriated thirty hectares of the city's central area and set out to create "nature" in the center of the city. The landscaping started in 1839 while the construction of the Royal Palace was still in progress, and ten years later the garden had expanded to its current area (Figure 5.d). For the final phase of landscaping, Amalia summoned the French chief-gardener Bareaud, whose assistant traveled all over Western Europe to collect seeds in order to enrich the Royal Garden with new species that could flourish on Greek soil.

Mpris[60] notes that the Queen's plans for the Royal Garden brought her into continuous debate with a professor of botany, Orphanidis, whose house was located inside the area of the garden. The substantial amount of water required for the creation of this new, royally fabricated urban nature (which at that time was assigned to the exclusive use of the royal family) was taken directly from the city's water supply system. For a city where water was a scarce good, this siphoning inevitably posed a serious social and political problem. In order to calm increasing public discontent, the

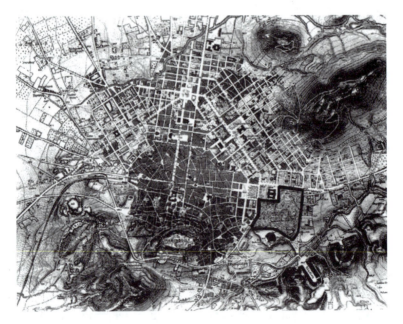

Fig. 5.d The J.A. Kaupert Plan for Athens. The area marked is the Royal Garden in 1875. Greek Ministry of Culture.

queen appointed the Bavarian engineer Rouf to drill for "her own" water so that she would not have to rely on the municipal water supply. However, groundwater resources were also scarce,[61] and the conflict between producing water as use value and producing water to create symbolic value reached a peak in the extremely hot and dry summer of 1843. During that summer, the public protested in the streets against the use of water to feed the plants in the Royal Garden while there was scarcely enough water to quench the thirst of the urban population.[62] This also represented the culmination of a broader social and political conflict, linked to the growing discontent with King Otto over his denial to concede a constitution to the Greek people, and finally resulted in an uprising against the Royal Palace on September 3rd.[63] The newspaper *Αθήνα* reports on July 1, 1843, that, in response to the public upheaval over water, the Mayor of Athens issued a pacifying statement "informing" the citizens of Athens that the inefficiency of water for the city was not the result of watering the Royal Garden, but was instead due to a "[l]ong term drought period and strong heat wave." This rhetorical identification between drought (a natural phenomenon) and water shortage (a socio-natural construction), and the conscious underplaying of the political and economic reasons behind water scarcity is a motif that has been used and is still being used over and over again when dealing with water issues up to the present day, not only in Greece, but also internationally, as we shall see in Chapter 7.

Despite social protest, work continued and the Royal Garden was completed in 1871. By that time, Otto had been deposed after a second rebellion against him in 1862. After the completion of the Royal Garden, there were many more empty areas in the city center which belonged to big landowners and which could, potentially, be landscaped, but were left instead to free land speculation practices. Moreover, there were no water, funds, or political will available to plan for more green spaces in the city. The controversy over the creation of the Royal Garden in Athens reflected a broader dilemma in the Western world between the allocation of land and resources towards the creation of "landscapes of consumption" (entertainment, leisure) and the creation of "landscapes of production" (agricultural land, residential land).[64] Gandy[65] describes for example, how this controversy was played out in the creation of Central Park, in the center of Manhattan, laid out by Frederick Olmsted in 1857. To be fair, however, despite the great controversy and arbitrary means of appropriating water in order to produce this piece of manufactured nature by royal decree, the Royal Garden of Athens (now renamed the National Garden and open to the general public) today remains one of the very few green spaces to be found in the center of Athens.

Modernizing as Reconnecting to a Classical Past

The preoccupation with reconnecting Athens to its ancient past also affected decisions over the construction of a water supply system for the city. Lack of funding for infrastructure development, combined with the desire to unearth the city's ancient past, made the local authorities promote the excavation and reconstruction of the city's ancient Roman aqueduct, Hadrian's Aqueduct, as the best solution available to the city's water problem. Crouch[66] gives a detailed history of the construction of the aqueduct, a major work carried out under the command of the Roman Emperor Hadrian and completed by his successor, Antonius Pius, in 140 AD (Figure 5.e). It was built from vaulted brick with a 25-km long channel laid at a depth between 2.5 and 40 meters. The aqueduct was feted throughout Renaissance Europe as a major feat of technology, progress, and civilization, but, according to the Historical Document of the Water Company of Athens, it had been rendered obsolete during the Ottoman period.[67] Now, the municipal authorities promoted the idea that, if restored, the aqueduct would serve the double purpose of providing a relatively inexpensive solution to Athens' water problem while at the same time it would reveal/restore an indisputably significant part of the city's

Fig. 5.e Hadrian's Aqueduct under restoration. An impressive ancient construction in the heart of Athens. Sorce: E.ΥΓ.ΑΓ. (the Water Company of Athens).

celebrated ancient past. Thus, its restoration became something of an obsession, an urban fetish whose myth was religiously pursued as part of the municipality's vision of modernizing 19th century Athens. This fascination was fuelled by the surge in humanistic archaeology in Western Europe and North America. Between 1833 and 1889, the vast majority of funds for the water supply of Athens were channeled into excavating and reconstructing this ancient Roman aqueduct, and reconnecting it to modern Athens (see Table 5.b).

Table 5.b Restoring Hadrian's Aqueduct

Date	Amount (drachma)	Funding Source	Works
1833	5,000	State funding	Repair works
1846	50,000	Interest free state loan	Cleaning and repair works (from Ampelokipi to Psyhiko)
1851–54	Data not available	Municipal funding	Replacement of old clay pipes with iron ones
1856	20,000	Interest free state loan	Channeling water from Ampelokipi Reservoir into the Royal Palace Purification plant at Aiolou Street
1860	150,000	APPLICATION FOR STATE LOAN	LOAN REFUSED
1860	300,000	LOAN FROM THE BANK OF GREECE	Repair works
1874–78	727,000	Loan from the Bank of Greece	Leveling works (from Kolonaki to Ampelokipi)
1879–87	Data not available	Loan from the Bank of Greece	Expansion of supply network
1887	110,000 390,000	State loan and loan from the Bank of Greece	Repair and drilling works
1889	MUNICIPAL DECISION TO SUSPEND ALL REPAIR WORKS ON HADRIAN'S AQUEDUCT		

Compiled by the author. Information based on: Gerontas and Skouzes (1963), Kalantzopoulos (1964), official Greek State Gazette.

After independence, and before the first municipal elections took place in 1835, the city of Athens was governed by an appointed Council of Elders. It was they who first raised a fund of 5,000 drachmas (dr.) in 1833 towards the restoration of Hadrian's Aqueduct. Additionally, part of the loan granted from the central government to Athens for general restoration purposes in July 1834 was used towards the same purpose. However, the funds were a miserable pittance compared to the cost for a full excavation and restoration works. Thus, the government granted the right to the council of elders to sell water to individual households who could afford to connect to the city's network. According to Gerontas and Skouzes, the connection charge was 200 dr. and the rate for use of water was 30 dr. for the first dram (approx. 95 liters) and 18 dr. for each additional dram consumed per annum.[68]

After the first municipal elections, repair works continued through a further 120,000 dr. loan which came out of the government's domestic budget.[69] A further 50,000 dr. loan was granted in 1846 by the Ministry of Internal Affairs on the condition that the whole amount would be used *exclusively* towards cleaning and repairing Hadrian's Aqueduct. As published in the *Official Greek State Gazette* in 1847,[70] the loan initially was granted at an 8% interest rate, but after pressure from strong local agents, it was eventually offered interest free,[71] although it was agreed that the revenue from the water supply would go to the state chest until the loan was fully repaid. At this point, the government appointed a committee to supervise the contracted works. The committee was also heavily involved in the long and deeply controversial process of drafting the official land use plan for Athens. This was a first strong intervention on the part of the state into a process which, until then, had been administered by the municipality alone (although the funds came from the central state).

Kalantzopoulos[72] reports that between 1851 and 1854, the aqueduct's old clay pipes were replaced with new iron ones. However, despite the money and labor put into it, the aqueduct remained only partially operational. Progress in bringing more water into the city (see Table 5.c) was frustrated by increasingly high levels of leakage due to the old masonry work, which also made the water muddy and potentially unsuitable for drinking, as Gerontas and Skouzes report.[73] According to Paraskevopoulos, while new parts were being restored, other stretches were falling into disrepair.[74] The report produced by the German architect Ernest Ziller stated that the enterprise was "a demanding process…both in terms of time and expenditure, since most of these projects are impossible to carry out without [expensive] excavation works."[75]

Table 5.c Water Supply of Athens between the Years 1879 and 1931

Year	Water Supply (m³/year)	Water Supply (m³/day, average)	Water Supply (L/capita/day, average)
1879	1,102,665	3,021	44
1888	876,000	2,400	18
1898	693,500	1,900	16.5
1923	2,920,000	8,000	10
1928	5,502,617	12,829	18
1929	8,204,308	22,477	30

After 1910 the figures correspond to the metropolitan areas of both Athens and Piraeus.
Compiled from: Koumparelis (1989: 75), Michalopoulos (1932), Kalantzopoulos (1964).

The policy and practice of pumping more money into the aqueduct enterprise was disputed for the first time in 1853. The municipality's request for yet another state loan took two years of discussions and dispute before it was finally approved.[76] This time, however, the loan was not spent on excavations, but went towards the construction of a purification plant (Aiolou Street) and a vaulted reservoir to be located behind the Royal Palace, which had a storage capacity of 500 cubic meters.[77]

In 1860, when the municipality requested yet another loan, the central government refused it outright and suggested that, on this occasion, the municipality should turn to the National Bank of Greece. The state would still act as a guarantor as long as the municipality supplied all public services with free water. A larger loan was granted by the National Bank of Greece (see Table 5.b).[78]

The end of state financial support for the municipal works was one of the first substantial blows to the municipality's power (see also Chapter 6). The municipality was now forced to assume a more entrepreneurial attitude towards finding solutions to the city's water problem. In 1866 the municipal council decided to increase municipal taxation, and use a quarter of the municipal income for establishing a fund for the improvement of water supply, while also increasing water charges. A study carried out by Kordellas compared the cost for water connection and consumption for individual customers in different cities. He found the sum charged in Athens was minimal compared with charges in other cities: five times less than Vienna, six times less than Paris, seven times less than London, and twenty times less than Marseilles.[79]

The results, however, were disappointing: the new scheme could only fund a few minor repair works on Hadrian's Aqueduct, while the municipality's finances were altogether worsening. An additional impediment was the traditional law linking water rights to land property rights, which made compensating landowners increasingly expensive as land speculation became more pervasive (land prices had increased by a factor of ten since the declaration of Athens as the capital of Greece).[80] This period encouraged a number of water entrepreneurs and water vendors to exploit the thirst of Athens and its citizens. In 1889, after half a century, the municipal council finally decided to suspend all works related to restoring Hadrian's Aqueduct and to look for other means of watering Athens (see Chapter 6).

An Interpretation

To be sure, the quest to establish the direct link between classical past and modern future, which became the leitmotiv of the vision for the "New Athens", can be interpreted as a form of nationalistic hallucination. However, as we have seen earlier, this link was neither a Greek invention nor an entirely Greek enterprise. It could be argued that Greece actually *imported* the idea of associating modernization with the excavation of its classical past from the West. It subsequently tried to fit into this reinvented Western imagery of what Greece meant for the Western world: from an obscure place at a remote corner of the Ottoman Empire, Greece was reinvented as the center of Western civilization's cultural heritage, the symbol of democracy and freedom. The Western mind's cognitive geography of Greece was re-drawn from being part of the Orient (the Ottoman Empire) to belonging to the West. It was precisely this image that the West had constructed for Greece to which the newly liberated Greek state tried to conform. Eager to connect to a Western capitalist future, yet unable to take off in a process of industrialization on its own, Greece used its buried classical past as a more direct means of dragging the cognitive geographical boundaries of "the West" towards its own position on the map. In this way, Athens became something of a 19th-century Cinderella, longing to be transformed by the hand of progress, in order to finally be embraced by her Western prince. First, however, she had to pay her dues to her past. The patronizing attitude of the West towards Greece, demanding her transformation in order to fit into the Western imagery, is exemplified in the paragraph written by the German archaeologist L. Ross, when he visited Athens in 1832:

> Your gaze falls upon the city.... [A]nd you wander about in sorrow, the way you do when you encounter a beloved old girlfriend whom

you have left in blooming beauty and who is now welcoming you with deformed face and plucked hair. This is not the glorious eastwards facing Athens. ... [I]f it were not for the temple of Theseus, and for the ruins of the Acropolis, one would find it hard to believe one is indeed in Athens.[81]

However, the project of linking Athens to its future by connecting it to its ancient veins proved to be unattainable. Despite optimistic aspirations, excavating Hadrian's Aqueduct proved not only difficult and more expensive than originally anticipated, but also insufficient to water a fast growing city. It soon became evident that the reconnection of Athens to its past alone was not enough to produce a modern city. The projection of beauty as the "modern truth" and the accompanying efforts to unravel or rediscover the ancient past as a means to modernize, although producing impressive results on a symbolic level (e.g., monumental neoclassical buildings and the baring of an impressive ancient aqueduct) did not produce equally impressive results on a practical level and proved inadequate to assist Greece in becoming a part of the industrialized Western world. With a population of 200,000 and growing, adorned with glorious neoclassical buildings, and partly reconnected to its ancient veins, Athens still lacked an adequate supply of potable water as it entered the 20th century.[82]

CHAPTER 6

Tamed Nature: Late 19th and Early 20th Century

Life has few pleasures to compare with dam-building. …The pleasure comes from the elegance of the compromise you strike between where the water wants to go (guided by gravity and the medium it's moving over), and what you want to do with it.

I. Banks, The Wasp Factory (1984: 84)[1]

The apotheosis of the "engineering era"—the process of modernizing Western cities—ran between the late 19th century through to the first three quarters of the 20th century. modernity's Promethean project culminated during this period with large-scale infrastructure projects taming nature and making it work for the benefit of capitalist expansion. And water was central to it: rivers were harnessed from miles away to feed the growing urban population or dammed to provide electrical power for industry, while mountains were pierced to provide transport routes for people and trade. These projects heralded a new relationship between human beings and nature, between nature and the city. Instead of being fearful and threatening, nature became tame and serviceable, a prerequisite for development. In turn, the city was reconceptualized as a realm outside the reach of nature's processes.

The analysis in this chapter juxtaposes the taming of nature in the industrialized world to similar projects in the colonies of the Western world and in Greece. Late 19th century Greece held a peculiar position within the international dynamics of capitalist expansion. Although an independent state, its economic dependence on Western capital placed it in a similarly submissive position within the geopolitics of capitalist expansion to that of the colonies. The production of the Marathon Dam, Greece's first big water infrastructure project, illustrates Greece's unique position within the world economy.

Capitalist Expansion in Search of New Territory (1880s–1930s)

Toward the end of the 19th century, the spread of industrialization and capitalist formation outside Britain gave rise to powerful new players in Europe and North America, and fierce competition commenced between the industrialized countries over international market shares. The intensification of international competition led to a reassessment of free trade principles, the development of state protectionism, and the imposition of trade barriers and tariffs. In particular, the Ottawa Agreements of 1932 marked the end of free trade between the industrialized nations until the formation of the General Agreement on Tariffs and Trade (GATT) in 1948. The emergence of the state as a key player in capitalist formation went hand in glove with the rise of nationalism, independence movements, and the continuous shifts in international alliances. North America, in particular the United States, emerged from this process as a new yet powerful geo-political and economic player. After 1900, the U.S. dollar began to replace the pound sterling as the reserve currency in international trade, culminating with the Bretton Woods agreement (1945) after World War II.

By the mid-19th century, Western metropolises had begun to compete with each other in the spheres of technological innovation, imperial grandeur, and luxury goods. World exhibitions provided a grand stage for this competition. New technologies and machinery could be found on display there, side by side with exotic colonial goods. London's 1851 world exhibition was hosted in the Crystal Palace, which was itself a display of technological achievement, while Paris celebrated its 1889 exhibition with the daring construction of the Eiffel Tower.

The competition amongst industrial powers was not only over industrial output and international trade shares, but also over the appropriation of new territory for the expansion of market operations and for overcoming the recurring crises of capital overaccumulation. This led to a new wave of colonization. The great scramble for Africa was completed in 1914 when the continent was divided between Belgium, Britain, France, Germany, Italy, Portugal, and Spain; only Ethiopia and Liberia were independent nations. Competition over new territory was also extended to neighboring areas within the European continent itself, where the once powerful Ottoman Empire was now crumbling. Despite efforts for domestic reform within the Ottoman Empire (the *Hatt-i-Sherif* reform in 1839, the Young Turk movement in 1889), the reactionary yet powerful Islamic institutions impeded capitalist formation and the introduction of technological change. The Ottoman Empire had become the "sick man of Europe", with its collapse accelerated by the intervention of the industrialized European countries, either directly through military action (as in the case of Egypt) or through financial support for independence wars (as in the case of Greece).[2] World War I was the final blow for the Turks, who lost all their possessions on the European continent, except for a small area around Constantinople.

A Selective Export of Modernity's Promethean Project

According to Mintz,[3] the taming of nature in plantation colonies was a precursor of the Industrial Revolution in Western Europe. Similarly, the taming of domestic nature played a pivotal role in furthering industrial development in the West. Railways, tramways, tunnels, gas pipes, and electrical networks transformed the physical landscape and made natural elements work for the benefit of capitalist expansion. Furthermore, large-scale urban infrastructure projects secured water and good sanitation for the growing urban population, thus supporting more industrial activity and urban sprawl.

Between 1901 and 1920, London's population nearly doubled from 4.5 to 8.6 million, and the physical area of the metropolis expanded outwards rapidly. As well, London had become the command and control center for trade and finance of an extensive colonial system. Hebbert[4] reports that in 1914 the city alone hosted around 40,000 firms that employed 350,000 people, mainly in the services sector. The Port of London held 29 percent of U.K. trade in 1913 and 38 percent by 1938.[5] The world's first power station was built by Thomas Edison in London in 1883, and the electrification of railways and tramways, combined with the expansion of the underground and innovations in road transport, encouraged the expansion of London both in physical space and in population.[6]

The taming of nature also played a pivotal role in enabling the international expansion of market operations. The export of the Western Promethean Project to the colonies not only increased dominance over nature, but also dominance over human beings in old and newly conquered land alike. However, the introduction of technology in non-Western territory was a highly eclectic process: technology that would assist the market expansion of industrialized countries, such as transportation and communication, received the full attention and funding of Western capital, while projects that could potentially trigger local independent development, such as irrigation or water supply, received little or none. Only the expatriate colonial communities, which sought prestige in relation to the home bourgeoisie, were often allocated special funding to develop restricted localized networks of water and electricity.

Thus, although colonies did modernize in a sense, with railways, roads and electrification, they remained underdeveloped in many other respects. This partial introduction of technology and infrastructure is termed by Headrick "selective modernization".[7] He contends that technologies introduced this way into non-industrialized countries operated "for decades as alien enclaves, linked to distant suppliers and customers with little or no local articulation".[8]

Finally, the introduction of western experts accompanied the introduction of western technologies into non-industrialized territory. A wide range of professionals (engineers, mechanics, medics) arrived along with technology as part of the same process of conquering people and landscapes. However, the importation of experts and technology was not accompanied by arrangements for the transfer of knowledge to local agents. Colonial powers feared the development of domestic import-substitution industries, as well as the breeding of a native bourgeoisie that would create potential competition in the future. Some degree of knowledge transfer developed inadvertently by the early 20th century, but it occurred mainly through local initiative rather than through colonial planning.

Water Resources Development as an Exemplary Case

The tensions inherent in the process of "selective modernization" become clear when one examines water supply, sanitation and irrigation projects. Although in the industrialized world such projects had taken off by the mid-19th century, in the colonies (old and new alike) such projects received little or no attention. Britain, France, Spain, and Belgium gave water supply and sanitation projects top priority and allocated public funding and efforts very early on, as we have seen in the previous chapter. London was able to accommodate increased urbanization and rising levels of industry thanks to the early centralization of decision making and the advancement of institutions related to water abstraction and allocation, amongst other factors. Abstractions became the object of regulation as early as the late 19th century,[9] ensuring not only that the population of the imperial capital could be supplied with safe drinking water, but also that the needs of water-consuming industries located in and around London could be met. The numerous wells bored through the London clay into London's huge chalk aquifer were used almost exclusively for private and manufacturing purposes: breweries, gas-works, public baths, factories, hotels, and large blocks of offices and services (see Table 6.a).[10]

While the amount of water available to London kept expanding, the situation in British colonies was quite different, and this was not only due to the different climatic conditions. In India, for example, while there was widespread investment in transport technologies, urban water supply and rural irrigation systems that would have been highly beneficial for feeding the population and initiating local independent development, were not of interest to the British colonizers. Sharma contends that: "the British gave priority to the construction of railways over the construction of canals, because the former facilitated British trade in India, whereas the latter benefited agriculture, for which the British trader had little or no concern."[11] Expenditure on irrigation in India began catching up with railway spending only after the 1930s,[12] partly as a response to the pressure from Indian nationalists (notably the Indian National Congress under the leadership of Mahatma Gandhi) and the voting of the Government of India Act in 1935.

Swyngedouw's insightful analysis in *Social Power and the Urbanization of Water*[13] further supports this argument. It was only after Ecuador became independent from Spanish rule in 1830 that urban infrastructure projects received attention and funding. Between 1850 and 1910, water-works and electricity in Guayaquil were mainly funded mainly through the development of mono-cultural cash crops, particularly cocoa.

Thus, while urban water supply and sanitation projects were prioritized and even naturalized in the industrialized world, such projects remained a

Table 6.a London Water Supply Sources (% of total abstractions)

Period	River Thames	River Lee	Springs and Wells
Before the 1860s	<50.0	20–30	20–30
After the 1860s	50.0	20–30	20–30
1888	50.0	38.0	12.0
1921	59.0	23.5	17.5
1947/1948	67.0	16.5	16.5
1980s–1990s	70.0	15.0	15.0

Source: Esteban Castro and Erik Swyngedouw. The case of London: Metropolitan areas and sustainable use of water (METRON). Final report to the European Commission, Environment and Climate Programme, Framework V. Oxford, November 2000. Elaborated from Bolton (1888), Garnett (1922), MWB (1949), MWB (1954), Perera et al. (1985), Sexton (1988), Connarton (1999).

low priority for colonial regimes. The taming of nature that had taken place in the industrialized world as an essential part of industrialization was only performed selectively in the non-industrialized world. As we will see in the following sections, the development of water projects in Greece—a nation on the margins of capitalist expansion—was closer to the experiences of colonial societies than to those of the industrialized West.

The Paradigm Shift

Chapter 5 examined how Greece's early 19th century archaeological project succeeded in attracting the attention of a great number of archaeological institutions, travelers and archaeologists, but failed to attract the desired capital investment that would trigger the country's industrialization and capitalist formation. However, towards the end of the 19th century, endowed with an enlightened leadership, Greece turned away from this archaeological modernization paradigm, and pursued its modernization through an engineering paradigm, a development strategy focused predominantly on the introduction of technology and big infrastructure projects. Liberal changes on the Greek political scene towards the end of the 19th century led to the election of Charilaos Trikoupis as Prime Minister (1882–1885, 1887–1890, and 1892–1895), a "reformist liberal"[14] determined to modernize the country by clamping down on traditional feudal structures and elites, and by paving the way for a domestic bourgeoisie to develop and flourish. Trikoupis pursued the initiation of industrialization through development loans. However, getting approval for such loans proved a difficult task. Greece's creditworthiness was undermined by its outstanding debt, which started with the first loans to finance the War of Independence (see Chapter 5). For this reason, Trikoupis introduced a series of strict measures, including raising indirect taxes and custom duties and exploiting state monopolies in matches and salt. He eventually succeeded in regularizing the country's debt, which allowed the state to secure new loans for the development of technology and infrastructure.

However, Trikoupis' efforts would not have been as effective had they not coincided historically with a period of recession in Western economies. Indeed, the paradigm shift from archaeological to engineering projects in Greece's modernization process owed as much to domestic reform as to the overaccumulation crisis of Western capital. Slackening demand for investment and falling domestic interest rates in western Europe turned investing abroad into an attractive option from the 1870s onwards.[15] Greece became one of the many fertile sites for Western capital in search of a "spatial fix"—an underdeveloped geographical site that offered investment opportunities, which could offset diminishing returns in regions already heavily invested in.[16] The favorable domestic and international political and economic configuration enabled Greece to raise six external loans for a total nominal value of 630 million drachmas between 1879 and 1890,[17] and to pursue a number of big technology infrastructure projects whose budget exceeded Greece's domestic budget.[18]

However, technology never "'flows' on its own accord from 'advanced' to 'backward' areas,"[19] and when it does, this 'flow' never comes for free. Thus, in Greece too, the type of development projects supported by foreign (predominantly English and French) capital bore many of the characteristics of colonial development and initiated a process very similar to colonial "selective modernization." Although a sovereign state and not a colony, Greece was economically dependent on advanced Western economies, which put it to a position similar to that of the colonies within the international division of labor and led a number of scholars, including Koronis, Psiroukis, and Leontidou to characterize Greece's development as "colonial".[20]

There are three key aspects to Greece's development through foreign loans towards the end of the 19th century, all of which support the argument for a selective modernization. First, like it did with its colonies, Western capital prioritized the development of railway and communication infrastructure in Greece over any other type of development.[21] The decade between 1883 and 1893 went down in Greek history as "the railway decade," since the length of railway track grew from 7 to 568 miles. Similarly, the steamship tonnage increased from 8,241 tons in 1875 to 144,975 tons in 1895.[22] By 1925, 92% of railway infrastructure and 100% of Greece's telecommunications projects were financed through foreign capital.[23] Second, the economic patronage was coupled by political patronage. Britain and France provided the bulk of foreign capital inflow to Greece, but both countries were also heavily involved in Greek politics, and had been Greece's allies in recent wars. Third, Greece had to import foreign expertise, along with foreign technology. A team of highly paid French engineers, known as the "Delegation of French Engineers", was in charge of most of the railway engineering projects in Greece during the 1880s. Vaxevanoglou reports that the foreign experts, educated under the banner of reason and rationalism, were unable to grasp the social reality in Greece, which was "far more complicated than their perfectly laid plans and unexpectedly irrational to their taste".[24]

The Case of Urban Infrastructure

The type of development that was pursued in Greece through foreign loans led to the oxymoron of a country which was both "modern and underdeveloped"[25]—barely industrialized, yet buzzing with modernizing railway projects, and with a capital city (Athens) that still lacked adequate water supply and sanitation. The lack of funding for water supply and sanitation projects supports further the selective modernization thesis. Water supply or irrigation projects that yielded neither money nor symbolic capital were not considered a desirable investment for colonial regimes. Referring to India, Headrick notes:

> An irrigation system is neither dramatic nor romantic. It takes much longer to build than any other public work and provides no return until it is almost completed. A layman finds it uninteresting to look at unless he remembers the waste lands it replaced… hence, irrigation has few poets and publicists to sing its praises compared to those other monuments of the Raj, the railways and the cities.[26]

Thus, given Greece's peculiar position in the international geopolitics of capitalist expansion, urban infrastructure projects were caught between the Scylla of not figuring on the list of interests of foreign capital, and the Charybdis of lying beyond the financial abilities of the Greek state. The Greek diaspora bourgeoisie had no interest in investing in a water supply system either. Although labeled "Greek", diaspora capital was closer in its interests to foreign capital and channeled investment mainly into trade and finance.[27] According to Tsoukalas[28] the diaspora Greeks "colonized" their own country of origin, either on their own or in alliance with foreign capital through the stock market and trade activities.[29]

In addition to the economic and political reasons that prevented foreign or diaspora capital from investing in water supply projects, the social-cultural perceptions around water also proved to be a significant barrier to attracting private investment in water infrastructure projects. Water was still perceived as a public good, as a sacred and awesome life-sustaining resource, which could not and should not be turned into a profit-making engine, and which traditionally had been managed and allocated through the local authorities. A case in point of the difficulty to commodify water and to hand it over to the private sector was the public outcry against a private Greek company that was established in 1839 to implement a small scale water supply project for Athens, and which became known as "the company of the four capitalists".[30] The company's proposal met with immediate public criticism and outrage. The municipality not only rejected it, but also characterized it as "an excessive and hideous speculation" because it sought to "profit from selling a public good".[31]

To complicate matters further, the link between water rights and land ownership that had existed since the Ottoman period made the design and implementation of large-scale collective water supply projects very difficult. Moreover, the dispute between the municipality of Athens and the central state over ownership and management of water resources went unresolved.

Given the circumstances outlined above, the development of urban infrastructure did not occur until the moment when an initial industrialization process allowed for the state to step in and develop institutions and infrastructure which would safeguard both production and reproduction. This moment coincided with the development of a strong central state as well as with another moment of crisis in the economies of Western Europe, which led to further expansion of Western capital investment abroad.

Towards Urban Oasis

The presence of foreign expertise and the selective choices for infrastructure development in Greece went not uncontested. Greek engineers, most of whom came from affluent families (domestic or diasporic), and were educated in Britain or France, were eager to assert their expertise by putting forward alterative engineering projects for the country's development. Many of their proposals were projects for irrigation and water supply, and directed technology towards an alternative type of development. Indeed, late 19th century and early 20th century saw a plethora of plans prepared by Greek engineers that would water Athens or develop national irrigation plans that intended to increase agricultural production. However, not a single one of these large-scale water supply project proposals attracted financial support, despite the rapid population growth and accentuation of the water problem of Athens as the city grew rapidly (see Table 6.b).[32]

As late 19th century Athens grew in both population and physical size, water shortages became even more acute. Excavations for Hadrian's Aqueduct continued, but were no longer uncontested, since what had previously been work in empty fields now included excavations in the middle of settlements, and the affected residents threatened to take up arms to stop the works.[33] It was at this point when authorities began looking for a solution to the water problem *outside* instead of *underneath* the city. The lack of capital and the absence of a coherent political program for watering Athens did not prevent the Greek engineering community, which was rapidly gaining kudos and influence, from proposing ambitious plans for solving the city's enduring water problem.[34] The plans were modeled after successful engineering projects in Western Europe and North America.

The first proposal for Athens was submitted to the municipality by the Greek public works engineer, Aggelopoulos, in 1889—a year of severe

Table 6.b The Population of Athens between the Years 1820 and 1940

Year	Population
1820	10,000
1830	20,000
1851	24,754
1853	31,122
1860	65,000
1879	68,677
1888	133,000
1890	114,355
1898	114,000
1900	200,000
1904	215,000
1910	190,000
1923	800,000
1928	704,247
1940	686,629

The figures after 1910 correspond to the joint population of Athens and Piraeus.
Compiled from; Mpiris (1939; 1996), Gerontas and Skouzes (1963), Kalantzopoulos (1964), Clogg (1984), Leontidou (1989), and statistical data from ΕΣΥΕΑ.

drought for Athens. The proposal suggested piping water to Athens from Lake Stymphalia located in the mountains of Corinth. In a response to the proposal, the Greek government summoned the French engineer Quellennec to investigate Athens' water supply. Quellennec was at the time head of the delegation of the French engineers in Greece,[35] and he had been involved in the construction of the Greek railroad network, the Corinth Canal, and the construction of several harbors.

Quellennec produced a report in 1890[36] that stated the obvious: the existing water resources were not sufficient. He too, like Aggelopoulos, proposed channeling water from Lake Stymphalia. The proposal acknowledged drawing its inspiration from the ancient Romans (!) who used water from Stymphalia to supply Corinth, but did not acknowledge or make any reference to Aggelopoulos' study, which had proposed the same solution a year earlier. The only difference between the two proposals lay in a slight variation in the planned course of the proposed aqueduct.[37] Quellennec's proposal promised the channeling of 2,000 liters per second of water from Lake Stymphalia, from which 900 liters per second would water Athens and

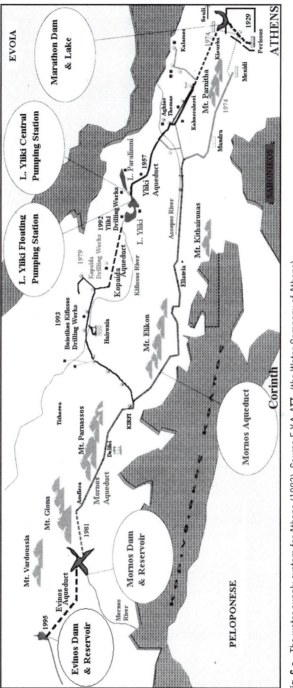

Fig. 6.a The water supply system for Athens (1993). Source E.ΥΔ.ΑΠ. (the Water Company of Athens).

Piraeus, with the rest irrigating 4,600 hectares of land (this was calculated for a projected population of 250,000 inhabitants by 1910). Less than a month after receiving the report, the Greek government announced a public competition for the project. Nevertheless, the Association of Greek Engineers, who felt that their scientific credibility and integrity were put into question, attacked Quellennec's report. Many expressed doubts regarding both the promised quantity of water, and the economic feasibility of Quellennec's proposal. The Greek Engineer Stratos calculated the supply of the springs at no more than 650 liters per second, as opposed to the 2,000 liters per second suggested by Quellennec's report.[38] Eventually, Quellennec admitted to having been "misled" by measurements carried out by previous researchers and that he had not carried out new measurements.[39]

The reasons behind the sloppiness and improvisation that more often than not characterized "scientific" reports by foreign experts did not stem from lack of adequate training or expertise. The majority of the foreign engineers (and Quellennec was no exception) had produced works of high quality in Greece and elsewhere, with a full sense of duty, but not without generous economic return. However, when it came to large-scale water projects, they were fully aware of the negative economic feasibility of such projects, and of the political rather than pragmatic-technical role their reports were called upon to play, i.e., providing "scientific justification" and granting "time credit" for delays in the implementation of water supply projects. Dutiful to the quasi-colonial regime by which they were employed, foreign experts agreed to produce water supply reports as a "courtesy" to the Greek government. However, they knew in advance that their reports would not be implemented and thus carried them through with the least possible effort. After a long debate, Quellennec's project was eventually abandoned.

Despite the fact that it did not produce any effect, the debate triggered a series of further suggestions and proposals.[40] Still, none of these ambitious engineering proposals received financial support, since the end of the glorious "railway decade" found Greece with 50 percent of the national budget allocated to servicing its external debt (1890s). This culminated in the bankruptcy of the Greek state in 1893.[41] Following this economic disaster, a major defeat for Greece in 1897 in their continuing war against Turkey resulted in Greece having to take yet another loan to pay for war damages. The development loans not only failed to initiate a process of industrialization, but the type of development pursued had detrimental effects on the agricultural sector. During the 1890s, one-sixth of the impoverished Greek agricultural population emigrated to the UK and Egypt. The political instability and discontent exploded in 1909 with an uprising in the army circles (the Military League). Confronted with the threat of a military *coup d' état*, the Royal Palace agreed to revise the constitution. At the end of this charged political period, Eleftherios Venizelos, leader of the Liberal Party, became Prime Minister and embarked on an extended policy of domestic renewal.

It was the sweeping changes in the domestic social, political, and economic configuration brought by Venizelos' liberal politics that encouraged, for the first time, a more ambitious outlook towards water supply and irrigation projects. One of the most important reforms was the land reform law, which granted the state the right to expropriate land and property in cases where it was deemed necessary to the national interest.[42] This had the effect of breaking up big estates, which dealt a substantial blow to the remains of the feudal system. It also had a major impact on water resource development. The land reforms that followed in 1917 and 1934 completed this task. On top of the land reforms, a number of liberal reforms were introduced in the economy and social policy, including the reduction of interest rates, the introduction of minimum wages, the official recognition of trade unions, and the declaration of company unions as illegal. Securing great popularity and a large degree of domestic consensus, the liberal government engaged in the Balkan Wars, by the end of which (1913) Greece had increased its territory by 70% (Figure 6.b) and its population from 2,800,000 to 4,800,000.[43] At the same time, a small but growing educated middle class was forming. As well, the Liberal Party openly supported the newly emerging, shipping-based commercial and industrial bourgeoisie, and was determined to realize its commitment to a state-aided acceleration of the establishment of a market economy, following the example of its Western European allies.

On the swiftly changing social and political scene, the dependency on foreign capital investment for development became more acute. However, the mechanisms through which foreign capital was channeled and invested into the country underwent major changes. At the beginning of the 20th century, Greek legislation for the first time allowed equity-based companies to form, and they were subsequently listed on the Athen's stock exchange market. Thus, 111 equity capital companies of a total capital value of 518,300,000 drachma were established in Greece between 1901 and 1919.[44] A large number of these companies were formed by foreign capital (see Table 6.c). Foreign capital also got involved in the main Greek banks via shareholding. Many economic activities were financed from loans taken from foreign banks. But the expansion of foreign capital investment was now predominantly facilitated by the introduction of state loans. It was the introduction of this particular economic instrument,

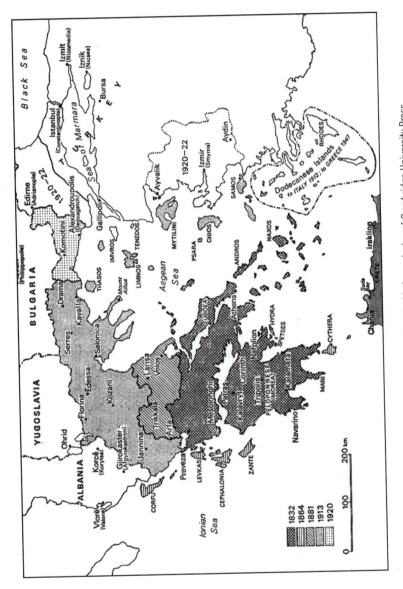

Fig. 6.b The growth of Greece since 1832. (Clogg, 1979: ix) Reproduced by kind permission of Cambridge University Press.

Table 6.c The Structure of External Trade for Greece in 1919

Country	Imports (in golden drachma)	Exports (in golden drachma)	Balance (in golden drachma)
United States	445,327,509	80,002,867	− 365,324,642
Great Britain	338,724,619	175,438,012	− 163,286,607
France	133,586,337	44,949,592	− 88,636,745
Italy	142,020,913	37,982,022	− 104,038,891
Turkey	76,305,715	80,448,552	+ 4,142,837
Egypt	83,819,995	48,204,947	− 35,615,048

From Psiroukis (1964: 73)

combined with the sweeping social, political, economic reforms mentioned above, as well as advances in engineering science, that opened up the possibility for large utility infrastructure projects to be financed and implemented in Greece for the first time from 1910 onwards.

Within this favorable climate, a number of projects were proposed for watering Athens. Amongst those, a project proposal for a dam and reservoir at Marathon (see Figure 6.a) was tendered in 1918. It was the first one accompanied by a comprehensive economic feasibility study (prepared by the Bank of Piraeus in 1919) and endowed with financial support from American capital. Earlier dam proposals had been rejected not only because of the lack of a supportive funding mechanism, but also because dam constructions were considered to be dangerous and risky.[45] This time, however, improved technological expertise and the experience of many successful dam constructions around the world (and in particular in the U.S.) eased the initial negative predisposition towards such solutions. Even the Greek medical community, which had adamantly opposed receiving the water supply from reservoirs, eventually succumbed to the pressures posed by chronic water shortages and related cholera epidemics.[46]

Thus, economic, engineering, and medical advancements all seemed to presage a successful completion to the proposed Marathon project. American engineering consultants drafted the initial report, and the Greek state, together with the Bank of Piraeus, reached an informal agreement for its implementation. However, the process was soon halted as a new war against Turkey in 1919 led to the electoral defeat of Prime Minister Venizelos, whose replacement, "Gounaris," declared the Marathon agreement illegal on the basis that there had not been a public bidding for the project.

Looking for Water Outside the City

The end of the war against Turkey had disastrous social, political, and economic consequences for Greece and became known in modern Greek history as the "Asia Minor Disaster". The treaty of Lausanne, signed in July 1923, announced the end of hostilities, redefined the borders of the Greek state (Figure 6.b), and imposed international financial controls on Greece. A subsequent convention ordered a "compulsory exchange of Turkish nationals of the Greek Orthodox persuasion resident in Turkish territory, and of Greek nationals of the Moslem religion resident in Greek territory."[47] This resulted in the inflow of 1.3 million people of Greek Orthodox religion from Asia Minor into Greece in exchange for half a million Greek Muslims, who resettled in Turkey. Predictably, this generated an explosive refugee problem. The population of Athens doubled to 704,247 inhabitants between 1920 and 1928 (see Table 6.b).[48]

The exchange of refugees changed not only the size of the population, but also its social composition. The cities in Asia Minor, from where the Greek Orthodox migrants originated, were important trading centers with a highly socially stratified population. Most of the migrants who resettled in the still semi-feudal Greece had been part of the merchant and entrepreneurial elites in their place of origin, and therefore had higher skill levels and class consciousness than the indigenous Greek population. The transformed social, political, and economic structure demanded innovations in administration, socio-spatial organization and infrastructure.[49]

The influx of refugees created even more acute water problems. Water supply per capita was falling (Table 6.d) while conflicts over it intensified,[50] and Athenians demanded an immediate solution.[51] However, the explosive political situation that followed the "Asia Minor disaster" did not allow for quick planning. Prime Minister Protopapadakis resigned in August 1922 and King Constantine decided to "appoint" Triantafyllakos as

Table 6.d Water Supply of Athens between the Years 1879 and 1931

Year	Water Supply (m³/year)	Water Supply (m³/day, average)	Water Supply (L/capita/day, average)
1879	1,102,665	3,021	44
1888	876,000	2,400	18
1898	693,500	1,900	16.5
1923	2,920,000	8,000	10
1928	5,502,617	12,829	18
1929	8,204,308	22,477	30

After 1910 the figures correspond to the metropolitan areas of both Athens and Piraeus.
Compiled from: Michalopoulos (1932), Kalantzopoulos (1964); Koumparelis (1989:75).

the new Prime Minister. This decision caused a rebellion in army circles (the Gonata-Plastira movement), and eventually resulted in King Constantine's stepping down in favor of his son, George, in September 1922. A new government was formed under Prime Minister Krokidas, which tried and sentenced to death the leaders of the movement. This caused great public upheaval and led to a new round of national elections, which were won by the Liberal party (December 1923). King George was sent into exile, while the self-exiled Venizelos returned to Greece in 1924. This put an end to a long period of high political volatility.

It was after the end of this period that the Marathon project re-emerged from limbo. In 1923, the executive director of the Ministry of Transport, Genidounias, was summoned to assess all projects for the water supply of Athens that had been proposed since 1889. A five-volume report was published, comparing all the proposals in terms of cost and annual yield. It concluded that: "the construction of a dam and an artificial lake for water collection at Marathon is beyond any doubt the optimum solution."[52] The report suggested that the Marathon Dam proposal presented "the last recourse" for Athens, and calculated that the cost of the project would be between 3.6 and 6 times less than that of an equivalent construction at any other possible location.

The report did not go uncontested. The engineer Korizis contended that there had not been an adequate study of rainfall levels at the site and calculated the actual annual yield from the reservoir to be half (40 Hm^3) of that predicted by the ministry's report.[53] Despite rising controversy, the report legitimized the only comprehensive study available that also carried the necessary financial guarantees. Thus, in 1923 the Ministry of Transport gave its final approval to the preliminary study for the Marathon project, and the Liberal government decided to proceed immediately with its implementation.

According to Gerontas' epic description, "it was the moment that signified the beginning of the end of a century-old water scarcity, which had tormented the capital of Greece and its inhabitants, who endured, patiently and resignedly, like a new Tantalus, the daily misery of lack of water."[54]

A restricted public competition was announced and the government assigned the project to Ulen & Co, a New York-based multinational construction firm with 30 years of experience, predominantly in developing countries. On December 22, 1924, the Greek government, Ulen & Co, and the Bank of Athens signed the contract for financing and constructing the water supply works at Marathon. This included the construction of a dam and artificial lake at the site of Marathon, a conveyance pipe of 21.5 km, a treatment plant, and a distribution network. The contractual agreement was approved by the Greek Parliament, which also ordered the establishment of the Hellenic Water Company for Athens, Piraeus, and Environs Limited (which we will refer to as *EEY* [*Ελληνική Εταιρία Υδρεύσεως*]). The role of the *EEY* was to financially manage the project, supervise the construction works, and oversee water supply.

Bonds and Knots

The Marathon project's total budget exceeded the stock and reserve funds of the National Bank of Greece,[55] but it was nothing more than an average size investment for Ulen & Co, which provided immediate cash flow for the project's implementation. However, the project was in effect financed by the Greek state in the form of a US$10 million loan to be repaid to Ulen & Co, worsening further the country's already considerable debt. The *EEY* was assigned to ensure the repayment of the loan through water charges in annual instalments of US$1 million. However, in order to preserve water's public good attribute, the *EEY* was allowed a profit margin that should not exceed 7.5% of its annual revenue. In order to guarantee steady flow of income for the *EEY*, connection to the water supply network became compulsory for all new households, as was the installation of a "security meter"[56] measuring individual household consumption.[57] The state maintained the right to define the rates for water charges. In addition to these arrangements, the Greek government issued bonds for the Greek state to a value of US$10 million for the markets of Athens, New York, and Cairo as a guarantee for the repayment of the loan. According to the contract, Ulen & Co shared both the loan and the company's shares with the Bank of Athens. The shares would be passed on to the Greek state only after the repayment.[58] On May 16, 1925, a further provisional contract for US$1 million in bonds was signed to finance the construction of a saline sewerage system, and the improvement of the existing fresh water systems.[59]

The Marathon contract was characteristic of the establishment of a new set of trade agreements (and economic dependency) between Greece and the U.S. that took place after the Treaty of Lausanne (1923). According to Psiroukis[60] the treaty weakened the relationship between Greece and its previous allies (France and the UK). Moreover, WWI turned Britain from an international creditor to a debtor.[61] After WWI it was New York and not London that became the "Center of the World."[62] This economic and geopolitical development paved the road for U.S. entry into the Near East at the expense of France and the UK, and assigned to the U.S. "the role of protecting the colonial regimes in the area."[63]

During that period, the UK directed its interest elsewhere and turned India into its "laboratory of hydraulic engineering" as part of its efforts to escape from its own financial crisis.[64] With no formal colonies of its own, the U.S. did the same through involvement in a great many projects in the Near East and South America. The operations of Ulen & Co typified this process. The company's contracts included building water and sewerage networks in Brazil and Colombia, public highway projects in South America, and railroads in Persia.[65] In Greece, along with U.S. capital, scientific know-how, and managerial expertise, U.S. working practices were also imported: of the 3,000 wage workers who were employed at the Marathon site, 900 were provided with accommodation by the company in:

> comfortable living quarters, gratis, in houses equipped with electric lights, screened doors and windows and heated by wood-fired stoves…. Palatable and nourishing meals are fed to the laborers at 20 drachmas (25 cents) for 3 meals a day.[66]

Ulen & Co's quasi-Fordist model was welcomed by the impoverished urban population. Although the company honoured its agreement to employ manual workers of Greek nationality only, the vast majority of the management and scientific personnel employed on the project remained North American.

Dams as Symbols of Modernization

The founding stone for the Marathon Dam was ceremoniously laid in October 1926 by Prime Minister Zaimis, while Venizelos participated in the ceremony.[67] A 13.4 km-long tunnel conveyed water from the reservoir into Athens (Figure 6.a). The construction took five years and a workforce of 450 people. The works were completed in May 1931,[68] when the existing aqueduct, reservoir, and distribution network were handed over to the *EEY.*

At the time, the Marathon Dam was the most important engineering project ever implemented in the Balkans, and one of the largest projects of this kind in all of Europe. It became a symbol for the new era of modernization in Greece. One year after the inauguration of the aqueduct, the supply of water for Athens reached 500 liters per second. As part of the same project for sanitizing Athens, municipal lorries were also assigned to collect garbage in 1924, while in 1928 the sewerage works of Athens were completed, thus relieving the city of its "black lake".[69] From 1926 onwards, all buildings were connected to the new water network. All new houses were fitted with bathrooms and toilets and water consumption rapidly increased (Table 6.e). However the symbolic character that the Marathon

Table 6.e Patterns of Domestic Water Availability for Athens

	No. of Households Connected	Patterns of Availability of Running Water to Connected Households (%)			
		Every 4 Days	Every 3 Days	Every 2 Days	Daily
1926 (June)	17,073	97	1.5	1.5	0
1926 (Dec.)	18,128 (1927)	88	10.5	1.5	0
1930	23,612	3	77	20	0
1931	48,043	0	0	15	85
1932	68,282	0	0	0	100

From Koumparelis (1989); newspaper Έθνος (April 6, 1956).

project acquired was the outcome of far more complex political, cultural, and social processes than the mere successful completion of a water supply system. The dam was emblematic because it denoted three key economic, political, cultural, and social processes. First, the choice of the dam's location and the morphology of the construction embodied Greece's peculiar modernization process. This, as we have seen in Chapter 5, involved connecting to the future and to the West through technology and development, but also reconnecting to the past through nourishing and consolidating the continuity between modern and ancient Greece. Second, the dam signaled the beginning of an era in modern Greek history in which Greeks ceased perceiving water as an awesome element—the lack of which impeded the city's growth and modernization—and started perceiving it as an element that could be manipulated to become a generator for development.[70] From that moment onwards, water resources management became one of the leading engines for the country's economic growth. Third, the dam symbolized the beginning of a socio-economic process in which the city's footprint expanded while nature became increasingly separated from the city. For the first time, the solution to the urban problem of watering Athens was looked for *outside* the city. In what follows, I will examine in greater detail the ways in which the Marathon Dam functioned as a signifier of the above three processes.

Connecting to the Future via Reconnecting to the Past

[T]he construction of the modern notion of the aesthetic artefact is...inseparable from the construction of the dominant ideological forms of modern class-society, and indeed from a whole new form of human subjectivity appropriate to that social order.

T. Eagleton, The Ideology of the Aesthetic (1997)[71]

The Marathon Dam (Figure 6.c) has been described as "a beautiful construction, unique world-wide."[72] Indeed, the beginning of the 20th century heralded a period when technology asserted its own aesthetic value, acquired its own aesthetic expressions and was fetishized and admired in and of itself (see Chapter 3). While cars embodied an individualized technological sublime, dams evinced a collective sublime. In his *Concrete and Clay*, Matthew Gandy[73] depicts the "magnificent approach" to the newly completed Kensico Dam via the "scenic utopia" of the Bronx River Parkway as a means to "inspire civic pride in the citizens of New York." However, the unique symbolic value of the Marathon project resided not only in it being an impressive engineering achievement, but also in it representing through its morphology and location the cultural links between modern and ancient Greek history, between the modern and ancient Greek state, between modern and ancient Greek achievements and civilization. Adopting a neoclassical aesthetic solution for a decidedly modern engineering construction pointed to a deeper effort to reconcile the tension between past and future that, as we have seen in Chapter 5, had long tantalized Greek politics, society, and culture.[74]

Fig. 6.c A glorious construction. The Marathon Dam after its completion. Notice the copy of the alter at the foot of the dam. Source: Ulen & Co., 1930, p. 29.

To start with, Marathon, the site that was chosen for the dam, already held a charged historical meaning as an ancient battlefield where the Athenians had won the final battle of a long war against the Persians. The site prompts a comparison between the victory of modern Greeks over nature to the victory of ancient Greeks over the "barbarians".[75] The erection of a temple at the foot of the dam in the form of a replica of the temple of the Treasure of the Athenians further accentuated the desire to establish this link (Figure 6.d). The original temple had been built by the ancient Athenians at Delphi in 490 BC to thank the gods for their help in securing victory at the battle of Marathon. In both cases, the temple signified the victory of civilization over wilderness, suggesting a comparison and continuity between the long battle that ancient Athenians waged and won against the Persians, and the century long battle that modern Athenians won against nature. Moreover, as if the location and symbolism of the temple were not enough, a sign, carved in marble and placed at the entrance of the replica of the Treasury, literally spells out the connection between past and future. The sign reads:

> To commemorate their victory in the battle of Marathon, Athens erected a treasury at Delphi. This building is a replica and commemorates a victory at Marathon in wresting from nature its life giving water for the citizens of Athens.

However, the attempts to connect past and future symbolically did not stop there. To further enhance the past–present–future link, all visible parts of the dam were covered with the same type of marble that was used for the construction of the Parthenon, thus inviting a comparison of the glory of these two structures: the Parthenon as the shrine of ancient Athens, the symbol of a great civilization, the cradle of Western culture; and the Marathon Dam as the shrine of modern Athens.

Although the shrine itself was located 42 kilometers outside Athens, the new link between antiquity and modernity also needed to be celebrated within the city itself. To this end, a marble public fountain was constructed in the center of Athens, next to the Arch of Emperor Hadrian and near the Ancient Temple of Zeus. The fountain received the first flow of water from Marathon during a public celebration staged next to it. To commemorate the moment, a document was signed by the Greek State and Ulen & Co, confirming satisfaction on both sides for the successful completion of the project. The document literally spells out the connection between ancient and modern Greek achievements, by directly comparing the Roman Emperor Hadrian, who undertook "the first great water supply works for Athens" (Hadrian's Aqueduct), to the modern Greek state, which, with the

Fig. 6.d Linking the past with the future: replica of an ancient alter at the foot of modern construction. Photograph: George Shoterioo.

aid of the private contractor, undertook the "second great water supply project for Athens." Quite a suitable metaphor, really, since in both cases, the process was linked to a process of colonization. The document, heavily adorned with images of ancient Greek figures and meanders, reads:

> On this day, in token of their completion, the first waters from the Lake of Marathon have been poured into a fountain constructed near the Arch of the Roman Emperor Hadrian, who constructed the first great water supply for Athens. Ulen and Company, having undertaken the second great water supply in the year one thousand one hundred and twenty five…feels pleased and honoured to have completed these works which will contribute largely to the future progress of the glorious and time honoured cities of Athens and Piraeus.[76]

Like many modern shrines, the Marathon Dam embodies in its form and aesthetics the co-existence of heterogeneous, contrasting, and often conflicting processes and manifestations in the process of modernization. It works almost as an allegory for a country caught between modernization and tradition, eager to modernize (Westernize), yet entangled in the persistent net of traditional social and cultural relations.

Turning Nature into the Prerequisite for Progress and Development

The Marathon Dam introduced state-of-the-art technology to Greece, and signaled a shift to large-scale modernizing projects that intensified the production of nature. Thus, it became a symbol of a new era in the relation between society and nature, whereby nature ceased to be a source of fear and anxiety and became instead the prerequisite for modernization and progress.[77] As with other expanding economies in the early 20th century, the management and exploitation of water resources became for Greece too part of a broader project of modernization and national development.[78]

The importance placed on managing and developing the country's agricultural sector via the development of water resources was related to the difficulties encountered by the Greek state in attracting capital investment in the industrial sector. With foreign capital focusing on selective large scale infrastructure projects, diaspora capital reluctant to invest in industry, and domestic capital limited to small-scale investment, the anticipated industrial take off proved very difficult, if not impossible, for Greece, despite a significant increase in the country's surplus labor due to the refugee inflow from Asia Minor.[79] The country's external debt accounted for 40 to 50 percent of the country's domestic budget, while the per capita debt was higher than the per capita income.[80] This prompted a feverish search for increased export earnings. Exporting agricultural products seemed like a viable solution to the country's debt problem, a decision that promoted water resource planning and management as an essential prerequisite for economic stability.

However, agricultural productivity was low, and social relations of production were still based on a semi-feudal system. The utilization of nature as a growth engine required the transformation of the social relations of production through political and economic reform and institutional changes. The law that implemented the Marathon project worked toward this direction. It heralded a shift in power relations and control over water resources and became the final act in a century-old dispute between the local and the central state over the ownership of and responsibility for water provision for the city of Athens. With the beginning of the Marathon works, control was transferred from the municipality to the *EEY*, which operated under the jurisdiction of the state. The aqueduct, the reservoir, and the distribution network—which used to belong to the municipality—were handed over to the *EEY*.[81] Once the contract was signed, the municipality became merely a client of the water company, and had to pay for its use of water.[82] This institutional blow to the local state, coupled with agricultural reforms that undermined the power of the rural landed elites, created space for a highly centralized, regulatory state that became the main interlocutor for planning and implementing large engineering and irrigation projects, and which could aid economic modernization. Extensive land redistribution programs in 1917 and 1923 opened up the agricultural sector to capitalist development, and dismantled the remnants of the conservative rural land élites. This was supported by the resettlement of 800,000 refugees into agricultural areas, where they would provide the necessary labor power.[83] These reforms dismantled the remnants of the conservative rural land élites, who had inherited 75% of the cultivated rural land from the Ottoman Christian landlords and had—ever since the formation of the modern Greek state—opposed both liberal changes and a more market-oriented development of the country.

Within this context, the Marathon Dam signaled the beginning of a new era of modernization through the production of nature as a theater for accumulation. Promoting the production of "second nature" as an engine for growth was a vision shared by liberal politicians, enlightened micro-entrepreneurs, small farmers, and the increasingly powerful engineering community. The fusion of the domestic state's interest with foreign capital investment forged the material basis for the realization of this vision, as demonstrated by the report produced by the American engineer Newmayer for the Ministry of Agriculture in 1948. The report presented water as the country's most important resource, which, with the right manipulation and management, could contribute greatly toward solving most of the country's development problems:

> Water resources constitute today the largest wealth-producing potential of the country, which is underdeveloped. Water comprises for Greece the most important source of domestic growth. Every inch of land which can be given over to cultivation and saved from erosion should be claimed.... The exploitation of the country's water capacity…will contribute more than any other resource towards the nation's economic growth and towards raising the currently low living standards of millions of Greeks…will render Greece more independent…will improve its Trade Balance by increasing exports and decreasing imports….will provide employment for many unemployed or underemployed people.[84]

The report bears a rather physiocratic attitude, by emphasizing the role of nature's water as the source of wealth and development. It presented the necessity to invest in labor power as a positive side effect rather than as a central component of the production process. However, there is no analysis of the means to finance the development of the country's hydraulic resource base. The discourse on the need to mobilize labor power towards this end was left to another supplementary report, prepared by the chief engineer of the Ministry of Agriculture. That report acknowledged the importance of labor power, but at the same time turned this acknowledgment into a powerful ideological tool to marshal broad societal support for transforming nature for the benefit of the nation. The report used yet another ancient example, that of the construction of the artificial Lake Kopaïda in 2000 BC by the ancient Minyes. It identified in this example the socio-political role model that modern Greece should follow in pursuit of its own modern development:

> It took an army of people and an intensive exploitation of human resources to carry out the works [for the construction of Lake Kopaïda]. To be sure, if those people were governed according to modern beliefs and swimming in the ocean of contemporary economic and social theories, they would not have achieved such a staggering technical civilisation so many thousands of years ago. One could compare such a society to that of bees and ants working towards a central aim with unrivalled discipline and diligence without having to resort to the help of external societies. Needless to say, the basic prerequisite for such an achievement was that, during those historical periods, people were not distracted by wars or social upheavals. To be sure, those societies were not structured around the unadulterated democratic principles or the political philosophical beliefs of the classical period; they were more practical societies and through their social organisation they secured self-sufficiency, prosperity, material wealth and power.[85]

Drawing on a remote ancient example, the report manufactured a "grand paradigm" for the social and political path modern Greek society should follow. To Xenos, the preparer of the report, the indisputable need to conquer nature dictated a nondemocratic social organization. Xenos' views are indicative of the argument later articulated by Wittfogel in *Oriental Despotism*[86]—namely, that the need to control water resources and to develop sophisticated irrigation systems necessitates the development of centralized bureaucratic states and hierarchical social structures. The environmentally deterministic character of this thesis met with much criticism[87] but Xenos' analysis used it as a policy instrument before Wittfogel offered his theoretical hypothesis. Xenos' plea for a more hierarchical social and political structure reflected not only a desire to transform Greece's physical landscape to serve the objectives of development, but also an attempt to deal with potential social unrest and the increasing threat of Communist insurrection. Indeed, at the time the report was published, Greece was embroiled in civil war between the Royalists and the Socialists/Communists (1946–1949) and had become "a key battleground in the Cold War".[88] The need to tame and control nature became intricately bound up with establishing the social and political stability necessary to accelerate industrialization and develop a healthy market economy. After the end of the World War II and the Greek civil war, the Greek state introduced a large number of engineering projects to supply Athens with water and to boost the Greek economy.

Developing an Hydrocephalus Athens

Following the end of World War II and the end of the Greek civil war in 1949, Athens underwent a period of "fierce urbanization".[89] The earlier ambitious plans for industrialization and for developing the agricultural sector through state investment in big infrastructure projects fell through, and most of the foreign aid that could have boosted the development of industry and agriculture was used up in funding the civil war. The new economic development model that prevailed after the end of the civil war was based on land speculation and on boosting the construction industry.[90] This process was supported and even led by the state[91] not only through institutional reforms, but also through financial incentives and tax breaks for investment into the booming housing market.[92] According to Mantouvalou and Martha's[93] excellent study, 90% of Athens housing was built between 1950 and 1975. The building materials industry became the fastest growing sector of Greek manufacturing, and many of these companies became monopolies or oligopolies. The investment, employment, and profiteering opportunities that were created made Athens a very attractive destination for people on the Greek periphery,[94] especially given the slow decline of the agricultural sector. In 1951, the water in the Marathon Lake and Reservoir reached its lowest level, and the construction of a new aqueduct bringing water from Lake Yliki (Figure 6.a) was deemed necessary. Construction works began in 1957 and were completed in 1958.[95] A series of subsequent projects between 1966 and 1978 increased the operational capacity of the Yliki pumping station (which ranks amongst the largest in Europe) to its current level of 750,000 m^3 of water per day with a total power of 20,700 HP.[96]

However, the capital's thirst for water was insatiable. As the population grew, Athens harnessed more rivers and lakes to serve it. The vertical swelling of the city's central areas (Figure 6.e) and the expansion of both illegal settlements and planned middle class suburbs demanded the capture of yet further water resources. The development of the water system followed the messy course of the city's "fierce urbanization".[97] Illegal

Fig. 6.e The vertical "swelling" of Athens. Photograph: Maria Kaika.

settlements would initially develop their own illegal local water networks. These would eventually be connected to the main water supply system, as part of a client-based deal that also "legalized" them. During the 1967–1974 dictatorship, the problem heightened due to the concessions and indirect subsidies given to the construction industry and the use of land as a direct source of profit.

Apart from the number of people served by the network, the per capita use of water also increased, since new households were equipped with plumbing and private bathrooms (see Table 6.f). The state subsidized water prices by further developing the network and resources. Ulen & Co, on the other hand, had no incentives to manage the system, or to intervene in the expansion of the network, since that would mean a loss of income (especially since the network expansion was not done at the company's expense).

The city's expanding need for water led to the construction of another large-scale infrastructure project. The Mornos Dam and Reservoir (Figure 6.a) completed in the 1980s, was one of the largest constructions

Table 6.f Water Consumption Levels per Capita per Day around the World

Country	Water Consumption (L/capita/day)
Austria	135
Australia	268
Belgium	122
Canada	326
Denmark	139
Finland	145
France	137
Germany	116
Greece	200
Hungary	102
Ireland	142
Italy	213
Japan	278
Korea	183
Netherlands	130
New Zealand	165
Norway	140
Portugal	119
Spain	210
Sweden	191
Switzerland	158
Turkey	195
England and Wales (UK)	150
United States	365

Source: The Environment Agency: *Demand Management Bulletin* 1999; 36:7.

in Greece. The project transferred water from water rich Western Greece to water poor Athens, further supporting the capital's development of hydrocephalic characteristics—in every meaning of the word.[98] Mornos was estimated to provide an extra 267 liters per capita per day for Athens[99] and, once again, it was expected to solve the city's water problem for good.

The implementation of big infrastructure projects was linked to a reorganization of the institutional framework for water management. Since the 1950s Ulen & Co's role in decision making had become marginal, and the state was now leading decision making and project implementation. Although the period of dictatorship delayed institutional reform, after this ended the Greek state (via the Bank of Greece) bought Ulen & Co's share of the Water Company of Athens (*EEY*) and proceeded to a *de facto* nationalization of this body. Law 1068/80 (1980) merged the Hellenic Water Company (*EEY*) and the Athens Sewerage Organization (ΟΑΠ) to form a unified water supply and sewerage authority, the Athens Water Supply and Sewerage Company (*EYΔAΠ*). The company's sole shareholder was the Greek state and it operated as a public utility company.[100] The company's responsibility began with raw water, and continued with its impoundment, transport, treatment, and final distribution to the consumers in the form of potable water. This was the first major institutional change in water management in Greece since the 1930s. However, the great breakthrough in planning and managing water resources came in 1987 with a legislation[101] that centralized water resource planning and allocation (this had previously been a matter of regional and local policy). The law, voted in by the Socialist government, annulled all previously existing rights over water linked to private property; sanctioned the right of the state to expropriate land, edifices, or settlements; restrained the use of water by individuals and companies (after compensation); created a new institutional framework for the management of water resources by dividing the country into 14 hydrological departments to be administered by their own water boards; declared water a "natural gift (*αγαθό*) to be used for the satisfaction of social needs" and the right to water as "the undeniable right of every individual"; and acknowledged domestic water supply as a priority over other uses of water.[102]

A Perfectly Tamed Nature: Abundance, Overflows, and Optimism

By the early 1970s, thanks mainly to huge state expenditure in engineering works and partly to the reorganization of the water sector, the water shortages that had previously threatened urban life in Athens receded, both in reality and in people's consciousness. Since 1926 the per capita consumption of water had been increasing steadily and today it ranks amongst the highest in the world (Table 6.f). In spite of the continuous growth of its population (3.5 million people at the beginning of the 1980s) Athens succeeded for the first time in its modern history in having more water than it actually needed.

In 1985, the city's main reservoir, Mornos, literally overflowed. This was hailed as a landmark and met with public and political enthusiasm. According to the spokesman of Athens' water supply company (*EYΔAΠ*), at this time Athens was the only place in the world that permitted irrigation of agricultural land with purified water![103] The optimistic mood was also reflected in a five-year project plan (1988-1993) issued by the Ministry of Environment, Physical Planning and Public Works (*ΥΠΕΧΩΔΕ*) in 1988. The document confidently stated: "the Mornos Reservoir will continue to cover the city's needs for water…. There is also scope for using the existing water supply system and available resources to cover the needs of areas which are not yet connected to the network."[104]

Athens entered the 1990s with confidence in the adequacy of its water resources despite the continuous rise in population and water consumption levels. This moment signaled the ultimate success of Greece's Promethean Project for taming nature, which finally brought ample water into Athens after a century of recurring water shortages. It was almost an act of revenge over an element that had been tormenting the city by its absence for centuries and which was now finally tamed. The now unproblematic and uninterrupted presence of water in people's households not only contributed to changes in cultural and social perceptions of nature's water, but also to experiencing the function of the city as independent from the function of a now tamed nature, thus positing the city as a realm separate from nature's processes[105] (see Chapter 2).

Consuming the Modernist Dream

Describing the relationship between water and the medieval city, Guillerme[106] contends that water had been "subjecting the city to its power by moulding it at will, forcing the streets and buildings to adapt to its winding path." The Marathon Dam signaled precisely the moment when nature's water could be controlled and channeled by human will and announced a new relationship between nature and the city: after a century of being subjected to water's power, Athens was freed finally from the constraints that nature's water posed over its form and function, and could expand in all directions and forms. And it did! The Marathon Dam represented the first instance of looking outside Athens for the solution to the city's water problems and signaled the beginning of the perpetual expansion of the city's ecological footprint. That same moment, however, also signaled the city's perpetual dependency on the production of (new) nature in order to sustain its life, form, and metabolism. Now water not only could be, but had to be tamed, managed, channeled, and redirected in order to sustain the city's growth and expansion over space and in time. Looking for solutions to urban water problems outside the urban became the norm, and water consumption levels kept rising (Figure 6.f) while turning the tap inside one's home became the natural thing to do to get water. The most recent development in Athens along these lines was a dam project for the transportation of water from Evinos River, located 500 km northwest of Athens (Figure 6.a); it became operational in 2001.

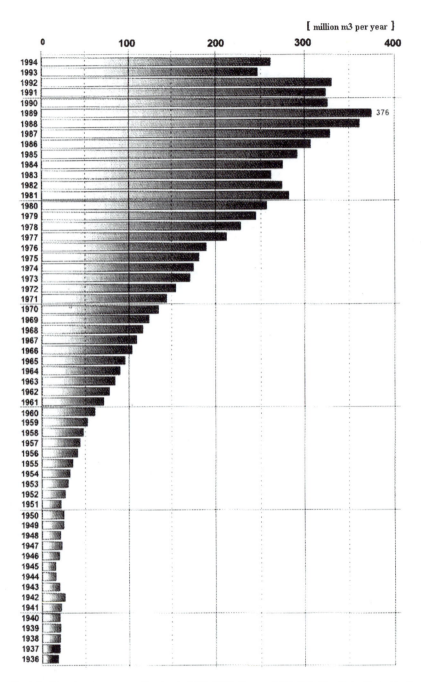

Fig. 6.f Athens' water consumption levels 1936–1994. Source: E.YΔ.ATT. (The Water Company of Athens).

This naturalization of the domestication and commodification of nature signaled the ultimate triumph of the process of mastering nature, but it also contributed further to the conceptual separation between nature and the city. While domesticated, tamed nature became increasingly naturalized, the complex network of social and material connections between nature and the city (networks of water, sewerage, electricity, telecommunications, gas, etc.) become increasingly opaque, hidden underneath and outside the city. In the case of dams, the connection between the reservoir's water and the water coming from the domestic tap is hidden in a subterranean maze of pipes and networks. This provides a case in point of Vidler's[107] assertion about modernity's dialectics between dark and light: reflecting modernism's fascination with flooding dark spaces with light, flooding modern cities with ample water is predicated upon the creation of a maze of dark, hidden spaces where this water can travel and rest. In this way, dams can be seen as embodiments of some of the contradictions that make modern urban life possible. As the production of water became mystified and fetishized, the Marathon Dam itself became an important cultural artifact, and a national symbol to which Athenians paid tribute by going on pilgrimage as tourists until well into the 20th century (the trend faded only towards the end of the 1970s).

These dam trips depicted a new way of experiencing the countryside and nature. Green[108] argues that, while the preferred object for visits during the 18th century were gardens and estates of the famous, the 19th century urban dweller traveled into the countryside in order to transcend his urban experience and "immerse himself into something else." For Green, this signified a qualitative shift in the way the countryside was experienced. It could be argued that the popular 20th century pilgrimages to dams signaled another shift in the way the urban dweller experienced and appropriated the countryside and nature: no longer in search of transcending his/her urban experience but as the son/daughter of Prometheus who arrived to supervise the now mastered land; no longer in search of the awesome beauty of a god-given, pristine nature, but in conscious pursuit of the splendor of man-made, pride-inducing "second" nature. The "new" experience of the countryside was rather that of tracing the origins of urban experience, tracing the signs and landmarks of the tamed countryside that made the city and the urban home tick, tracing the connection between the dam's (and Man's) domination over nature and the functioning of the modern city. It should be noted that, unlike 18th and 19th century countryside visits, which were a predominantly a middle class activity, 20th century dam visits featured factory workers who were taking *en masse* dam trips, often organized and funded by their employer, to witness what human labor—their labor—was capable of producing. Dam constructions provided a materialization of what Benjamin called "dream images" of modernity[109] testifying that the modernist emancipatory Promethean dream was about to come true, ready to be consumed and subsequently fetishized.

The splendor of this altered nature also provided a new image around which national ideologies could be constructed. While 18th and 19th century ideological constructions of nationhood were centered on the land and the region, technological transformations of nature now entered the list of things the nation should be proud of.

The palimpsest of contradictory meanings and symbols etched into the fabric of the Marathon dam supports an understanding of modernity as a complex and contested process, of which the production of nature constitutes a major parameter. The Marathon Dam embodies in its form, function and symbolism, the culmination of contested visions of modernization. By being a modern project draped in neoclassical forms, veneered with the same marble as that which had been used for the Parthenon and completed with a modern neoclassical altar at its foot, the dam embodies the contradictions of a country dedicated to its future yet strongly bound to its past; a country eager to modernize, yet caught in the persistent nets of traditional social, political, and cultural relations. An archetypal example of people looking for solutions to endemic urban problems *outside* the city, the dam became a landmark to the successful conquest of nature and the ongoing physical expansion of the city.

However, the celebration of the success of the Promethean Project and of the urbanization of the countryside was short lived. The act of mastering and controlling nature would soon turn on its head, as the expansion of the footprint of the modern city led to recurring socio-political and environmental crises. Modernity's Promethean project would be challenged wholesale. The last chapter will examine the political ecology of this repeal.

CHAPTER 7

Late 20th Century:
Tamed Nature as a Source of Crisis

The period 1950–1970 witnessed the apogee of modernity's Promethean project, when advances in urban environmental infrastructure in Western states allowed for greater control over nature. Although highly contested, particularly with respect to the democratic deficit it created, the centralization of power over water resource management after World War II did deliver many of the promised material goods. Between 1950 and 1970 the majority of urban households in the Western world had access to drinking water. By 1990, 100% of the urban population in Europe and Northern America enjoyed full access to water supply and sanitation services.[1] It was the apogee of modernity's Promethean project. Despite differences in hydrological and institutional configurations, as Western cities became increasingly thirsty, the networks bringing water to them grew and their ecological footprints expanded yet further.[2] While Athens succeeded in overflowing its main reservoir at Mornos, in other parts of the Western world the results were even more impressive. In London, the increase in domestic water availability was coupled by a successful campaign for cleaning up the tidal Thames. By the late 1970s, more than 90 varieties of fish had returned to the Thames.[3]

As water became controlled, tamed, and domesticated, its presence and availability became "normalized" and taken for granted. The fierce quest for water transformed landscapes often hundreds of miles away from cities, and increased tension between rural and urban users.[4] In some cases, this quest extended to international/interstate water transfers, such as: the (in)famous North American Water and Power Alliance (NAWPA),[5] a US$10 billion project for water transfers from Canada and the northern US to the south; the Texas Water Plan, which included large imports from the Mississippi basin across the state of Louisiana; or inter-regional (Spain, Greece, Belgium) transfers. In less than a century, urban water supply had become the guarantor for urban sanitation and the basis for urban expansion. The development of urban infrastructure became part of a powerful redistribution mechanism[6] in postwar Keynesian Western states and was integral to the dominant Fordist system.[7]

However, this process soon resulted in serious public deficits that impeded further public spending. By the late 1970s, the once fetishized urban infrastructure was aging and in need of serious re-investment (see Chapter 3). The slack in public spending increased socio-environmental inequalities and undermined the foundations of the great modern dream. Western metropolises, whose growth seemed to have defied nature, now became the hub of socio-environmental disasters: from water shortages to floods and from devastating hurricanes to electricity blackouts. In 1980, the toll of natural disasters in the US was calculated at 10,000 deaths with an estimated cost of US$44 billion, rising to $56 billion in 1998.[8] After the triumphant conquest of nature, the end of the 20th century cast nature, once again, as a threat and a source of crisis. The discourse paralleled that of the early 19th century (see Chapters 3 and 5). The similarity is striking: in the 19th century, nature was awesome and threatening, an impediment to urban development; in the late 20th century, the once tamed nature again becomes discursively constructed as vengeful and threatening, a potential impediment to progress. However, despite the similarities in the discursive construction of nature then and now, the *materiality* of nature in the late 20th and early 21st century is undoubtedly very different from that of the 19th century. 21st-century nature is no longer the pristine, wild, whimsical nature that must be tamed and conquered through progress; rather, it is a socially constructed hybrid, the outcome of intense interaction between human beings and the natural environment.

But, to what extent does this discrepancy between the discourse and the materiality of nature in the 21st century matter? Drawing on the contemporary politics of urban water supply in London and Athens, this chapter examines how this discrepancy leads to incongruous practices and policies. The discursive construction of resources as *external* to human societies and independent of them in fact justifies further developmental practices, while at the same time it pays lip service to the need to address the adverse effects of modernity on the environment. The solutions promoted to "save" Western cities from discursively constructed or real imminent environmental disasters (e.g., water scarcity) are, oddly enough, very similar to those offered during the early 20th century. New development projects (dams, reservoirs) have been promoted as the best way to deal with nature's scarcity, while demand management strategies are confined mainly to price hikes.

However, there *is* a difference in the way water supply and development projects are pursued in the 21st century, and it is a significant one. In the first three quarters of the 20th century water supply and infrastructure development was part of the provision of what Castells[9] termed the "collective means of consumption". Along with transport, health services, education etc., it belonged to a category of services produced, managed, and distributed not through the market (given their lower than average profitability rate) but through the state. The provision of water was deemed essential for the smooth function of the market, the reproduction of labor power and the growth of national economies. Today, in contrast, the supply of water is taken away from the public sphere and functions more than ever as an engine for capital expansion and for the promotion of private enterprise. After the 1980s, the increased pressure to find new ways of financing infrastructure provision,[10] combined with the rise of the neoliberal state[11] and the demand to reduce budget deficits and public spending, led many countries towards the pursuit of privatization strategies. This practice was conveniently in tune with both the desire to expand the investment base for capital and the acceptance of the market logic in environmentalist discourse.[12] This crucial shift has important socio-cultural implications that are epitomized by the change in the socio-cultural perception of water. Water, which used to be perceived and treated as a *public good*, and which used to be provided to almost everyone in the Western world at subsidized low prices, has now become discursively and materially constructed as scarce and valuable, and thus an inevitably expensive *commodity* to be bought and sold in the market. Even where water services remain public, water becomes commodified in one way or another.[13] Public awareness campaigns around the Western world from the 1980s onwards alerted the public to the fact that the overabundance and optimism of the 1950s–1970s was nothing but a mirage, a miscalculation. Resources are now to be treated as rare and costly, and thus the public can expect to pay dearly for them. This chapter critically investigates how the discourse on "nature as crisis" has affected post-1980s politics and practice of urban water supply in London and Athens.

London: Prometheus vs. Adam Smith

The centralization of power in water management in England and Wales started in earnest in the 19th century, was intensified during World War II and culminated in 1973 with the Water Act.[14] Despite receiving fierce criticism for marginalizing local authorities, this state-led water management system proved able to deal with emergencies and recurrent crises, such as, for example, the 1975–1976 drought.[15] Nevertheless, in the late 1980s, the water sector in England and Wales underwent a process of total restructuring and privatization. The 1989 Companies Act *de facto* privatized the assets and management of water supply in England and Wales, and transferred responsibility for water supply and sewerage to ten private Water Service Companies (WSCs), which replaced the Regional Water Authorities (RWAs) (Table 7.a). The 29 Statutory Water Companies that had survived the reorganization of the water sector in 1974 were allowed to continue their operations as Water-only Companies (WoCs). The privatization act also created a new public body, the National Rivers Authority (NRA),[16] which was given responsibilities previously held by the RWAs: pollution control; water resource management, fisheries, flood protection and alleviation, and land drainage. In order to regulate the new industry, a number of public bodies were established: the Directorate General of the Office of Water Services (OFWAT); the Drinking Water Inspectorate (DWI); and the National River Authorities (NRA). Certain responsibilities were also taken on by the Monopolies and Mergers Commission (MCC), HM Inspectorate of Pollution, the District Health Authorities, and local authorities.[17] In 1995 the roles of the NRAs were amalgamated to form the Environment Agency (EA), which became the main environmental regulator.

After privatization, the metropolitan area of London was serviced mainly by Thames Water Utilities Ltd. It is the largest WSC, with operations expanding to a much larger area of south-central England. Also, an important share of the metropolitan population continued to be served by Water-only Companies (WoCs) (Table 7.b). The average daily amount of water supplied by Thames Water in 2001 was 2,090 million liters to an estimated population of over 7.8 million people.[18] Until 1994, no single individual or company could hold more than 15 percent of WSC shares, and the government retained an absolute veto over the activities of the privatized utilities.[19] However, this protection was removed in 1994, resulting in a surge of takeovers and mergers by local and foreign investors. Thames Water became the target of aggressive competitors, such as the French groups Vivendi and Saur, and was eventually taken over in September 2000 by the German multi-utility company RWE.

Table 7.a Water Holding Companies (WHCs) and Water Service Companies (WSCs) in England and Wales (1999)

WHCs	WSCs	Water Supply		Sewerage	
		Population	Area km²	Population	Area km²
Anglian Water Plc	Anglian Water	4,058,000	22,000	5,425,000	27,500
Hyder Plc	Dwr Cymru	2,824,000	20,400	2,961,000	21,300
United Utilities Plc	North West	6,871,000	14,415	6,816,000	14,445
Northumbrian W. G.	Northumbrian	2,537,000	8,993	2,590,000	9,400
Severn Trent Plc	Severn Trent	7,355,000	19,745	8,250,000	21,650
South West Water Plc	South West	1,523,000	10,300	1,418,000	10,800
Southern Water Plc	Southern	2,250,000	4,450	3,999,000	10,450
Thames Water Plc	Thames	7,679,000	8,200	11,871,000	13,750
Wessex Water Plc	Wessex	1,179,000	7,350	2,431,000	10,000
Yorkshire Water Plc	Yorkshire	4,534,000	13,900	4,766,000	13,600
Total		40,810,000	129,753	50,526,000	152,895

From Castro, E. and E. Swyngedouw. 2000. *Metropolitan Areas and Sustainable Use of Water: The Case of London*. Final Report, European Commission, Environment and Climate Programme, DG XII, Human Dimension of Environmental Change. School of Geography and the Environment, University of Oxford, Oxford. Also available online: http:// www.feweb.vu.nl/re/regional/Metron/metronlit.html

Table 7.b Companies Serving London Metropolitan Area (1998–1999)

	Water Supply			Sewerage	
Company	Population	Area (km²)	mL/d	Population	Area Covered (km²)
Thames Water	7,679,000	8,200	2,515	11,871,000	13,750
North Surrey	481,000	500	129	—	—
Mid Southern	692,000	1,502	205	—	—
Sutton and East Surrey	637,000	833	165	—	—
Three Valleys	2,441,000	3,213	700	—	—

From Castro, E., M. Kaika, and E. Swyngedouw. London: structural continuities and institutional change in water management. *European Planning Studies* 2003; 11(3):283–298. Elaborated by Dr. Esteban Castro from OFWAT report (2001).

According to Castro et al.,[20] two main objectives were set by the Conservative administration who implemented the privatization of the water sector in the UK: to solve the chronic under-funding of the water sector (economic), but also to upgrade environmental standards and pollution control (environmental). More specifically, economic targets were set: promoting competition and enterprise; reducing the size of the public sector; involving staff in companies; spreading shares ownership; and freeing enterprise from state control. With respect to environmental protection, privatization was expected to upgrade water systems after decades of under-investment, and to satisfy the need to comply with the tighter environmental and quality regulations driven by the European Community's directives. With privatization, water provision was turned from a public good to a private service, and water supply became a private enterprise. What is important to note, however, is that this happened, amongst other reasons, in the name of "nature" and "environmental protection". Maloney et al.[21] argue that the centralization of decision making in water management after the 1950s and the destruction of preexisting networks of power actually facilitated the privatization process in the 1980s. The decades-long practices of stripping discourses on nature and water management of their socio-political dimension turned water supply into a technical-managerial issue. Water became something "out there", beyond the city's boundaries, external to society, something which could/should/would be dealt through scientific and technical means and managed by a technocratic elite. A majority of this technocratic elite eventually came to support the liberalization of the water sector.[22] Their support, combined with the discourse on nature as a source of crisis, further facilitated the political decision to privatize in the 1980s. But to what extent did privatization achieve the aims set by the government, i.e., help reduce public deficit while improving environmental standards?

To be sure, Thames Water inherited an ageing infrastructure system and was expected to reverse the situation. Between 1989 and 1999, Thames Water relined about 10 percent and renewed a further 12 percent of the main trunks (of a total of 3,232 km).[23] However, the Thames Water Authority (the public board that had preceded Thames Utilities Ltd. in managing the resource in the Thames basin) had already achieved high service standards before privatization and had developed a sound system for integrated watershed management.[24] Moreover, most of the projects that were carried out by Thames Water Plc (TW) had been designed by the public Thames Water Authority and were in line before privatization: the cleaning of the River Thames; the construction of the London Ring Main; and the North London Artificial Recharge in the Lee River basin.[25] According to Maloney et al.[26] the board of the Thames Water Authority actually promoted privatization, which they saw as an opportunity to transform a well-managed and well-resourced public company into a profit making private undertaking.

Leakage control figured highly among the environmental objectives of the privatization scheme. With the inauguration of the London Water Ring Main in 1994, Thames Water expected to reduce leakage significantly, as the new system would decrease pressure from the old trunk mains. However, this did not happen and leakage in the areas served by Thames Water reached a peak in 1996–97, with over 30 percent of water in the system lost. Important improvements have since been made, but Thames Water remains a poor performer in this respect.[27] While failing to meet leakage control standards—which are essential in achieving the much desired environmental protection and demand management standards—Thames Water proposed instead to develop further the resource base through the construction of the Upper Thames Reservoir, a 14 square km project in South Oxfordshire in order to deal with rising demand. For years, the plan met with opposition from environmental NGOs and the water regulator, who insisted on meeting leakage control standards rather than expanding the resource base. However, recent debates indicate that the scheme might go ahead after all. It resurfaced and received a great deal of media attention immediately after a particularly dry summer in England in 2003.[28]

Despite its reluctance to invest in leakage control and infrastructure improvement, the water industry has nevertheless been increasing its profit rates steadily.[29] In 1998, Thames Water Plc had a turnover of £1.39 billion, 74.1 percent of which was derived from the U.K. water operation, while the rest was composed by international operations (12.4 percent) and other activities (13.5 percent). The industry's profitability owes much to the natural monopoly character of the water market. While gas, electricity and telecommunications competition has helped to improve services and cut down tariffs, the private monopoly of the water market resulted in substantial increases in water prices, uneven performance between companies and low levels of investment. After privatization, consumers in England and Wales were paying an additional 44 percent to 99 percent for their water bills compared to the period 1989–1990.[30] The combination of rises in water price with the announcement of the companies' high profit rates and the managing directors' six-figure salaries led to intense media scrutiny and a public outcry.[31]

Moreover, despite efforts to disassociate discourses on nature's water from socio-political practices, the privatized water regimes in England and Wales were inevitably faced with a number of socio-environmental problems. The 1995 drought in the UK exposed the inefficiency of some water operators[32] and the inability of the private water market to resolve *of its own accord* the social and environmental dimensions of water management,[33] including those stemming from the disconnection of poorer households' water supplies due to unpaid bills. Over 3,000 households had their water supply cut off in 1996/7 in England and Wales after privatization[34] (Table 7.c). The new Labor administration addressed the problem at its Water Summit in 1999, where it decided to make it illegal for water companies to disconnect users.[35]

To counteract the adverse social, economic, and environmental effects of a natural monopoly market, the regulator in England and Wales resorted to using yardstick competition, a process whereby regulators fix water prices in order to provide incentives for companies to become more efficient and make better investment choices. Thus, in its 1999 revision of the tariff system, the regulator (OFWAT) ordered a reduction in water prices for all companies as an incentive for them to reduce operation costs.[36] The companies' reaction, however, was to cut staff numbers, reduce investment programs, and halt leakage control management programs. This reaction illustrates vividly that there is no escape from the financial cost implicated in developing a sound environmental and social policy.[37] It also shows how inflexible social and environmental planning can become under a privatized system. As long as the ultimate aim of every

Table 7.c Number of Household Disconnections by Company for the Period 1996–1997

Water Company	No. of Household Disconnections
Anglian	72
Bournemouth and W. Hampshire	14
Bristol	100
Cambridge	33
Chester	8
Cholderton	0
Dwr Cymru	81
Essex & Suffolk	14
Folkestone	15
Hartlepool	27
Mid Kent	208
Mid Southern	0
N. Surrey	17
N. West	410
Northumbrian	66
Portsmouth	464
Severn Trent	457
S. East	0
S. Staffordshire	108
South West	0
Southern	34
Sutton and E. Surrey	73
Tendring Hundred	40
Thames	213
Three Valleys	314
Wessex	0
Wrexham	18
York	34
Yorkshire	348

From OFWAT published in BBC News Water Week [10 October 2003]
http://news.bbc.co.uk/hi/english/static/waterweek/issues08.html

private company is profit making, social and environmental concerns are secondary and will be addressed only within specific regulatory regimes, never through the incentive of the market itself. Often, the favoring of one will work against the other, as in this case, where the call for better financial performance with lower prices and sounder environmental control had a significant cost in job losses.[38]

Athens: From Overflow to Scarcity

Only one year after the publication, in 1988, of the optimistic five-year project plan for the future of Athens' water supply by the Greek Ministry of the Environment (see Chapter 6), the situation was turned on its head. A severe drought hit Athens in 1989 and lasted for almost 3 years, turning water from an abundant resource, a source of optimism, into a scarce resource, a source of crisis and conflict. The drought threatened to disrupt the function of the "eternal" city and created great anxiety for its residents. The Mornos Reservoir, which was overflowing in the late 1980s, reached unprecedentedly low levels in 1990, a situation that attracted the attention of the media and the general public. But the low levels at the Mornos Reservoir were neither as sudden nor as unexpected a phenomenon as was reported by the government and presented in the media at the time. In fact, the water level had been falling steadily for a number of years (Figure 7.a). A number of reports published by non-governmental bodies (academics, independent researchers, environmental NGOs, and the Technical Chamber of Greece) had repeatedly predicted that the city's

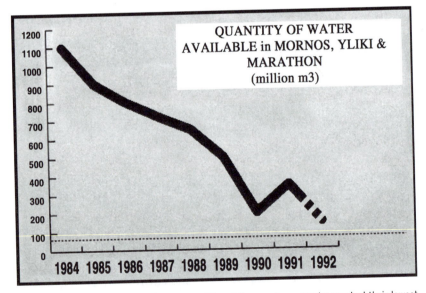

Fig. 7.a In 1990 the resources available in Athens' three main reservoirs reached their lowest point. Source: E.YΔ.ATT. (The Water Company of Athens).

demand for water would eventually exceed the storage capacity of the reservoir.[39] However, it was only in May 1990 that the crisis went public, generating sensationalized media coverage and heated debates in parliament and in everyday life. Nobody seemed to know exactly how much water was available in the reservoirs. Each ministry published different figures defending its own interests and strategies.[40]

Interviews conducted with the administration of the water company indicated that it was socio-political rather than natural processes that had led to the moment of crisis: the expansion of the network and the increase in the numbers of users without any accompanying increase in the available volume of water; illegal extractions from the aquifer by individuals through local springs and wells; lack of strategic planning; and low prices (15 drachmas [€0.04] per cubic meter in 1985).[41] Added to the above were the scandalous technical flaws in the construction of the Mornos Dam, and the subsequent bad management which resulted in an estimated loss of 400 Hm³ of water between 1981 and 1989.[42] Arguably, the drought would not have produced severe water shortage had it not been for the bad management of the network.[43] Still, the panic that followed the first months of the drought eventually led to the implementation of three controversial acts in 1990 that promised to quench the city's thirst but which also sparked major changes in water pricing, supply, and management. The acts stipulated:

1. the retroactive implementation of a new tariff and pricing system, to be combined with a public awareness campaign, and the prohibition of activities which led to heavy domestic water consumption (e.g., car washing, watering gardens, filling swimming pools)
2. the construction of a new dam on the Evinos River (Figure 7.b)
3. the transportation of water from Lake Trihonida to the Mornos Reservoir (by means of tankers and a pipeline), and from Lake Paralimni to the Yliki Reservoir (through the construction of a pipeline) (Figure 7.b)

The retroactive increase in water prices by up to 300%, as well as the construction of a large scale dam project with a serious socio-environmental impact, were projects that would normally have produced great public debate. However, despite their considerable social, economic, political, and environmental implications, these projects[44] were voted in by the Greek Parliament under the form of "Emergency Acts," a procedure that only permits very brief discussion and demands an immediate vote and implementation. Public debate was sacrificed in the name of "saving the city from thirst".[45]

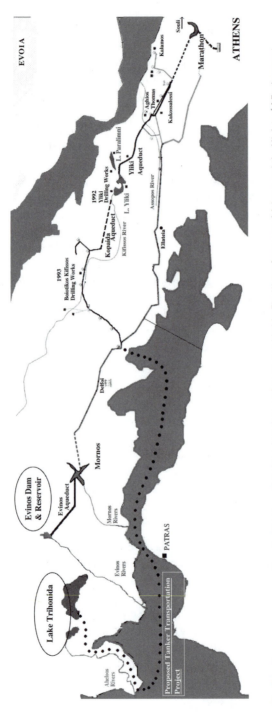

Fig. 7.b Emergency measures. Compiled by the author, based on data and maps provided by The Water Company of Athens and the Ministry of Environment, Planning and Public Works.

The 1989–1991 drought coincided with one of the most turbulent periods in modern Greek politics. An economic and political scandal in which the socialist government was allegedly involved while at the height of its popular support led to a prolonged period of political crisis. Three rounds of national elections took place within a period of less than two years.[46] The first two failed to give a majority to any one party, and the third, in April 1990 with the trials of former Socialist ministers pending, led to a Conservative party victory. It was the newly elected Conservative government that brought the Emergency Acts before Parliament for immediate implementation.[47]

This fusion of a political crisis with a natural crisis (drought) facilitated the almost uncontested implementation of the Emergency Acts that would change the culture, politics, and management of water in Athens in a decisive manner. However, public response and debate over the controversial "Emergency Measures" was numbed not only by their swift implementation in the midst of a political crisis, but also by the systematic cultivation of public anxiety through government reports and the media. In May 1990, the water company announced that there were only 170 days of water left for Athens, an authoritative yet easily digestible statement which was taken on by the media in the form of a countdown to the day the city would "die of thirst" (Figure 7.c). The anxiety around the "170 days of water" often took the form of competition and conflict over water consumption among the citizens of Athens. Instances of washing a car or watering a garden met with verbal abuse or worse. Residents would shout at each other for "looting their water" or even call the police to report uncivil behavior. Interestingly, but not surprisingly, such incidents had a clear class character. They occurred only in the poorest neighborhoods of Athens, where high housing densities[48] and blurred boundaries between private and public space allow for a much closer "policing" of other people's activities. Similar acts of "water policing" were difficult, if not impossible, to perform within the spatial and social configuration of secluded suburban areas, where high volume water consumers and swimming pools abound, and where the privacy of green, security-guarded estates is zealously protected.

During the drought, the water company imposed frequent disruptions in water supply as a demand management strategy. The public anxiety created when the taps—symbols of a comfortable modern life—refused to provide their services (Figure 7.d) was partly due to the *expectation* that domestic water would always "naturally" be there in an era which had tamed nature, filled the reservoirs to overflowing, and officially declared its confidence in the adequacy of water resources (see Chapter 6).

Fig. 7.c *"The 170 days of water" NEPO* became a key theme for sensational media coverage. Source: The author's impression (collage) of media coverage of the water scarcity crisis.

The naturalization of water supply and the reification of the social relations of its production played an important role in influencing the public reaction to this crisis, turning the dry taps in Athenian households into what is described in Chapter 4 as the *domestic uncanny*, a threat to domestic comfort which challenged the naturalized character of water supply.

Nature's Crisis as a Source of Exchange Value

Casting nature as a source of crisis and defining water resources as scarce provided the context in which the dominant neo-liberal rhetoric and attitude towards water resource management (i.e., demand management through pricing) could be further applied. The first step towards reestablishing Athens' blissful relationship with nature was to "reassess" (i.e., increase) the "economic" (i.e., exchange) value of water.[49] The pair—scarcity/exchange value—coupled with the public anxiety and fear over the disruption of water services played a central role in facilitating the implementation of the first of the emergency proposals: the decision for a *retroactive* increase in water prices. This act, which aimed to reduce consumption (see Table 7.d), raised the price of water by between 105 percent

Fig. 7.d When the taps—symbols of a comfortable modern life—refused to provide their services. Source: E.YΔ.ATT. (The Water Company of Athens), 1990 water scarcity awareness campaign.

and 338 percent, and water bills by between 40 percent and 140 percent, through a complex system of rates related to consumption levels.[50]

The new rates system offered higher volume consumers a much greater price reduction for water savings than that offered to lower volume consumers (Table 7.d).[51] The alchemy introduced in the pricing system was contested by the water company itself, which had suggested a rise of no more than 18 percent in water rates, while the company's trade union characterized the new pricing policy as "inefficient, socially unjust, profiteering, and perplexing".[52] Nevertheless, the complex pricing system was implemented immediately, and actually resulted in an average 20 percent decrease in water demand. Notably, however, the public response to the water saving campaign and price incentives was stratified socially.[53] Despite the fact that the new pricing system was designed to give the greatest financial incentives to heavy users, in the end it was the lower volume consumers (corresponding to lower income households) who achieved the greatest savings and reduced their consumption by up to 30 percent. The top 3 percent of consumers ended up using 40 percent of the total water supplied. To illustrate the difference in water consumption, large consumers were using four times more water per month than the average family of four.[54]

Table 7.d The Stratification in Water Pricing Introduced in 1990

Consumption Level (m³/month)	New Prices per m³ (drachma/euros)	Consumption Level (m³/month)	Price Reduction for 30% Saving in Water Consumption	
			% of Total Bill	In drachma/ euros per m³ saved
0–5	102/0.3	15	38.16	132/0.39
5–20	154/0.45	20	44.67	176/0.51
20–27	428/1.25	30	47.65	192/0.56
27–35	600/1.76	45	49.56	196/0.57
>35	750/2.20	60	49.31	203/0.59
		80	65.37	393/1.15
		100	67.62	544/1.59
		120	67.75	675/1.98

Compiled by the author from data provided by Water Company of Athens (E.Y.Δ.Α.Π).

These figures testify to a clear class stratification not only in water consumption, but also in public sensitivity and responsiveness to the call for environmental protection and demand management strategies. The new pricing system was not only unsuccessful in targeting high volume consumers, but it also punished lower volume consumers by virtually excluding them from price discounts. On the basis of this injustice, one of the poorest municipalities of Athens, Lavrion, sued the government at the time, claiming that the imposed increase in water prices was unconstitutional and illegal.[55]

The pricing system, however, was successful in forging public acceptance of water as an economic resource and, finally, as a valuable commodity. Cunningly, however, while the "scarce" character of water resources was invoked to create public consensus over price hikes, there was silence about the very process that actually makes water a commodity, i.e., its production process. Ironically, even the president of the Water Company's Trade Union, arguably the person most fit to talk about the labor power expended in the production of water, opted to stress the natural, non-produced character of the resource, when arguing against the increase in water prices and against rumors of plans to privatize the company:

> Market competition cannot be applied to the case of the water
> company since the product this company delivers (i.e., water) *is not
> produced* as is, for example, electricity…water is a natural good;
> moreover, it is scarce; therefore, it cannot be privatized.[56]

This discourse elucidates the fact that, once taken out of the social and
political nexus, the production, consumption and conservation of nature
can be used to support almost any argument: for or against privatization;
for or against the commodification of water.

Nature's Crisis as Justification for More Development

The construction of a new dam at the Evinos River (250 km from Athens;
see Figure 7.b) was the second of the emergency measures responding to
the drought crisis. The proposed dam was expected to provide an extra
annual average yield of 200 million m^3 and was estimated to cover the
city's water needs until the year 2020.[57] The cost of the project was initially
estimated at 55 billion dr. (€160.8 million), 85 percent of which was
funded through the European Union's Cohesion Fund.

The dam proposal was not entirely new. It had been originally suggested as a possible future addition to the Mornos project (1969–1981)
(see Figure 7.b) and had been awaiting the go ahead.[58] In 1991, the right
conditions prevailed: economic (funding available from the EU Cohesion
Fund); socio-environmental (drought presented as water scarcity); and
socio-political (consensus due to crisis and rising water prices combined
with a turbulent political period). Although studies for alternative solutions were submitted to the government by environmental NGOs, academics and private engineering companies (see Table 7.e), they never
received serious attention.[59] An interviewee from the higher ranks of the
Ministry of Development noted that "under drought situations…deci-
sions for large scale projects, which are clearly political, are normally
favored as the quickest and (in the short term) 'cheapest' solutions."[60]

The proposed dam project followed a development/resource base
expansion logic that totally contradicted the demand management/conser-
vation logic behind the price hikes.[61] However, dams are no longer greeted
with the same public enthusiasm as in early 20th century,[62] and are no
longer objects of worship or agents of social consensus. Thus, consensus
around their construction has to be forged through means other
than mere references to "progress". In the case of the Evinos Dam, the
threat of dry taps and of further increases in water prices was used as a justification for expanding the resource base (Figure 7.e). The promise of
more and cheaper water was coupled with the promise for continuous

Table 7.e Alternative Solutions Proposed During the Drought Period

Sealing Lake Yliki's sinkholes	235
Underground water from the river valleys of Boiot, Kifissos, Kalamos, and Assopos	211
Repair of the Mornos system leakages	75
Recycling	180–200
Total	701–721

Note: Estimated yield in million m³.
From Water Company of Athens (E.Y.Δ.Α.Π).

development and economic growth and worked as a very effective consensus building mechanism.

Indeed, the Evinos project promised growth and guaranteed employment for at least five years at high wages[63] for a region whose people struggle financially and are often structurally dependent on agricultural subsidies provided by the government and the EU. These were very significant factors in fostering social consent.[64] The president of one of the communities that would be affected by the dam stated that the Evinos project would cause a number of problems, including: land expropriation with low (and often delayed) financial compensation; loss of water for the area; continuous dynamite explosions and dust; and destruction of the area's flora and fauna. Yet, he concluded that "we [the local community] would be happy to consent to the implementation of the project, provided that we, too, got something out of it."[65] This phrase captures the naturalization of the clientalist character of political and economic relations and indicates how the promise of development had become part of a consensus-generating mechanism.

Of course, this kind of growth would be as short-lived as the construction period of the dam itself. To compensate for this, political promises were made to channel further funding (national or EU) and implement more projects in the area.[66] According to this logic, the solution to socio-environmental problems caused by progress resided in promises of more progress, and a "further boosting of the construction industry."[67]

Nature's Crisis as a Source of Direct Profit

The third emergency measure to alleviate the Athenian drought was the project for water transportation from Lake Trihonida (Figure 7.b), which ended up as one of the most notorious water supply scandals of the 20th century in Greece. The idea was that, with state permission, public water could be freely appropriated from Lake Trihonida by private companies,

Fig. 7.e The Engineer is scaring the ghost of water scarcity (ΛΕΙΨΥΔΡΙΑ) by expanding the resource base. Source: E.Υ.Δ.Α.Π. (The Water Company of Athens), 1990 water scarcity awareness campaign.

who would then have the right to sell it back to the (public) water company at a price per cubic meter which was set at double the price the consumer paid for it. Each cubic meter flowing into the Mornos Reservoir in this way would cost over 200 dr. (€0.58) to the public water company, while the average price that the consumer paid at the time was 102 dr. (€0.29) per m³.[68] However, with nationalized water resources, water-related private enterprises could only be established and thrive with strong state support and approval. Thus, the relevant Emergency Act amended earlier laws that banned the appropriation of water from lakes and rivers by private companies.[69] It also ordered the *continuous* supply of water for a period of three to five years (1993–1996/98), *irrespective* of any changes in environmental conditions (drought) or in the structure of water demand or supply, thus ensuring a guaranteed income for the contractors independent of the availability of water resources. In sum, if the contracts were to be honored, it would mean that for a period of two to four years, large quantities of probably *unneeded* water would be transported at a very high public cost, imposing a significant financial burden on the already indebted public water company. This cost would correspond to over 65 billion dr. (€190.6 million) over a two-year period for what would in all likelihood be a superfluous extra daily supply of 450,000 cubic meters of water. The Amending Act stated clearly that this extra cost would be covered through state subsidies and, therefore, the government's attempt to sanitize the water company's financial structure would not be jeopardized. Of course, the great losers would be the citizens, since, in effect, they would subsidize the new prices and projects either way. The procedure was characterized by the spokesman of the Socialist party, Sgouridis, as "colonial,"[70] while agricultural cooperatives, local authorities, the Technical Chamber of Greece (a powerful politically body) and the water company itself were also opposed to the proposal.[71]

However, it was not the public outcry against the contested Amendment Act and the Trihonida project that prevented it from materializing, but rather the fact that the Conservative party, which had put together the proposal, lost its majority to the Socialist party a few months after the proposal in the 1993 elections. The new government refused to act as guarantor for the appointed contractor's request for a loan from foreign banks, while the water company stated that it could no longer cooperate with the contractor. Eventually, the public tender for the project was cancelled and the project was dropped altogether.[72]

Although, nature's "crisis" seemed to be over, the higher water rates remained as a relic of the process of part-privatization of the water company, which went ahead as part of Greece's commitment to a "third way" between socialism and the market ideology.

Paving the Road to Privatization

The one *immediate* positive outcome from the implementation of the emergency projects in Athens was the 20% saving in water consumption, and an extra yield of 100,000 to 200,000 m^3 per day from additional drilling works. These quantities, however, were far from the originally estimated extra need of 1,000,000 m^3 per day (Table 7.f), supporting the argument for a discursively constructed rather than actual water scarcity during the drought period. Moreover, once the decision for the price rise was confirmed and all four Emergency Acts had been voted in, the discourse about water scarcity both in Parliament and in the media stopped abruptly, as if the mere act of adopting emergency measures had been sufficient to chase the ghost of water scarcity away. Indeed, by August 19, 1990, only three months after passing the Emergency Acts and before any concrete results had been achieved, the apocalyptic prophesies about imminent disaster had disappeared and the Minister of Environment,

Table 7.f Estimated Available Water Resources in Attica in 1990; Estimated Needs for 1990; and Projected Needs for 2001

1990: Estimated Existing Available Water Resources for Attica (in million m³)		1990: Estimated water needs for Attica (in million m³)		2001: Projected water needs for Attica (in million m³)
From Mornos	200–250	Domestic water supply	380	500
Boiotikos Kifissos River	160	Irrigation and industry of Attiki	13	55
From Lake Yliki and Lake Paralimni	220	Irrigation of Kopaida and Theba valleys	160	400
TOTAL	580–630	TOTAL	553	955

Data from Water Company of Athens (ΕΥΔΑΠ); compiled by the author.

Planning and Public Works asserted that "there will not be a water problem this year for Athens".[73]

However, the measures adopted—and in particular the price increases—were part of a much bigger project than the one that provided emergency relief from drought. The value that the 1987 law assigned to water as a "common good and a human right" had to be imbued with the assertion of its exchange value before embarking on the "liberalization" (i.e., privatization) of the public water company. Ironically, it would be the reelected Socialist government that would finalize the privatization process, partly responding to pressures from the European Union.

The new price schemes contributed an extra 16 to 17 billion dr. (€47 to €50 million) per year to ΕΥΔΑΠ's budget (Table 7.g). This became the first step towards the public company's financial "sanitization." In 1989, the company's total debt was 100 billion dr. (€293.5 million) and its annual deficit over 25 billion dr. (€73.3 million). After the implementation of the new pricing system, the company's financial situation turned around, and annual net profit amounted to 2.7 billion dr. (€7.9 million) by 1992, thus making the company attractive to investors for the first time.[74]

Furthermore, as a public utility company, ΕΥΔΑΠ was at the time eligible for soft loans from both the government and the European Union in order to finance its deficit. For example, the company's five-year plan (effective as of 1993) to gradually replace old network pipes was financed through a 35 billion dr. (€102.6 million) loan from the European Union's Cohesion Fund. Thus, the company's pending privatization was in effect subsidized directly by the government and, indirectly, by the European Union.

Table 7.g Net Profit for ΕΥΔΑΠ (1989–1998)

Net Profit for ΕΥΔΑΠ (in billion drachma)	
1989	−25
1992	+2.7
1997	+5.4
1998	+6

Source: Οικονομικός, Review (July 29, 1993); newspaper Το Βήμα (March 12, 1998).

In 1992 the capitalization of 130 billion dr. (€381.2 million) worth of the water company's shares went ahead "in order to deal with the company's outstanding debt".[75] In 1996, a new law[76] authorized a public competition for the post of the company's managing director (previously a state appointee), who, since 1997, is appointed by a consortium of private management consultancy companies (although the president and members of the administrative council still remain state appointees).[77] The changes in the company's administration and financial management were presented as part of a broader project for the modernization of public utility companies.[78] In 1999, a public tender was opened and 49 percent of the company's shares were sold to the private sector. This tender was accompanied by a bill[79] that sanctioned the division of *ΕΥΔΑΠ* into two companies: "*ΕΥΔΑΠ–A.E.*", a company with private shareholders that would be responsible for water and sewerage services; and "*ΕΥΔΑΠ*—Fixed Assets Company", which would remain a public company, in charge of the infrastructure, land, and buildings, and responsible for the protection and environmental management of water sources.

The same bill sanctioned the subsidizing of the newly privatized company by the government during the period 1999–2004 (Table 7.h), and ordered the establishment of a national committee to regulate *ΕΥΔΑΠ–A.E.* (and other possible future private water and sewerage companies).[80] The strategic sale of the company's shares was highly contested by the company's employees, who, during the six months preceding the procedure, engaged in strikes and protest campaigns.[81]

The changes in the management of the water sector in Athens and its part-privatization were partially attributed to the inefficiency of the public sector and its inability to deal with a crisis caused by nature. However, the analysis in this chapter shows that London's "successful" management model underwent a very similar practice of privatization and price hikes to that of its "unsuccessful" counterpart in Athens. In both cases, the use of nature as crisis was marshaled to justify the change, and the discourse and media attention around pending environmental disasters became powerful tools for bringing about public consensus over the restructuring of the status and ownership of water supply.

Table 7.h State Subsidies Announced in 1999 for EYΔAΠ–A.E. for the Period 1999–2004

Year	Amount (in billion drachma)
1999	14
2000	15.8
2001	12.6
2002	9.5
2003	6.3
2004	3.1

From Newspaper Επενδυτής (Aug. 22, 1999).

"Valuable" Nature

The intricate political, economic, and socio-environmental dialectics of scarcity and water management in London and Athens exemplify the fact that contemporary water crises can no longer be understood merely as the caprice of an untamed, unpredictable nature, but need to be addressed instead as part of the dynamics of a complex and, at times, vulnerable socio-environmental and economic system. Yet, the call to take environmental issues seriously is repeatedly buried in scarcity discourses. These often result in the assertion of the economic value of natural resources, while the social, cultural, and political issues around the production of nature remain silenced. The drought crisis in Athens is a case in point, where the discourse around the scheme "scarce = valuable = expensive" asserted that the increase in water's exchange value was an inevitable social response to an otherwise natural phenomenon. In this way, the inevitability of a *natural* phenomenon (drought) is translated into the *self-explanatory* inevitability of a *socially constructed* [82] phenomenon (i.e., water scarcity).

If, instead, we were to view nature not as *external* to society (or indeed to the socio-natural hybrids called modern cities), but as *socially produced*, [83] water shortages would no longer feature only as the direct outcome of a prolonged dry period; rather, they could be understood as the outcome of long periods of interaction between available resources, human labor, and the economics, politics, and culture of urbanization and water use. In London, the discourse around nature's crisis and the need to protect the environment was marshaled to support the privatization of the water sector; however, the new privatized management scheme did no more or less to protect the environment than the state-led scheme that preceded it. In the case of Athens, the Emergency Measures of the 1990s provided less of a solution to an *environmental problem*, and more of a means to sustain the *socio-environmental transformation* of an ever expanding urban system.

In both cases, the discourse on environmental protection co-existed with the continuation of not-so-environmentally-friendly developmental practices and discourses: the Evinos Dam and Reservoir in the case of Athens, and the Upper Thames Reservoir in the case of London. It seems that both projects remained pending until favorable political and socio-natural configurations were able to push their implementation forwards. In both cases, a natural "crisis" was used as a justification for perpetuating a contested development logic. Moreover, both projects represented cheaper (for the operator) solutions to accommodating increasing demand or falling supply, in contrast to simply repairing and updating the network system. In both examples, the *raison d' être* of the rise in water prices and of the proposed reservoir constructions was to sustain the existing socio-economic order of things, including the existing economic and cultural patterns of water use and capital expansion. Finally, in both cases the role of the state within the "free", market-led configuration remained very important, and very far from Adam Smith's preaching of *laissez-faire*. Indeed, the state mechanism remained as active as ever (if not even *more* active than ever) in order to ensure environmental protection and just resource allocation, while securing the smooth operation of the market. In the case of the UK, in order for a natural-monopoly "free" market to operate, the state has to regulate extensively. Moreover, state subsidies have not disappeared, although they are now indirect and come mainly in the form of tax breaks, such as the ones that had been allocated to the UK water industry to help it meet the quality standards set by the European Union's Drinking Water Directives.[84] Moreover, the unprecedented regulatory apparatus developed to make the privatized water market operational also makes a great claim on public budgets. In the case of Athens, the subsidies to the privatized industry were more direct. By maintaining its responsibility for the management of networks, the public sector takes on the high maintenance cost, while the profitable part of the system (water supply and management) is sold off to the private sector.

In the cases of both London and Athens we witness the development of what Graham and Marvin[85] term a "utility patchwork," an entangled network of regulators and private operators, which depletes public resources while not allowing for reinvestment of profits in public services. Such a utility patchwork stands is stark contrast to modernity's dream for a highly rational, organized, controlled and functional urban space.[86] The contemporary fragmentation of the city's veins is, interestingly enough, reminiscent of early 19th century urban infrastructure, which also used to be a hodgepodge of service providers administering water of varying quality and prices. Modernity's programmatic visions tried to administer the irrationality of that early system in the name of urban social order. However, these efforts were dissolved again through socio-economic and cultural processes driven by the expansion of the market economy. This historical geographical process of continuous creative destruction endorses modernization as an ongoing process, despite post-modern accounts declaring its death. True enough, modernity constantly "sets the scene for its own downfall,"[87] but modernization as a social, economic, and cultural process is not over yet. As Charles Baudelaire put it in his famous declaration: "Modernity is the transitory, the fugitive, the contingent, the half of art of which the other half is the eternal and the immutable."[88]

Epilogue

Now that we have coaxed the lightning to curl round our feet like a
kitten and, fearless as eagles have counted the freckles on the face of
the sun...other blind forces are born to us, other major fears.

L. Aragon, The Paris Peasant (1926/1994: 117)[1]

When Louis Aragon wrote *Paris Peasant* in 1926, his aspiration was to
produce a myth of an era—modernity—while the era was still alive and
while he was still living in it. Unlike the romantic poets who preceded him,
and who sang the sagas of times past and lamented lost glories, Aragon
wished to sing the legends of his own era, to celebrate the glory of modernity *en vivant*, for the benefit of the modern man and woman.

However, modernization did not rely on its poets alone for promoting
its legendary image. The production of myths and dream images (Chapters 2, 3, and 4) was an integral part of the process of creative destruction
called modernization. This book has shown that the production of urban
landscapes and the taming of nature was subject to the exercise of power
and the investment of money, technology, and human labor, but it was
also conditioned by the construction of geographical imaginations and
ideologies of what nature is and how it should be treated, of what a
modern city is and how it should function. The materiality of London's
sewers (Chapters 5 and 6) developed through funds generated from industrialization and from the enterprise called "The British Empire". However,
this great achievement was conceived first as part of the geographical
imagination that envisioned London as The "Great Imperial Capital", a
clean, sanitized Western metropolis that could not afford to be "smelly".

167

Moreover, the allocation of public funds for this project was contingent on the collapse of the previously dominant "miasmatic" conjecture.

Although the Western world shared common visions of modernization, nevertheless these visions were transmuted within different geographical contexts. The construction of particular wish images and their materialization were geographically specific processes. Notwithstanding the similarities between the modernizing vision as it applied to both Athens and London, the specific geo-political configuration in Athens led to the pursuit of a very different type of modernization. Lack of funding and a strong dependency on Western capital allowed only for "selective" modernization, a process similar to the one that colonial regimes underwent. This selective modernization promoted large scale transport and communication projects, but neglected the development of basic urban infrastructure, of water supply and sanitation projects, which nevertheless constituted one of the main social and political priorities for Athens at the time. The pursuit of the modernizing vision for Athens was further complicated by the geographically specific wish image that combined the desire to produce a modern city with the vision to reconnect this city to its ancient past. The superimposition of these two different, if not antithetical, geographical imaginations for modern Athens resulted in the promotion of a century long enterprise for the restoration of the city's ancient aqueduct. This enterprise, it was hoped, would supply the modern city with water, while at the same time reconnect it to its ancient veins. The decision to restore Hadrian's Aqueduct (Chapter 5) was born as much out of the desire to pursue this twofold modernizing vision for Athens, as it was out of sheer material necessity (i.e., a lack of funding to pursue new water supply projects). However, the enterprise failed to improve the supply of water to an ever growing city. It was only when the material circumstances could match the compound wish-images (i.e., when adequate funding was made available through external loans) that Greece could finally make its first step towards the materialization of its modernizing vision. The construction of the Marathon Dam (Chapter 6) was a decisive step in this process. While the restoration of Hadrian's Aqueduct had been no more than a process of rescuing ancient technology and trying to put it to the service of the contemporary city, the construction of the Marathon Dam was a full blown modernist project, a process of creative destruction that changed irrevocably the physical landscape around the dam, but also contributed to further changes in the urban and social landscape of Athens itself. It also induced the euphoria and optimism linked to the belief that a better society was emerging.

Across the Western world, the lining of cities with networks and technology went hand in glove with the promise for a better society.

Modernity's sweeping creativity destroyed preexisting social and physical landscapes, but in return, it promised improved living conditions and human emancipation. To be sure, the modern hero—in the guise of the engineer, the architect, the planner, or the developer[2]—helped fulfill many of the promises of the modernist project: building cities, supplying them with adequate water and sanitation facilities, piercing mountains to make way for aqueducts, railroads and highways. Through both persuasion and crude power modernization did deliver many of the promised goods in the West, and did live up to the legend that Aragon had mused about: it did coax the lightning "to curl round [man's] feet like a kitten"; it did harness rivers to feed urban and domestic dreams of glory and prestige; it did deliver water and electricity to everyone's (or almost everyone's) doorstep. The modernist dream of taming nature in the West did not just materialize; it became "normalized" and "naturalized" as well.

However, the delivery of the material goods did not necessarily contribute to building a more just and egalitarian society. For the promised paraphernalia were delivered in the form of commodities and thus were subject to the rules and power relations of the market economy. The materialization of a consumers' paradise in which we all are supposed to participate equally, was accompanied by the diffusion of political and social power into all aspects of everyday life. The realization of modernity's sparkling wish images was accompanied by a series of nightmares, from environmental degradation to increasing social inequality and poverty worldwide. The generations who were bred and fed with the material goods of development now look incredulously at the benefits of progress. The Western world has stopped admiring technology the way it did a century ago. Dam constructions are no longer objects of admiration or places of pilgrimage. Development projects are today greeted with great skepticism. The public consensus over progress is no longer guaranteed.

Still, alongside a thriving global capitalist market, and glittering global cities, the developing world still awaits to receive the full benefits of modernization. Although the Western corners of the world have grown distrustful and skeptical of the modernist myth, its less developed quarters are only just beginning to construct their own modernist dreams, to formulate their own modernist wish images, and to pursue their own agendas of creative destruction. Who can deny them the right to do so? The recent completion of the Three Gorges Dam project at China, which includes promises of "water and electricity for all," produced a transmuted physical landscape and displaced 700,000 people whose livelihoods and lifestyles "stood in the way of progress." Although the Western world launched a fierce critique of the project, the logic of this development was in fact identical to that of similar projects which were splashed all over the Western world during the late 20th and even the 21st century. The Three Gorges Dam project never received funding from the World Bank. Still, after its completion the mutated landscapes that the project produced became a major tourist attraction, and attract daily pilgrimages, similar to those that the Westerners used to attend in the first half of the 20th century. According to an article published in *The Guardian* on October 30, 2003,[3] many amongst the area's displaced farmers have now become gondoliers, taking visitors on boat trips over their inundated houses. Contrary to the expectations of the West, the peasants-turned-gondoliers are not embittered; once sustaining a livelihood by cultivating vegetables on the banks of the Yangtze River, their lives were probably already too bad to get any worse: "I may float over my old home every day, but I never think about it. What's the point? … [L]ife is better now. We have a new home, more space and more money. The dam has been good for us."[3] Likewise, the towns that have sprung up along the newly engineered Yangtze landscape constitute an eyesore to Westerners. Most locals, however, perceive the skyscrapers that tower the new skylines as an improvement of the landscape. Chances are that some 50 years ago, the Western eye would have reacted in exactly the same way.

But what is more astonishing is that, even today, despite the criticism of large scale development projects, the Western world continues to develop in the same logic as it did back in the 19th and early 20th centuries. More often than not, the response to desolation caused by development is: "more development"—from the Spanish national hydrological plan, one of the most ambitious dam projects ever undertaken, to the re-branding of derelict industrial landscapes as "brownfields" and promptly "redeveloping" them, the process of creative destruction lives on. Despite the discourses on "sustainability", more rivers are harnessed (like the Evinos River in Greece) and more reservoirs are built (like the Upper Thames Reservoir in England) to feed the ongoing process of urbanization. Either through long-term large scale projects, or through smaller scale ephemeral "urban pulsars" (International Expositions, Olympic Games, Cultural Capitals) urban and non-urban landscapes exist in a state of perpetual transformation.

Athens' successful bid for the 2004 Olympic Games produced a unique chance (or excuse?) for the implementation of more large scale development projects. In pursuit of the production of Athens as an Olympic Capital, the development practices of the 19th and early 20th centuries remain largely the same. However, it is not only contemporary material practices that are comparable to those of earlier periods of modernization; the wish-images that are promoted at present are also astonishingly similar to those of the past. In 2004, Athens marketed itself worldwide as an Olympic city where the ancient and the modern come together. The old ideal of producing a link between ancient and modern Athens lurked around the corner of every new "Olympic" development. The frantic race to build more dams and reservoirs, faster railroads, highways, metropolitan lines, more stadiums, and more accommodation to cater to the needs of an Olympic city, brought new archaeological findings to light on a daily basis. With each new finding, the completion of the projects was further delayed, given the requirement for an official archaeological assessment before the projects could proceed any further. Beyond this, however, each new finding gave rise to new opportunities for asserting the link between Athens' past and present.

The official promotional campaign for Athens 2004 (sponsored by the Greek National Tourism Organization and Organization Athens 2004) was based on a playful, at times semi-ironic, engagement with the dialectics between the city's past and future. Half of the advertisements started by stating the importance of the city's past, only to play it down in the next sentence, in favor of the city's "modern" present. The other half did the reverse: they started by renouncing the city's devotion to its past, only to reassert the importance of this past in lines that followed.

The advertisement in Figure 8.a starts by declaring Athens' past as the city's most important asset: "In ancient times, the best were sent to Athens to be enlightened."

However, this assertion is immediately played down in the lines that follow: "Times have changed, though, and so have we. Hundreds of award winning beaches, dozens of cosmopolitan islands, theatres, nightclubs…are the rewards Attica has to offer today." The message is that in the end, it all comes together: past and present.

"Naturally, museums and ancient ruins are still there as a constant inspiration from the past. But with nearly 300 days of sunshine per year, there's more than one way to be enlightened in [modern] Attica."

Another advertisement, shown in Figure 8.b, follows the reverse trajectory, but nevertheless reaches the exact same conclusion. It starts by declaring provocatively: "In Athens, transportation is stuck in the past." However, the text that follows undermines the original statement: "We tried to build the new subway system as fast as possible, but we simply had to make a few stops along the way. You see, we unearthed some fascinating ancient findings." The interplay culminates in the final sentence, which brings the city's past and future together, recalling 19th century discourses: "The new subway system moves at the speed of today. But we never forget the glory of the past."

In ancient times, the best were sent to Athens to be enlightened.

Fig. 8.a Past and Present come together in *Athens 2004*.
The advertisement from the promotional campaign for *Athens 2004* starts by declaring Athens' past as the city's most important asset: "In ancient times, the best were sent to Athens to be enlightened", only to immediately play down this assertion: "Times have changed, though and so have we. Hundreds of award-winning beaches, dozens of cosmopolitan islands, theatres, nightclubs are the rewards Attica has to offer today". In the end, past and present come together: "Naturally, museums and ancient ruins are still there as a constant inspiration from the past. But with nearly 300 days of sunshine per year, there's more than one way to be enlightened in [modern] Attica".
Source: Campaign *Athens 2004* sponsored by the 'Greek National Tourism Organisation' and 'Organisation Athens 2004'.

Fig. 8.b Past and Present come together in *Athens 2004*.
The advertisement for the new Athenian Subway Line starts by declaring provocatively: "In Athens, transportation is stuck in the past". However, the text that follows undermines the original statement: "We tried to build the new subway system as fast as possible, but we simply had to make a few stops along the way. You see, we unearthed some fascinating ancient findings". This interplay culminates in the final sentence, which brings the city's past and future together, resonating 19th century discourses: "The new subway system moves at the speed of today. But we never forget the glory of the past".
Source: Campaign *Athens 2004* sponsored by the 'Greek National Tourism Organisation' and 'Organisation Athens 2004'.

The big gift box that lay at the heart of the newly constructed Olympic Village awaiting the opening ceremony of the Olympic Games also illustrates this point. The box contained a freshly excavated part of the old Hadrian's Aqueduct, which had come to light while digging for the foundations of the Olympic Village. Once the box was opened, the athletes and visitors were able to admire both modern and ancient Athens at one single glance.

It seems that, despite all the rhetoric about the end of modernity, the Western world is not through with producing wish-images, ideologies, and dreams of modernization, and with relentlessly pursuing their materialization. Modernization remains a project still under way, an ongoing process in which nature, cities, and people are woven together in an inseparable dialectic of creation and destruction, pursued through both ideological and material means. This book used water as a vehicle to examine the flows that administer this process: flows of social power, money, labor, technology, and resources that produce modern urban landscapes. Of course, there are more channels through which one can explore this process. As Foucault asserted:

A whole history remains to be written of spaces—which would at the same time be history of powers (both these terms in the plural)—from the great strategies of geo-politics to the little tactics of the habitat, institutional architecture from the classroom to the design of hospitals, passing via economic and political installations.

M. Foucault, "The Eye of Power"; cited in A. Vidler,
The Architectural Uncanny (1992: 168)[4]

Endnotes

Chapter 1

1. Plaskovitis, S. 1961. *The Dam (Το Φράγμα)*, Kedros, Athens.
2. See Heynen, H. 1999. *Architecture and Modernity: A Critique*, MIT Press, Cambridge MA; Harvey, D. 2003. *Paris: Capital of Modernity*, Routledge, New York.
3. Foster, J. B. 1997. Marx and the environment, in *In Defense of History: Marxism and the Postmodern Agenda*, Wood, M., Foster, E., and Bellamy, J., Eds. Monthly Review Press, New York, 150–162.
4. Smith, N., 1984. *Uneven Development Nature Capital and the Production of Space*, Blackwell, Oxford.
5. This is a rework of an earlier book chapter, co-authored by Erik Swyngedouw and published under the title: "The Environment of the City or ... The Urbanisation of Nature", in *A Companion to the City*, Bridge, G. and Watson, S., Eds., Blackwell, Oxford, 2000, 567–580. Many thanks to Erik Swyngedouw, the editors and to Blackwell publishing for granting copyright permission.
6. This is a rework of an earlier publication, co-authored by Erik Swyngedouw and published under the title: "Fetishising the Modern City: the Phantasmagoria of Urban Technological Networks", *International Journal of Urban and Regional Research*, 24, 120–138, 2000. Many thanks to Erik Swyngedouw and to the journal editors for granting copyright permission.
7. This is a rework of an earlier publication authored by M. Kaika, titled "Interrogating the Geographies of the Familiar: Domesticating Nature and Constructing the Autonomy of the Modern Home", *International Journal of Urban and Regional Research*, 28, 265–286, 2004. Many thanks to the journal editors for granting copyright permission.
8. Part of the material on Athens that appears in this chapter comes from Kaika, M. "Constructing Scarcity and Sensationalising Water Politics: 170 Days that Shook Athens", *Antipode*, 35, 919–954, 2003. Many thanks to the journal editors for granting copyright permission.

Chapter 2

1. Phelan, S. 1993. "Intimate Distance: The Dislocation of Nature in Modernity", in *In the Nature of Things: Language, Politics, and the Environment*, Bennett, J. and Chaloupka, W., Eds. University of Minnesota Press, Minneapolis, 45–62.
2. Guirand, F. 1959. *Larousse Encyclopaedia of Mythology*, Graves, R., Ed. Paul Hamlyn, London.
3. See Toulmin, S. 1990. *Cosmopolis: The Hidden Agenda of Modernity*, The Free Press, New York; Johnston, R. J., Gregory, D., and Smith, D. M., Eds. 1994. *The Dictionary of Human Geography*, Blackwell, Oxford; Bauman, Z. 1991. *Modernity and Ambivalence*, Polity Press, Cambridge; Berman, M. 1983. *All that is Solid Melts into Air: The Experience of Modernity*, Verso, London.

175

4. Foster, J. B. 1997. "Marx and the Environment", in *In Defense of History: Marxism and the Postmodern Agenda*, Wood, M., Foster, E., and Bellamy, J., Eds. Monthly Review Press, New York, 150–162.

5. Bewell, A. J. 1989. *Wordsworth and the Enlightenment: Nature, Man, and Society in the Experimental Poetry*, Yale University Press, New Haven, CT.

6. Glacken, C. J. 1967. *Traces on the Rhodian Shore: Nature and Culture in Western Thought from Ancient Times to the End of the Eighteenth Century*, University of California Press, Berkeley.

7. Latour, B. 199.3 *We Have Never Been Modern*, translated by C. Porter, Harvester Wheatsheaf, New York.

8. Katz, C. and Kirby, A. 1991. "In the Nature of Things: The Environment and Everyday Life" *Transactions, Institute of British Geographers*, 16(3), 259–271; Anderson, K. 1995. "Culture and Nature at the Adelaide Zoo: At the Frontiers of 'Human' Geography", *Transactions, Institute of British Geographers*, 20(3), 275–95; Katz, C. 1998. "Whose Nature, Whose Culture?: Private Productions of Space and the "Preservation" of Nature", in *Remaking Reality: Nature at the Millennium*, Braun, B. and Castree, N., Eds., Routledge, London, 46–63; Gerber, J. 1997. "Beyond Dualism—the Social Construction of 'Nature' and the Natural and Social Construction of Human Beings", *Progress in Human Geography*, 21(1), 1–17

9. Kropotkin, P. 1972. (1902) *Mutual Aid, A Factor of Evolution*, Allen Lane, London; Stoddart, D. R. 1975. "Kropotkin, Reclus and 'Relevant' Geography", *Area* 7, 180–190.

10. Marcuse, H. 1986. (1964). *One Dimensional Man: Studies in the Ideology of Advanced Industrial Society*, Ark, London.

11. Marx, K. 1976. (1859). Capital Vol. I 474–475, cited in Grundmann, R. 1991. *Marxism and Ecology, Marxist Introductions,* Clarenton Press, Oxford, 78.

12. Eckersley, R. 1992. *Environmentalism and Political Theory: Toward an Ecocentric Approach*, UCL Press, London; Redclift, M. 1987. *Sustainable Development: Exploring the Contradictions*, Routledge, London.

13. Foster, J. B. 1997. "Marx and the Environment" in *In Defense of History: Marxism and the Postmodern Agenda*, Wood, M., Foster, E., and Bellamy, J., Eds. Monthly Review Press, New York, 150–162.

14. Seminal works include: Bird, E. 1987. "The Social Construction of Nature: Theoretical Approaches to the History of Environmental Problems", *Environmental Review*, 11, 260–71; Castree, N. 1995. "The Nature of Produced Nature: Materiality and Knowledge Construction in Marxism", *Antipode*, 27 (1), 12–48; Fitzimmons, M. 1989. "The Matter of Nature", *Antipode*, 21, 106–120; Harvey, D. 1996. *Justice, Nature and the Geography of Difference*, Blackwell, Oxford; Katz, C. and Kirby, A. 1991. "In the Nature of Things: The Environment and Everyday Life", *Transactions, Institute of British Geographers*, 16 (3), 259–271; Simmons, I. G. 1993. *Interpreting Nature: Cultural Constructions of the Environment*, Routledge, London; Smith, N. 1984. *Uneven Development: Nature, Capital and the Production of Space*, Blackwell, Oxford.

15. Lefebvre, H. 1994. (1974) *The Production of Space*, Blackwell, Oxford.

16. Katz, C. 1998. "Whose Nature, Whose Culture?: Private Productions of Space and the 'Preservation' of Nature," in *Remaking Reality: Nature at the Millennium*, Braun, B. and Castree, N., Eds. Routledge, London, 46–63.

17. Braun, B. and Castree, N., Eds. 1998. *Remaking Reality: Nature at the Millennium*, Routledge, London.

18. Gregotti, V. 1993. (1966) "Architecture, Environment, Nature," in *Architecture Culture 1943–1968*, Ockman, J., Ed. Rizzoli, New York, 399–401.

19. Smith, N. 1984. *Uneven Development: Nature, Capital and the Production of Space*, Blackwell, Oxford.

20. Oelschlaeger, M. 1991. *The Idea of Wilderness: From Prehistory to the Age of Ecology*, Yale University Press, New Haven, CT; Wilson, A. 1992. *The Culture of Nature: North American Landscape from Disney to the Exxon Valdez*, Blackwell, Cambridge, MA.

21. Pollution is, of course, also a strongly politicized concept whose meaning changes with time and place, as the seminal work by Mary Douglas has demonstrated: Douglas, M. 1970. *Purity and Danger: An Analysis of Concepts of Pollution and Taboo*, 2nd ed. Penguin, Harmondsworth; first edition 1966, Routledge, London.

22. Thompson, K. 1993. *Emile Durkheim*, Routledge, London. Tönnies, F. 2002, 1887. *Community and Society*, Dover, New York.
23. Buckingham, J. S. 1849. *National Evils and Practical Remedies with a Plan of a Model Town, Accompanied by an Examination of Some Important Moral and Political Problems*, London.
24. Carter, H. 1983. *An Introduction to Urban Historical Geography*, Edward Arnold, London, 128.
25. Howard, E. 1996. (1898) "Garden Cities of Tomorrow," "Author's Introduction," and "The Town-Country Magnet," in *The City Reader*, LeGates, R. and Stout, F., Eds. Routledge, London, 345–353.
26. Olmsted, F. L. 1996. (1870) "Public Parks and the Enlargement of Towns," in *The City Reader*, LeGates, R. and Stout, F., Eds. Routledge, London, 337–344.
27. Fishman, R. 1982. *Urban Utopias of the Twentieth Century*, MIT Press, Cambridge, MA.
28. Le Corbusier. 1925. *Urbanisme*, Crés, Paris; Le Corbusier. 1929. *The City of Tomorrow and its Planning*, John Rodker. London.
29. Ibid.
30. Wright, F. L. 1996. (1935) "Broadacre City: A New Community Plan," in *The City Reader*, LeGates, R. and Stout, F., Eds. Routledge, London, 376–381.
31. LeGates, R. and Stout, F., Eds. *The City Reader*, Routledge, London, 376–377
32. Mumford, L. 1938. *The Culture of Cities*, Secker & Warburg, London.
33. Alexander, C. 1996. (1965) "A City is Not a Tree," in *The City Reader*, LeGates, R. and Stout, F., Eds. Routledge, London, 119–131.
34. Berman, M. 1983. *All that is Solid Melts into Air: The Experience of Modernity*, Verso, London.
35. Calvino, I. 1979. (1974) *Invisible Cities*, translated by Weaver, W. , Picador, London.
36. Gottlieb, R. 1993. *Forcing the Spring: The Transformation of the American Environmental Movement*, Island Press, Washington, D.C.; O'Connor, J. 1998. *Natural Causes: Essays in Ecological Marxism*, Guilford Press, New York, 118.
37. Davis, M. 1990. *City of Quartz: Excavating the Future in Los Angeles*, Verso, London.
38. Archer, K. 1998. Imagineering Nature: The Post-Industrial Political Ecology of Florida, paper read at RGS-IBG Annual Conference.
39. McHarg, I. 1969. *Design with Nature*, Doubleday, New York.
40. Cronon, W. 1991. *Nature's Metropolis: Chicago and the Great West*, W W Norton and Company, New York.
41. Davis, M. 1990. *City of Quartz: Excavating the Future in Los Angeles*, Verso, London; Davis, M. 1995. "Los Angeles After the Storm: The Dialectic of Ordinary Disaster," *Antipode*, 27 (3) 221–241; Davis, M. 1998. *Ecology of Fear: Los Angeles and the Imagination of Disaster*, Metropolitan Books, New York.
42. Swyngedouw, E. 1999. Modernity and Hybridity: nature, regeneracionismo, and the production of the Spanish waterscape, 1890–1930. *Annals of the American Association of Geographers* 89(3): 443–465; Swyngedouw, E. 2004. *Social Power and the Urbanization of Water: Flows of Power*. Oxford: Oxford University Press; Gandy, M. 2002. *Concrete and Clay: Reworking Nature in New York City*. Cambridge, Massachusetts: MIT Press; Desfor, G., and R. Keil. 2004. *Nature and the City: Making Environmental Policy in Toronto and Los Angeles*. Tucson, Arizona: The University of Arizona Press.
43. Harvey, D. 1996. *Justice, Nature and the Geography of Difference*, Blackwell, Oxford.
44. Swyngedouw, E. 1999. "Modernity and Hybridity: Nature, Regenerationism, and the Production of the Spanish Waterscape, 1890–1930," *Annals of the American Association of Geographers*, 89 (3), 443–465.
45. Swyngedouw, E. 1996. "The City as a Hybrid: On Nature, Society and Cyborg Urbanisation," *Capitalism Nature Socialism*, 7 (25 (March)), 65–80.
46. Smith, N. and O'Keefe, P. 1980. "Geography, Marx and the Concept of Nature," *Antipode* 12 (2), 30–39; Swyngedouw, E. 1999. "Modernity and Hybridity: Nature, Regenerationism, and the Production of the Spanish Waterscape, 1890–1930," *Annals of the American Association of Geographers*, 89 (3), 443–465; Swyngedouw, E. 2004. *Social Power and the Urbanization of Water: Flows of Power*, Oxford University Press, Oxford; Gandy, M. 2002. *Concrete and Clay: Reworking Nature in New York City*, MIT Press, Cambridge, MA; Keil, R. 1998. *Los Angeles: Globalization, Urbanization, and Social Struggles*, John Wiley & Son, New York.

47. See, among others, Smith, N. 1996. "The Production of Nature," in *FutureNatural—Nature/Science/Culture*, Robertson, G. Mash, M. Tickner, L. Bird, J. Curtis, B. and Putnam, T., Eds. Routledge, London, 35–54; Castree, N. 1995. "The Nature of Produced Nature: Materiality and Knowledge Construction in Marxism," *Antipode*, 27 (1), 12–48.
48. Haraway, D. 1997. *Modest_Witness@Second_Millennium.FemaleMan_Meets_Oncomouse*, Routledge, London.
49. Swyngedouw, E. and Kaika, M. 1999. "Hybrid Worlds: On Nature, Society and Cyborgs," (in french) in *Discours Scientifiques et Contextes Culturels: Geographies Britaniques et Françaises a l' epreuve postmoderne*, Chivallon, C., Ragout, P., and Samers, M., Eds. Maison des Sciences de l'Homme d'Aquitaine, Talence, 271–284.
50. Giddens, A. 1997. "Risk Society: The Context of British Politics," in *The Politics of Risk Society*, Franklin, J., Ed. Polity Press, Cambridge, MA, 23–34.
51. Latour. 1996. Cited in Castree, N. 1995. "The Nature of Produced Nature: Materiality and Knowledge Construction in Marxism," *Antipode*, 27 (1), 12–48.
52. Lewontin, R. 1997. "Genes, Environment, and Organism," in *Hidden Histories of Science*, Silvers, R. B., Ed. Granta Books, London, 115–139.
53. Calvino, I. 1979. (1974) *Invisible Cities*, translated by Weaver, W., Picador, London, 122.
54. Haraway, D. 1997. *Modest_Witness@Second_Millennium.FemaleMan_Meets_Oncomouse*, Routledge, London. Latour. 1996. Cited in Castree, N. 1995. "The Nature of Produced Nature: Materiality and Knowledge Construction in Marxism," *Antipode*, 27 (1), 12–48.
55. Skeat, W. W. 1898. *An Etymological Dictionary of the English Language*, Clarendon Press, Oxford, 278; *Encyclopaedia Britannica, Vol. V*, 179.
56. Swyngedouw, E. and Kaika, M. 1999. "Hybrid Worlds: On Nature, Society and Cyborgs," (in french) in *Discours Scientifiques et Contextes Culturels: Geographies Britaniques et Françaises a l' epreuve postmoderne*, Chivallon, C., Ragout, P., and Samers, M., Eds. Maison des Sciences de l'Homme d'Aquitaine, Talence, 271–284.
57. Ibid.; see also Haraway, D. 1997. *Modest Witness—Second-Millennium. FemaleMan Meets Oncomouse*, Routledge, London.
58. Williams, R. 1985. (1973) *The Country and the City*, Chatto & Windus, 1973; this Hogarth edition offset from the original Chatto edition, *Hogarth Critics*, Hogarth Press, London.
59. Harvey, D. 1996. *Justice, Nature and the Geography of Difference*, Blackwell, Oxford, 94.
60. Latour, B. 1993. *We Have Never Been Modern*, translated by Porter, C., Harvester Wheatsheaf, New York, 121.

Chapter 3

1. Aragon, L. 1926. *The Paris Peasant*. Boston: Exact Change.
2. Castells, M. 1985. *High Technology Space and Society*. Beverly Hills, CA; Harvey, D. 1996. *Justice, Nature and the Geography of Difference*. Oxford: Blackwell; Merrifield, A. The struggle over place: redeveloping American Can in Southeast Baltimore. *Transactions of the Institute of British Geographers* 1993;18:102–121; Sennett, R. 1994. *Flesh and Stone: the Body and the City in Western Civilization*. London: Faber and Faber.
3. Deleuze, G. and Guatlan, F. 1997. City state. In: Leach, N. Ed. *Rethinking Architecture*. London: Routledge, 313–316.
4. Russell, N. W., L. McKnight, and R. J. Solomon. 1999. *The Gordian Knot: Political Gridlock on the Information Highway*. Cambridge, MA: MIT Press.
5. Castells, M. 1985. *High Technology, Space, and Society*. Beverly Hills, CA: Sage; Chant, C. 1989. *Science, Technology and Everyday Life 1870–1950*. London: Routledge (in association with The Open University); Franklin, U. 1990. *The Real World of Technology*. C. Enterprises, ed. CBC Massey Lectures Series CBC Enterprises, Toronto; Graham, S. and S. Marvin. 1996. *Telecommunications and the City: Electronic Spaces, Urban Places*. London: Routledge.
6. Marx, K. 1976 (1859). *Capital*. Vol I.
7. Pietz, W. 1993. Fetishism and materialism: The limits of theory in Marx. In: E. Apter, Ed. *Fetishism as Cultural Discourse*. Ithaca: Cornell University Press, 119–151.
8. Marx, K. 1859/1976. *Capital*. Vol. I. B. Fowkes, trans. Harmondsworth: Penguin; see also: Mitchell, W. J. T. 1986. *Iconology: Image, Text, Ideology*. Chicago: University of Chicago Press; Best, S. 1994. The commodification of reality and the reality of commodification:

Baudrillard, Debord, and postmodern theory. In: Kellner, D., Ed. *Baudrillard: A Critical Reader*. Oxford: Blackwell, 41–65.

9. Eagleton, T. 1991. *Ideology: An Introduction*. London: Verso, 37.

10. Marx, 1859/1976: 165.

11. Buck-Morss, S. 1995. *The Dialectics of Seeing: Walter Benjamin and the Arcades Project*. Cambridge, MA: MIT Press.

12. Ibid.: 181.

13. On the commodification of urban space, see Harvey, D. and L. Chatterjee. Absolute rent and the structuring of space by governmental and financial institutions. *Antipode* 1973; 6(1):22–36; Harvey, D. 1982. *The Limits to Capital*. Oxford: Blackwell; Lefebvre, H. 1991. *Critique of Everyday Life*. London: Verso.

14. See Fainstein's excellent analysis: Fainstein, S. 1994, *The City Builders: Property, Politics & Planning in London and New York*. Oxford: Blackwell.

15. Castells, M. 1977. *The Urban Question: a Marxist Approach*. London: Edward Arnold.

16. Illich, I. 1986. H_2O *and the Waters of Forgetfulness*. London: Marion Boyars; Swyngedouw, E. Power, nature, and the city. The conquest of water and the political ecology of urbanization in Guayaquil, Ecuador: 1880–1990. *Environment and Planning*, A 1997; 29(2):311–332; Swyngedouw, E. 2004. *Social Power and the Urbanization of Water: Flows of Power*. Oxford: Oxford University Press.

17. For an analysis of the history of water privatization in the UK, see Castro, E., M. Kaika, and E. Swyngedouw. London: structural continuities and institutional change in water management. *European Planning Studies* 2003; 11(3):283–298.

18. Marx, K. 1859/1976. *Capital*. Vol. I. B. Fowkes, trans. Penguin, Harmondsworth.

19. Buck-Morss, S. 1995. *The Dialectics of Seeing: Walter Benjamin and the Arcades Project*. Cambridge, MA: MIT Press.: 181.

20. Ondaatje, M. 1988. *In the Skin of a Lion*. London: Picador.

21. Waites, B. 1989. Social and human engineering. In: Chant, C., Ed. *Science, Technology and Everyday Life 1870–1950*. London: Routledge (in association with The Open University), 316–361.

22. Headrick, D. R. 2000. *When Information Came of Age: Technologies of Knowledge in the Age of Reason and Revolution, 1700–1850*. New York: Oxford University Press.

23. Gympel, J. 1996. *The Story of Architecture: From Antiquity to the Present*. Koln: Konemann, 72.

24. Marx, L. 1964. *The Machine in the Garden: Technology and the Pastoral Ideal in America*. New York: Oxford University Press; McLuhan, M. and Q. Fiore. 1967. *The Medium is the Massage*. New York: Bantam Books.

25. Goubert, J. P. 1989. *The Conquest of Water*. Cambridge: Polity Press.

26. Burchell, S. C. 1970. The age of progress. Krieger, L., Ed. *Great Ages of Man*. Amsterdam: Time-Life International, 39.

27. Gympel, 1996: 76.

28. Chant, C. 1989. *Science, Technology and Everyday Life 1870–1950*. London: Routledge (in association with The Open University).

29. See Coley, N. 1989. From sanitary reform to social welfare. In: Chant, C. 1989. *Science, Technology and Everyday Life 1870–1950*. London: Routledge (in association with The Open University), 271–293.

30. Ibid.

31. Corbin, A. 1994. *The Foul and the Fragrant*. London: Picador; Rindisbacher, H. J. 1992. *The Smell of Books: A Cultural-Historical Study of Olfactory Perception in Literature*. Ann Arbor: University of Michigan Press; Suskind, P. 1986. *Perfume*. London: H. Hamilton.

32. Aragon, L. 1994/1926. *Paris Peasant*. Boston: Exact Change, 117.

33. Portaliou, E. 1998. Alienation from Urban Space and the Crisis of Collective Memory: the Historical Centres of Cities and the Spatial Constraints. Space, Inequality and Difference. Athens: Aristotle University of Thessaloniki/National Technical University of Athens/ University of the Aegean, 284–289.

34. Ondaatje, M. 1988: 109.

35. Becher, B. and H. Becher. 1988. *Water Towers*. Cambridge, MA: MIT Press.

36. Plaskovitis, S. 1961. *The Dam* (Το Φράγμα). Athens: Kedros.

37. See Gandy, M. The Paris sewers and the rationalization of urban space *Transactions of the Institute of British Geographers* 1999; (24):23–44; Reid, D. 1991. *Paris: Sewers and Sewermen: Realities and Representation.* Cambridge, MA: Harvard University Press.
38. Buck-Morss, 1995: 82.
39. Ibid.: 115.
40. Ibid.: 118.
41. Ibid.: 181.
42. See Waites, B. 1989. Social and human engineering. In: Chant, C., Ed. *Science, Technology and Everyday Life 1870–1950.* London: Routledge (in association with The Open University), 316–361.
43. Franklin, U. 1990. *The Real World of Technology.* C. Enterprises, Ed. CBC Massey Lectures Series CBC Enterprises, Toronto.
44. Forty, 1995; Lupton and Miller, 1996.
45. Davis, M. *Beyond Blade Runner; Urban Control—The Ecology of Fear.* Open Magazine Pamphlet Series. 1992;23. New Jersey: Open Media.
46. Richard, G. 1988. On the assembly line. In: Roberts, G. K., Ed. *Sources for the Study of Science, Technology and Everyday Life 1870–1950. Vol. 1: A Primary Reader.* London: Hodder and Stoughton (in association with The Open University).
47. Waites, B. 1989. Social and human engineering. In: Chant, C., Ed. *Science, Technology and Everyday Life 1870–1950.* London: Routledge (in association with The Open University), 316–361.
48. Richard, G. 1988: 140–145.
49. Kern, S. 1983. *The Culture of Time and Space, 1880–1918.* Cambridge, MA: Harvard University Press.
50. Verne, J. 1863/1994. *Paris au XXe Siecle.* Paris: Hachette.
51. Lahiji, N. and D. S. Friedman. 1997. *Plumbing: Sounding Modern Architecture.* New York: Princeton Architectural Press.
52. Gandy, M. The Paris sewers and the rationalization of urban space. *Transactions of the Institute of British Geographers* 1999;(24):23–44; Gandy, M. 2002. *Concrete and Clay: Reworking Nature in New York City.* Cambridge, MA: MIT Press.
53. Ibid; also, Stern, R. A., M. T. Mellins and D. Fishman. 1995. *New York 1960.* New York: The Monacelli Press.
54. One of the main problems with the construction of Athens' new Metropolitan subway lines, was the lack of information about the exact location of water and sewage networks. The difficulty with identifying the network's lines, which had to be relocated in order to allow for the new subway to be constructed, resulted in big delays in the completion of the subway project. Similarly, one of the problems that Thames Water is faced with while relining London's water supply network (as part of the leakage control exercise) is the lack of detailed information and mapping of the actual network.
55. Latour, B. and J-P Le Bourhis. 1995. *Donnez-moi de la bonne politique et je vous donnerai de la bonne eau.* Paris: Centre de Sociologie de l' Innovation, Ecole Nationale Superieure des Mines de Paris.
56. Boyer, C. 1994. *The City of Collective Memory.* Cambridge, MA: MIT Press.
57. Debord, G. 1970. *The Society of the Spectacle.* Detroit: Black & Red.
58. Swyngedouw, E. and M. Kaika. 2000. The environment of the city or ... The urbanization of nature. In: Bridge, G. and Watson, S., Eds. *A Companion to the City.* Oxford: Blackwell, 567–580.
59. Williams, R. 1973/1985. *The Country and the City.* Hogarth critics, Eds. London: Hogarth Press. (First published by Chatto & Windus, 1973; this Hogarth edition offset from the original Chatto edition.)
60. Harvey, D. 1996. *Justice, Nature and the Geography of Difference.* Oxford: Blackwell, 94.
61. Katz, C. 1998. Whose nature, whose culture?: Private productions of space and the "preservation" of nature. In: Braun, B. and Castree, N., Eds. *Remaking Reality: Nature at the Millennium.* London: Routledge, 46–63.
62. Buck-Morss, 1995: 93.
63. Merrifield, A. 1998. *Somewhere Between Tyranny and Freedom: The Dialectics of Dystopia.* (Mimeographed paper.)

64. Davis, M. 1998. *Ecology of Fear: Los Angeles and the Imagination of Disaster*. New York: Metropolitan Books.

Chapter 4

1. Sennet, R. 1990. *The Conscience of the Eye: The Design and Social Life of Cities*. New York: Knopf.
2. Heidegger cited in Wigley, M. 1996. *The Architecture of Deconstruction: Derrida's Haunt*. Cambridge, MA: MIT Press, 104.
3. See Gay, P. 1973. *The Enlightenment: An Interpretation: Vol 2: The Science of Freedom*. London: Wildwood House.
4. Studies on the political, economic, and cultural processes behind the separation between private/public space include: Massey, D. 1984. *Spatial Divisions of Labor: Social Structures and the Geography of Production*. London: Macmillan; Harvey, D. 1996. *Justice, Nature and the Geography of Difference*. Oxford: Blackwell; Sennett, R. 1990. *The Conscience of the Eye: The Design and Social Life of Cities*. New York: Knopf; Jacobs, J. 1961. *The Death and Life of Great American Cities*. New York: Random House; Vidler, A. 1992. *The Architectural Uncanny: Essays in the Modern Unhomely*. Cambridge, MA: MIT Press; Wigley, M. 1996. *The Architecture of Deconstruction: Derrida's Haunt*. Cambridge, MA: MIT Press.
5. Katz (1998) as well as Braun and Castree (1998) argue that, despite the intense study of the nature/society separation in academic literature, a systematic analysis of the spatial implications of this separation is yet to be undertaken. Katz, C. 1998. Whose nature, whose culture?: private productions of space and the "preservation" of nature. In: Braun, B. and N. Castree. 1998. *Remaking Reality: Nature at the Millennium*. London: Routledge.
6. Lefebvre, H. 1968. *Le droit à la ville*. Paris: Anthropos.
7. Lahiji N. and Friedman D. 1997. *Plumbing: Sounding Modern Architecture*. New York: Princeton Architect Press.
8. For the importance of women's labor in the transport of water, see Curtis, V. 1986. *Women and the Transport of Water*. London: Intermediate Technology Publications; Cleaver, F. and D. Elson. 1995. *Women and Water Resources: Continued Marginalisation and New Policies*. London: International Institute for Environment and Development.
9. For an excellent sociological and aesthetic analysis of this process, see Forty, A. 1995. *Objects of Desire: Design and Society Since 1750*. London: Thames and Hudson; Lupton, E. and J. A. Miller. 1996. *The Bathroom, the Kitchen and the Aesthetics of Waste: A Process of Elimination*. New York: Kiosk (Princeton Architectural Press).
10. Coley, N. 1989. From sanitary reform to social welfare. In: Chant, C. 1989. *Science, Technology and Everyday Life 1870–1950*. London: Routledge (in association with The Open University), 271–293.
11. Buisson. 1991. *L' usage domestique de l' eau*. Mouans-Sartoux: Publications de l'ecole Moderne Francaise.
12. Gerontas, D. and D. Skouzes. 1963. *The Chronicle of Watering Athens* (Το χρονικόν της υδρεύσεως των Αθηνών). Athens
13. Lupton, E. and Miller, J.A. 1996. *The Bathroom, the Kitchen and the Aesthetics of Waste*. New York: Kiosk (Princeton Architect Press), 23.
14. Wescoat, J. L. The 'right of thirst' for animals in Islamic law: a comparative approach. *Environment and Planning D: Society and Space* 1995;13:637–654.
15. *The Observer*, 20–01–2002; The *Sunday Morning Herald*, January 2, 2003
16. Interview with club owner by Jamie Pietras in online magazine, http://www.columbusalive.com/2000/20000224/feature.html. [June 10, 2003].
17. Although for two of them, the Walbrook and the Fleet, the covering began much earlier, in 1463 and 1732, respectively. See Halliday, S. 1999. *The Great Stink of London: Sir Joseph Bazalgette and the Cleansing of the Victorian Metropolis*. Stroud: Sutton.
18. Keil, R. 1998. *Los Angeles: Globalization, Urbanization, and Social Struggles*. New York: Wiley; Latour, B. and E. Hermant. 1998. *Paris ville invisible*. Paris: La Decouverte.
19. Illich, I. 1986. *H₂O and the Waters of Forgetfulness*. London: Marion Boyars.
20. See Hill, P. 1972. *Rural Hausa: A Village and a Setting*. Cambridge: Cambridge University Press; Kendie, S. B. Some factors influencing effective utilization of drinking water

facilities: Women, income, and health rural in north Ghana. *Environmental Management* 1996;20:1–10.

21. Seager, J. 1997. The earth is not your mother. In: McDowell, L. and J. P. Sharp. *Space, Gender, Knowledge: Feminist Readings.* London: Arnold.

22. Iordanidou, M. 1987. *The Twirling of the Circle* (Στου κύκλου τα γυρίσματα). Athens: Hestia.

23. Rose, G. 1993. *Feminism and Geography: The Limits of Geographical Knowledge.* Cambridge: Polity Press, 121.

24. Excellent accounts on domestication and feminism also include: McDowell, 1983; Rose, G. The geography of women: An historical introduction. *Antipode* 1974;6:1–19; Pollock, G. 1988. *Vision and Difference: Femininity, Feminism and the Histories of Art.* London: Routledge; Young, I. M. 1990. *Throwing Like a Girl and Other Essays in Feminist Philosophy and Social Theory.* Bloomington: University of Indiana Press.

25. Swyngedouw, E. 2004. *Social Power and the Urbanization of Water: Flows of Power.* Oxford: Oxford University Press; also: Swyngedouw, E. Power, nature, and the city. The conquest of water and the political ecology of urbanization in Guayaquil, Ecuador: 1880–1990. *Environment and Planning* 1997; A29:311–332.

26. Sibley, D. The binary city. *Urban Studies* 1992; 38:239–250.

27. Pile, S. 1996. *The Body and the City: Psychoanalysis, Space and Subjectivity.* London: Routledge.

28. Lefebure, H. 1994/1974. *The Production of Space.* Oxford: Blackwell.

29. Wigley, M. 1996. *The Architecture of Deconstruction: Derrida's Haunt.* Cambridge, MA: MIT Press, 105.

30. Tafuri, M. 1973/1999. *Architecture and Utopia: Design and Capitalist Development.* La Penta, B. L., trans. Cambridge, MA: MIT Press, 18.

31. Wigley, 1996: 107.

32. Davis, M. 1992. *Beyond Blade Runner; Urban Control—The Ecology of Fear.* Open Magazine Pamphlet Series. 1992;23. New Jersey: Open Media; Deutsche, R. 1996. *Evictions: Art and Spatial Politics.* Cambridge, MA: MIT Press.

33. Anderson, K. and J. M. Jacobs. Geographies of publicity and privacy: residential activism in Sydney in the 1970s. *Environment and Planning* 1999; A31:1017–1030.

34. On the reproduction of social power relations and division of labor in the domestic sphere see Millett, K. 1977. *Sexual Politics.* London: Virago; Massey, D. 1984. *Spatial Divisions of Labor: Social Structures and the Geography of Production.* London: Macmillan; Sennett, R. 1990. *The Conscience of the Eye: The Design and Social Life of Cities.* New York: Knopf.

35. Bachelard, G. 1942/1963. L'eau et les rêves; essai sur l'imagination de la matière. Paris: J. Corti

36. Heidegger cited in Wigley 1996: 109.

37. Gilloch, G. 1996. *Myth and Metropolis.* Cambridge: Polity Press, 25.

38. Vidler, A. 1992. *The Architectural Uncanny: Essays in the Modern Unhomely.* Cambridge, MA: MIT Press, 4.

39. Freud, S. 1919/1990. *Art and Literature.* Vol. 14. London: Penguin, 342–344.

40. Ibid.

41. Ibid: 345.

42. Ibid: 345–47; original emphasis.

43. Ibid: 347.

44. The political cultural process of "normalization" of the original uncanny character of this building is beyond the scope of this chapter. For a "biography" of the Centre Pompidou, see Silver, N. 1994. *The Making of Beaubourg: A Building Biography of the Centre Pompidou, Paris.* Cambridge, MA: MIT Press.

45. Heidegger cited in Wigley, 1996: 109.

46. Wigley, 1996.

47. Heidegger, cited in Wigley 1996: 109.

48. Bachelard, 1942/1963.

49. Wigley, 1996.

50. On the rationalization and sanitation of urban space, see Boyer, C. 1986. *Dreaming the Rational City.* Cambridge, MA: MIT Press.

51. Sennett, R. 1994. *Flesh and Stone: The Body and the City in Western Civilization.* London: Faber and Faber; Harvey, D. 1996. *Justice, Nature and the Geography of Difference.* Oxford: Blackwell.

52. Oliver, S. The Thames Embankment and the disciplining of nature in modernity. *The Geographical Journal* 2000; 166:227–238.
53. Gandy, M. 2002. *Concrete and Clay: Reworking Nature in New York City*. Cambridge, MA: MIT Press.
54. Tournikiotis, P. (1985) Vassileos Konstantinou Avenue versus Ilissos: On the genealogy of urban form (*Βασιλέως Κωνσταντίνου versus. Ιλισός: περί γενεαλογίας της αστικής μορφής*). In: *Athens in the 20th Century: Athens As It Appears (Not), 1940–1985 (Η Αθήνα στον 20° αιώνα η Αθήνα οπως (δεν) φαίνεται 1940–1985)*. The Ministry of Culture and the Architectural Association of Greece (Eds.) Athens; Papadakis, M. (1997) *Ilissos: The Town's Sacred River which Disapeared(Ιλισός: το ιερό του άστεως ποτάμι που εξαφανίστηκε)*. Technical Chamber of Greece, Athens.
55. Swyngedouw, E. 2003. *Flows of Power*. Oxford: Oxford University Press.
56. Gandy, M. The making of a regulatory crisis: restructuring New York City's water supply. *Transactions of the Institute of British Geographers* 1997; 22:338–358; Nevarez, L. Just wait until there's a drought: mediating environmental crises for urban growth. *Antipode* 1996; 28:246–272.
57. Sibley, D. The binary city. *Urban Studies* 1992; 38:239–250.
58. Bloomer, J. 1993. *Architecture and the Text: The (s)crypts of Joyce and Piranesi*. New Haven, CT: Yale University Press.
59. Vidler, A. 1992. *The Architectural Uncanny: Essays in the Modern Unhomely*. Cambridge, MA: MIT Press.
60. Richter, H. 1997. *Dada: Art and Anti-Art*. London: Thames and Hudson; Ball, H. 1996. *Flight Out of Time: A Dada Diary*. Raimes, A., trans. John, E., Ed. Berkeley: University of California Press; Huelsenbeck, R. 1998. *The Dada Almanac*. Green, M., trans. Green, M. and A. Brotchie, Eds. London: Atlas Press.
61. Giddens, A. 1998. *The Third Way: The Renewal of Social Democracy*. Cambridge: Polity Press, 24, 43.
62. Douglas, M. 1970. *Purity and Danger: An Analysis of Concepts of Pollution and Taboo*. Harmondsworth: Penguin.

Part II

1. Smith, N. 1984. *Uneven Development: Nature Capital and the Production of Space*. Oxford: Blackwell.

Chapter5

1. Hall, P. 1996. *Cities of Tomorrow: An Intellectual History of Urban Planning and Design in the Twentieth Century*. Mumford, L. 1961. *The City in History: Its Origins, Its Transformations, and Its Prospects*.
2. Saïd, E. 1995. *Orientalism*. Harmondsworth: Penguin.
3. Schorske, C. E. 1981. *Fin-de-siecle Vienna: Politics and Culture*. Cambridge: Cambridge University Press, 42
4. Etlin, R. A. 1994. *Symbolic Space: French Enlightenment Architecture and Its Legacy*. Chicago: University of Chicago Press.
5. See Middleton, R. and D. Watkin. 1987. *Neoclassical and 19th Century Architecture/2: The Diffusion and Development of Classicism and the Gothic Revival*. New York: Rizzoli; Hersey, G. 1988. *The Lost Meaning of Classical Architecture: Speculations on Ornament from Virtruvius to Venturi*. Cambridge, MA: MIT Press; Etlin, R. A. 1994. *Symbolic Space: French Enlightenment Architecture and Its Legacy*. Chicago: University of Chicago Press.
6. Williams, R. 1990. *Notes on the Underground*. Cambridge, MA: MIT Press, 38.
7. Gympel, J. 1996. *The Story of Architecture: From Antiquity to the Present*. Koln: Konemann.
8. Schorske, C. E. 1981. *Fin-de-siecle Vienna: Politics and Culture*. Cambridge: Cambridge University Press, 43.
9. Ibid.; see also Picon, A. 1992. *French Architects and Engineers in the Age of Enlightenment*. Cambridge, MA: Cambridge University Press.

10. Schorske, 1981: 45.
11. Halliday, S. 1999. *The Great Stink of London: Sir Joseph Bazalgette and the Cleansing of the Victorian Metropolis.* Stroud: Sutton.
12. Reported in the foreword to the IWW pamphlet, "Sabotage: its history, philosophy, & function." Republished on: http://cat.tao.ca/dwu/sabotage.html#9 [Oct. 18, 2003]
13. Pouget, E. 1913. *Sabotage.* Translated from the French. Original introduction by Arturo M. Giovannitti. Cleveland, OH: Charles H. Kerr & Company. I.W.W. publishing bureau. Republished on: http://cat.tao.ca/dwu/sabotage.html#9 [Oct. 18, 2003]
14. Luckin, 1986 (cited in Oliver, S. The Thames Embankment and the disciplining of nature in modernity. *The Geographical Journal* 2000;166(3):227–238.)
15. Halliday, 1999.
16. Oliver, S. The Thames Embankment and the disciplining of nature in modernity. *The Geographical Journal* 2000;166(3):227–238.
17. Halliday, 1999.
18. For a longer analysis of the debate see Halliday, 1999.
19. Psiroukis, N. 1974. *The Greek Diaspora Phenomenon (Το Ελληνικό Παροικιακό φαινόμενο).* Athens: Epikairotita; Psiroukis, N. 1964. *The Asia Minor Disaster: 1918–1923.* Athens: Korontzi.
20. Agriantoni, C. 1986. *The Beginning of Industrialization Process in Greece During the 19th Century (Οι Απαρχές της Εκβιομηχάνισης στην Ελλάδα τον 19ο αιώνα).* Athens: Commercial Bank of Greece.
21. Tsoukalas, K. 1981. *The Greek Tragedy (Η Ελληνική Τραγωδία).* Athens: Nea Synora-Livani.
22. Karydis, D. 1990. *Reading Urban Planning: The Social Meaning of Spatial Forms (Πολεδομίας Ανάγνωση: η κοινωνική σημασία των χωρικών μορφών).* Athens: National Technical University of Athens.
23. Vergopoulos, K. 1975. *The Agricultural Question in Greece (Το Αγροτικό Ζήτημα στην Ελλάδα).* Athens: Hexantas, 41.
24. Karydis, 1990.
25. Agriantoni, 1986: 28.
26. Clogg, R. 1984. *A Short History of Modern Greece.* Cambridge: Cambridge University Press; Koliopoulos, J. S. and T. M. Veremis. 2003. *Greece: The Modern Sequel.* London: Hurst and Company.
27. Mpiris, K. 1996. *Athens from 19th to the 20th Century (Η Αθήνα απο τον 19ο στον 20ο αιώνα).* Athens: Melissa.
28. Wordsworth, C. 1837. *Athens and Attica: Journal of a Residence There.* London: J. Murray; Marcellus, V. D. 1839. *Souvenirs de l'Orient.* Vol. II. Paris; Karydis, 1990: 33.
29. Michaud, M. and Poujoulat. 1830. *Correspondance d'Orient.* 9
30. Mpiris, 1996: 21.
31. See Scott, A. J. 1998. *Regions and the World Economy: The Coming Shape of Global Production, Competition, and Political Order.* Oxford: Oxford University Press.
32. Diaspora bourgeois included Soutsos in Moldavia and Syggros in Odessa. For a detailed account see Moskoph, K. 1974. *Ethnic and Social Consciousness in Greece 1830–1909: The Ideology of the Comprador Space (Η εθνική και κοινωνική κοινωνική συνείδηση σιην Ελλάδα 1830–1909: ιδεολογία του μεταπρατικού χώρου).* Athens: Olkos, 115.
33. Ibid.
34. Tsoukalas, 1981.
35. Moskoph, 1974: 152.
36. Moskoph, 1974: 63.
37. Koliopoulos and Veremis, 2003.
38. Clogg, R. 1984. *A Short History of Modern Greece.* Cambridge: Cambridge University Press.
39. See also Koliopoulos and Veremis, 2003.
40. Excerpts from the speech of Kleomenis, president of the Committee for the Construction of Athens, September 15, 1834; cited in Mpiris, 1996: 40–41.
41. Gregory, D. Between the book and the lamp: imaginative geographies of Egypt, 1849–50. *Transactions of the Institute of British Geographers* 1995; 20:29–56; Godlewska, A. Map, text and image: The mentality of enlightened conquerors—A new look at the "Description de l' Egypte" *Transactions of the Institute of British Geographers* 1995;20(1):5–28.
42. Athens, September 15, 1834. Cited in Mpiris,1996: 40–41 [Author's translation].

43. Gerontas, D. and D. Skouzes. 1963. *The Chronicle of Watering Athens* (*Το χρονικό της Υδρεύσεως των Αθηνών*) Athens: 62–63.
44. Gandy, M. 2002. *Concrete and Clay: Reworking Nature in New York City.* Cambridge, MA: MIT Press.
45. Mpiris, K. 1996. *Athens from 19th to the 20th Century.* (*Η Αθήνα απο τον 19° στον 20° αιώνα*) Athens: Melissa, 170.
46. Illich, I. 1986. *H_2O and the Waters of Forgetfulness.* London: Marion Boyars, 47.
47. Ibid.: 47–48.
48. Goubert, J. P. 1989. *The Conquest of Water.* Cambridge: Polity Press.
49. Cited in Mpiris, 1996: 164–165.
50. Illich, I. 1986. *H_2O and the Waters of Forgetfulness.* London: Marion Boyars, 28.
51. Ibid.: 47.
52. Cited in Halliday, S. 1999. *The Great Stink of London: Sir Joseph Bazalgette and the Cleansing of the Victorian Metropolis.* Stroud: Sutton, 127.
53. Anninos, M. 1872. *Athens During the 1850s.* (*Αι Αθήναι κατα το* 1850) Athens: 3; Paraskevopoulos, G. 1907. *The Mayors of Athens 1835–1907.* (*Οι δήμαρχοι των Αθηναίων 1835–1907)* Athens, 203, 207.
54. Gerontas, D. and D. Skouzes. 1963. *The Chronicle of Watering Athens* (*Το χρονικό της Υδρεύσεως των Αθηνών).* Athens.
55. As reported in Paraskevopoulos, G. 1907. *The Mayors of Athens 1835–1907.* (*Οι δήμαρχοι των Αθηναίων 1834–1907)* Athens: 381–387.
56. Ibid.
57. Ibid: 92.
58. Kairofylas, G. 1978/1983. *Athens and the Athenians: 1834–1934* (*Η Αθήνα και οι Αθηναίοι 1834–1934).* Athens: Filippotis.
59. Ibid.
60. Mpiris, 1996: 37.
61. Kairofylas, 1978/1983.
62. Mpiris, K. 1939. *Athenian Studies.* Vol. II. (Αθηναϊκαϊ Μελὲται- Τόμος Ι) Athens.
63. Clogg, 1984.
64. Gandy, 2002.
65. Ibid.
66. Crouch, D. P. 1993. *Water Management in Ancient Greek Cities.* New York and Oxford: Oxford University Press; Gerontas and Skouzes, 1963.
67. Water Company of Athens (*ΕΥΔΑΠ*). 1995. *Photographic Review.* Athens: Water Company of Athens.
68. Gerontas and Skouzes, 1963: 58.
69. Gerontas and Skouzes, 1963: 63, footnote 18.
70. March 13, 1847, Issue 8.
71. *Proceedings of the Greek Parliament,* July 25, 1846; *Official Greek State Gazette,* March 13, 1847, Issue 8.
72. Kalantzopoulos, T. 1964. *The History of Water Supply of Athens* (*Το ιστορικόν της Υδρεύσεως των Αθηνών).* Athens: Palamari Kathrogianni and Co.
73. Gerontas and Skouzes, 1963: 78.
74. Paraskevopoulos, 1907: 229–230.
75. Cited in Gerontas and Skouzes, 1963: 91
76. Paraskevopoulos 1907: 211
77. Kordellas, A. 1879. *Athens Examined from an Hydraulic Perspective* (*Αι Αθήναι εξεταζόμεναι από υδραυλικήν άποψιν).* Athens.
78. Gerontas and Skouzes, 1963; Paraskevopoulos, 1907: 270–271, 228.
79. Kordellas, 1879: 148, footnote 1.
80. Boϊbondas, A., B. Kizilos, R. Kloutsiniotis, and S. Kontaratos. *City and Regional Planning in Greece: A Historical Survey* (Ρύθμιση του χώρου στην Ελλάδα: μια σύντομη ιστορική επισκόπηση). *Architecture in Greece* (*Αρχιτεκτονικά Θέματα*) 1977;11:128–151.
81. Rosa, S. 1832. Cited in: *Review,* September 16, 1960: 14.
82. Kairofylas, G. 1987. *Romantic Athens* (*Η ρομαντική Αθήνα).* Athens: Filippotis.

Chapter 6

1. Banks, I. 1984. *The Wasp Factory*. London: Macmillan.
2. Although Britain and France had supported Turkey against the Russians in the Crimean War (1853–1856), during World War I (1914–1918) they allied with the Russians against Turkey (who was supported by Germany and Austria-Hungary). France also intervened in the "independence" of Egypt under Napoleon, and, as we have seen, Britain and France aided the independence of Greece.
3. Mintz, S. W. 1986. *Sweetness and Power: The Place of Sugar in Modern History*. New York: Penguin.
4. Hebbert, M. 1998. *London: More by Fortune than Design*. Chichester: John Wiley, 138.
5. Castro, E. and E. Swyngedouw. 2000. The case of London: Metropolitan areas and sustainable use of water (METRON). Final report to the European Commission, Environment and Climate Programme, Framework V. Oxford, November 2000; see also Castro, E., M. Kaika, and Swyngedouw, E. London: structural continuities and institutional change in water management. *European Planning Studies* 2003; 11(3):283–298.
6. Hebbert, 1998: 52.
7. Headrick, D. R. 1988. *The Tentacles of Progress: Technology Transfer in the Age of Imperialism, 1850–1940*. New York: Oxford University Press.
8. Ibid.: 12.
9. The Thames Conservancy Act in 1932 tightened abstraction controls. See Castro and Swyngedouw. 2000. The case of London: Metropolitan areas and sustainable use of water (METRON). Final report to the European Commission, Environment and Climate Programme, Framework V. Oxford, November 2000.
10. Castro and Swyngedouw, 2000.
11. Sharma, S. R. 1951. *The Making of Modern India*. Bombay: Orient Longmans (cited in Headrick, D. R. 1988. *The Tentacles of Progress: Technology Transfer in the Age of Imperialism, 1850–1940*. New York: Oxford University Press, 195.)
12. Headrick, 1988.
13. Swyngedouw, E. 2004. *Social Power and the Urbanization of Water: Flows of Power*. Oxford: Oxford University Press.
14. Clogg, R. 1984. *A Short History of Modern Greece*. Cambridge: Cambridge University Press.
15. Ibid.
16. See Harvey, D. 2001. *Spaces of Capital: Towards a Critical Geography*. New York: Routledge; Harvey, D. 1985. *The Urbanization of Capital*. Oxford: Blackwell; Armstrong, W. and T. G. McGee. 1985. *Theatres of Accumulation: Studies in Asian and Latin American Urbanization*. London: Methuen.
17. Clogg, 1984.
18. Vaxevanoglou, A. 1996. *The Social Reception of Novelty: The Example of Electrification in Greece During the Interwar Period* (*Η κοινωνική αποδοχή της Καινοτομίας: το παράδειγμα του εξηλεκτρισμού στην Ελλάδα του Μεσοπολέμου*). Athens: Center for Modern Greek Studies, National Research Foundation of Greece; Agriantoni, C. 1986. *The Beginning of Industrialisation Process in Greece During the 19th century* (*Οι Απαρχές της Εκβιομηχάνισης στην Ελλάδα τον 19° αιώνα*). Athens: Commercial Bank of Greece.
19. Ibid.: 9. See also Headrick, D. R. 1981; 1998; 2000. *The Tools of Empire: Technology and European Imperialism in the Nineteenth Century*. New York: Oxford University Press.
20. Koronis, S. 1944. *Labor Policy Between the Years 1909–1918* (Η εργατική πολιτική των ετών 1909–1918). Athens; Psiroukis, N. 1974. *The Greek Diaspora Phenomenon* (*Το Ελληνικό Παροικιακό Φαινόμενο*). Athens: Epikairotita; Leontidou, L. 1982. *Athens: Economic, Social and Residential Structure of the Modern Urban Complex*. Athens: Papyros-Larousse-Britannica, 388–414.
21. Tsotsoros, S. N. 1995. *Energy and Development During the Post-War Period: The National Electricity Company, 1950–1992* (Ενέργεια και Ανάπτυξη στη Μεταπολεμική περίοδο: η Δημόσια Επιχείρηση Ηλεκτρισμού, 1950–1992). Athens: Center for Modern Greek Studies, National Research Institute.
22. Clogg, 1984.
23. Tsotsoros, 1995.
24. Vaxevanoglou, 1996: 92.

25. Headrick, 1981.
26. Headrick,1988: 194.
27. Agriantoni, 1986.
28. Tsoukalas, K. 1977. *Dependency and Reproduction: The Social Role of the Educational Mechanisms in Greece (1830–1922)* (*Εξάρτηση και αναπαραγωγή: ο κοινωνικός ρόλος των εκπαιδευτικών μηχανισμών στην Ελλάδα* (1830–1922)). Athens: Themelio, 266.
29. See also Psiroukis, 1974; Leontidou, L. 1989. *Cities of Silence: Working Class Colonisation of Urban Space, Athens and Pireaus 1909–1940.* (Πόλεις της σιωπής: εργατικός εποικισμός της Αθήνας και του Πειραιά, 1909–1940). Athens: Cultural and Technological Institution of the National Bank of Industrial Development of Greece (ETBA), 54.
30. Gerontas, D. and D. Skouzes. 1963. *The Chronicle of Watering Athens* (*Το χρονικον της υδρεύσεως των Αθηνών*). Athens.
31. Paraskevopoulos, G. 1907. *The Mayors of Athens 1835–1907.* Athens: 30.
32. See Leontidou, 1989.
33. For a beautiful account of the European "culture" of excavation and the conflict it created, see Williams, 1990; see also Gerontas and Skouzes, 1963.
34. For a detailed account of the projects proposed during this period see Kaïka, M. 1999. Modernity and the urban spaces of produced nature: The politics and culture of the urbanisation of water in Athens (1834–1999). DPhil thesis, School of Geography and the Environment University of Oxford, Oxford: 218–223.
35. Kalantzopoulos, T. 1964. *The History of Water Supply of Athens* (*Το ιστορικόν της Υδρεύσεως των Αθηνών*), Athens: Palamari Kathrogianni and Co.
36. Quellenec estimated the capacity of the existing water supply system at 75,000 cubic meters per day (300 liters per capita per day). Kalantzopoulos, T. 1964. *The History of Water Supply of Athens* (*Το ιστορικόν της Υδρεύσεως των Αθηνών*). Athens: Palamari Kathrogianni and Co., 55.
37. Bulletin, Ministry of Transport of Greece, 1889: 184; Kalantzopoulos, 1964.
38. Kalantzopoulos, 1964.
39. Bulletin, Ministry of Transport of Greece, 1890: 188.
40. Kaika, 1999.
41. Clogg, 1984.
42. Sloulatos, B., N. Dimakopoulos, and S. Kondis. 1984. *History of Greece: Modern and Contemporary, Volume 3.* Athens: Publishing House for Tutorial Books.
43. Clogg, 1984.
44. Psiroukis, N. 1964. *The Asia Minor Disaster:* (*Η Μικρασιατική Καταστροφή 1918–1923*) Korontzi, Athens: 72.
45. Murphy, J. S. and C. Keeping. 1963. *Dams: How They Were Built.* Oxford: Oxford University Press; McCully, P. 1996. *Silenced Rivers: The Ecology and Politics of Large Dams.* London: Zed Books.
46. Ktenas, K. A. The water supply of Athens (*Η ύδρευσις των Αθηνών*). Medicine (*Ιατρική*) 1923: 8.
47. Clogg, 1984: 120.
48. Leontidou, 1989: 132.
49. Mpiris, K. 1996. *Athens from 19th to the 20th Century*(*Αι Αθήναι: από τον 19° στον 20° αιώνα*). Athens: Melissa, 287.
50. Genidounias, T., A. Koumousis, and P. Loprestis. 1923. *The Water Problem of Athens* (*Το υδατικό πρόβλημα της Αθήνας*). Athens: Ministry of Transport; newspaper *Χρονικά*, May 11,12, 1922; Ktenas, 1923; Kalantzopoulos, 1964: 55.
51. Leontidou, L. 1990. *The Mediterranean City in Transition: Social Change and Urban Development.* Cambridge: Cambridge University Press.
52. Genidounias, Koumousis, and Loprestis, 1923: 175.
53. In fact, Korizis' prediction is justified today, since the actual yield from the reservoir is in the region of 10 Hm^3. See Koutsogiannis, D. and Th. Xantopoulos.1990. *Reliability and Security of Athens' Water Supply System.* Paper presented in workshop: "Prospectives for the solution of the water supply problem of Athens." Athens: EEDYP, October 17, 1990.
54. Gerontas and Skouzes, 1963: 132.
55. National Bank of Greece, budget report, 1926.

56. The explanatory "security" attached to the word "meter" suggested that these devices were installed with the primary objective of controlling levels of consumption; at the same time, they facilitated accurate billing, which was essential for the repayment of the loan to Ulen & Co.

57. Water Company of Athens. *Photographic Review* 1995. Athens: Water Company of Athens.

58. Contrary to the initial aspirations that water charges would fund the repayment of the loan, the water supply system has been in fact continuously subsidized by the state. When the water company became public in 1980 (and was renamed "*Ε.ΥΔ.Α.Π'*), that initial loan was still not repaid in full. When, in 1999, as part of a privatization process, *Ε.ΥΔ.Α.Π.* was floated on the stock market it still carried a US$2.4 million debt from the loan. See Kaika 1999; Kallis, G. and H. Coccossis. 2000. *Metropolitan Areas and Sustainable Use of Water: The Case of Athens.* Athens: University of the Aegean.

59. Ulen and Co. 1930. *The New Water Supply for Athens, Piraeus & Environs.* Athens: Pallis.

60. Psiroukis, N. 1974. The Greek Diaspora phenomenon (*Το Ελληνικό Παροικιακό Φαινόμενο*) Epikairotita, Athens: 174

61. Hebbert M 1998 *London: More by Fortune than Design.* John Wiley, Chichester: 139

62. Ibid.: 139

63. Psiroukis, 1974: 174.

64. Headrick, 1988: 196.

65. Ulen and Co, 1930.

66. Ibid.: 13.

67. Kairofylas, G. 1988. *Interwar Athens* (*Η Αθήνα του Μεσοπολέμου*). Athens: Filippotis.

68. Mpiris, 1996.

69. Ibid.: 300.

70. Smith, N. 1984. *Uneven Development: Nature, Capital and the Production of Space.* Oxford: Blackwell.

71. Eagleton, T. 1997. *The Ideology of the Aesthetic.* Oxford: Blackwell, 3.

72. Koumparelis, S. G. 1989. *The History of the Water/Sewerage Works of the Capital* (*Ιστορία έργων υδρεύσεως και αποχετεύσεως Περιοχής Πρωτευούσης*). Athens: The Sewerage Company of Athens and The Water Company of Athens, 75.

73. Gandy, M. 2002. *Concrete and Clay: Reworking Nature in New York City.* Cambridge, MA: MIT Press.

74. Greece's ideological preoccupation with its past, although dominant, was not uncontested. During the 1930s it lay at the heart of the schism between "modernists" and "traditionalists" and manifested itself in the political (conservatism vs. progressivism, monarchists vs. liberals), economic (petty capitalism and the informal sector vs. the emerging industrial and shipping bourgeoisie), and cultural arenas ("indigenous aesthetics" vs. "the international style") alike. See Tziovas, D. 1989. *The Transformations of Nationalism and the Ideology of the Greek Character 1920–1940* (*Οι μεταμορφώσεις του εθνισμού και το ιδεολόγημα της ελληνικότητας στο Μεσοπόλεμο, 1920–1940*). Athens: 73–93; Kotidis, A. 1993. *Modernism and Traditionalism in Greek Art: 1920–1940* (*Μοντερνισμός και Παράδοση στην Ελληνική Τέχνη, 1920–1940*). Thessaloniki: University Studio Press; Cholevas, N. T. 1998. *The Architecture of 'Transition' in Athens During the Interwar Period* (*Η Αρχιτεκτονική της μετάβασης στην Αθήνα κατα το Μεσοπόλεμο*). Athens: Libro.

75. The war of ancient Greeks against ancient Persians was known in the ancient world as the war of the Greeks against the "barbarians"; in ancient Greek, the word *barbarian* (*βάρβαρος*) signified anyone who was *non-Greek.*

76. Agreement of Completion of the Works, signed by the Greek State and Ulen & Co. [Author's translation.]

77. See Smith, 1984; Harvey, D. 1996. *Justice, Nature and the Geography of Difference.* Oxford: Blackwell; Castree, N. The nature of produced nature: materiality and knowledge construction in marxism. *Antipode* 1995;27(1):12–48.

78. Swyngedouw, E. Modernity and hybridity: Nature, regenerationismo, and the production of the Spanish waterscape, 1890–1930. *Annals of the American Association of Geographers* 1999;89(3):443–465.

79. Agriantoni, 1986.

80. Tsoukalas, K. 1981. *The Greek Tragedy* (*Η Ελληνική Τραγωδία*). Athens: Nea Synora-Livani, 36.

81. Ulen and Co, 1930.
82. Gerontas and Skouzes, 1963.
83. See Vergopoulos, K. 1975. *The Agricultural Question in Greece* (*Το Αγροτικό Ζήτημα στην Ελλάδα*). Athens: Hexantas; Tsoukalas, 1981.
84. Xenos, G. N. 1948. *The Water Problem of Greece* (*Το υδατικό πρόβλημα της Ελλάδας*). Athens: Greek Ministry of Agriculture, General Direction of Agriculture, 3–4.
85. Ibid.: 9–10.
86. Wittfogel, K. A. 1957. *Oriental Despotism: A Comparative Study of Total Power*. New Haven: Yale University Press; see also Worster, D. 1985. *Nature's Economy: A History of Ecological Ideas*. 2nd ed. 1994. *Studies in Environment and History*. Cambridge: Cambridge University Press.
87. For the most comprehensive criticism of Wittfogel's work within the context of the development of China, see Wheatley, P. 1971. *The Pivot of the Four Quarters*. Edinburgh: University of Edinburgh Press (especially pages 256–298).
88. Clogg, 1984: 162.
89. Leontidou, 1982: 388–414.
90. Vaiou, D., M. Mantouvalou, and M. Mavridou. 2000. *Postwar Greek Planning Between Theory and Chance*. Proceedings: 2nd Conference of the Greek Society for Urban History and Planning. "Planning in Greece 1949–1974." Volos: University of Thessaly; Vaiou, D., M. Mantouvalou, and M. Mavridou. Social inclusion and urban development in a united Europe. *Social Sciences Forum* (*Το Βήμα των Κοινωνικών Επιστημών*) 1995;16:29–57.
91. Burgel, G. 1981. *Croissance urbaine et developpement capitaliste: le "miracle" athenien*. Paris: Editions du Center national de la Recherche scientifique.
92. Giannakourou, G. 2000. The institutional framework of urban development in Greece: historical transformations and contemporary demands (*Το θεσμικό πλαίσιο του σχεδιασμού των πόλεων στην Ελλάδα: ιστορικές μεταμορφώσεις και σύγχρονα αιτήματα*). In: Oikonomou, D. and G. Petrakos, Eds. *The Development of Greek Cities: Interdisciplinary Approaches for Urban Analysis and Politics* (*Η Ανάπτυξη των Ελληνικών Πόλεων. Διεπιστημονικές προσεγγίσεις αστικής ανάλυσης και πολιτικής*). Volos: University of Thessaly, 457–480.
93. Mantouvalou, M. and L. Martha. The economic 'wonder' and its traps (*Το οικονομικό 'θαύμα' και οι παγίδες του*). *Αντί* 1982;199:25–28.
94. Burgel, 1981.
95. Raftopoulos, T. 1948. *Preliminary Study for Water Supply from Lake Yliki* (*Προμελέτη Υδρεύσεως εξ' Υλίκης*). Athens: Ministry of Public Works; Sinos, A. and T. Raftopoulos. Summary of the preliminary study for water supply and irrigation from Lake Yliki (*Περίληψις Προμελέτης Υδρεύσεως και Αρδεύσεως εξ' Υλίκης*). *Technika Chronika* (*Τεχνικά Χρονικά*) October–December 1947.
96. Water Company of Athens. *Photographic Review* 1995.
97. Leontidou, 1990.
98. Burgel, 1981.
99. Kallis and Coccossis, 2000.
100. Water Company of Athens. *Photographic Review* 1995.
101. Law 1739/87.
102. Official Gazette of the Greek State, Issue A201, 1987.
103. Personal communication. July 28, 1997.
104. Ministry of Environment, Physical Planning and Public Works, 1988. *Report and Five Year Plan for Water Resources Management*. Athens: (*ΥΠΕΧΩΔΕ*): 69. [Unless otherwise stated, all translations from Greek are the author's own.]
105. Kaika, M. and E. Swyngedouw. Fetishising the modern city: The phantasmagoria of urban technological networks. *International Journal of Urban and Regional Research* 2000;24(1):120–138.
106. Guillerme, A. Water for the city. *Rassegna: Themes in Architecture* 1994;57:6–21.
107. Vidler, A. 1992. *The Architectural Uncanny: Essays in the Modern Unhomely*. Cambridge, MA: MIT Press, 168.
108. Green, N. 1990. *The Spectacle of Nature: Landscape and Bourgeois Culture in Nineteenth Century France*. Manchester: Manchester University Press, 80.
109. Buck-Morss, S. 1995. *The Dialectics of Seeing: Walter Benjamin and the Arcades Project*. Cambridge, MA: MIT Press.

Chapter 7

1. Global Water Supply and Sanitation Assessment 2000 Report. Available at: http://www.who.int/docstore/water_sanitation_health/Globassessment/Global2.1.htm [October 10, 2003]
2. See Hundley, N. 1992. *The Great Thirst*. Berkeley and Los Angeles: University of California Press; Wackernagel, M. and W. E. Rees. 1996. *Our Ecological Footprint: Reducing Human Impact on the Earth*. Gabriola Island, BC: New Society Publishers.
3. Freeman, L. Old Father Thames clean-up complete by 1980? *Water* 1977;13:2–5; see also Castro, E. Metropolitan areas and sustainable use of water (METRON): final report. Available at: http://www.feweb.vu.nl/re/regional/Metron/metronlit.html [November, 10 2003]
4. Swyngedouw, E., M. Kaïka, and E. Castro. Urban water: A political-ecology perspective. *Built Environment* 2002;28(2):124–137; Castro, E., M. Kaika, and E Swyngedouw. London: Structural continuities and institutional change in water management. *European Planning Studies* 2003;11(3):283–298.
5. The NAWPA was put together in 1964 by Ralph M. Parsons Company of Los Angeles. The project suggests collecting surplus water from the high precipitation areas of the northwestern part of the North American continent and distribute it to water-deficient areas in Canada, the United States, and northern Mexico. Much of the "excess" water will be transferred from Canada to be used in the United States. Given the scale cost and socio-environmental impact of the project, it has never been implemented, but the US government has not given up on the idea to date. For a detailed critical account see Biswas, K., A. Z. Dakang, J. E. Nickum, and L. Changming. 1983 *Long-Distance Water Transfer: A Chinese Case Study and International Experiences*. Tokyo: United Nations University Press.
6. Castells, M. 1977. *The Urban Question: A Marxist Approach*. London: Edward Arnold.
7. Moulaert, F. and E. Swyngedouw. A regulation approach to the geography of the flexible production system. *Environment and Planning D: Society and Space* 1987;7:327–345; Amin, A. 1994. *Post-Fordism: A Reader*. Oxford: Blackwell.
8. http://lwf.ncdc.noaa.gov/img/reports/billion/timeserieslg2002.jpg [October 10, 2003]
9. Castells, M. 1977.
10. Swyngedouw, E. 1998. Homing in and spacing out: re-configuring scale. In: Gebhardt, H., G. Heinritz, and R. Weissner, Eds. *Europa im Globalisierungsprozess von Wirtschaft und Gesellschaft*. Stuttgart: Franz Steiner Verlag, 81–100.
11. Castells, M. 1988. High technology and urban dynamics in the United States. In: Dogan, M. and J. Kasarda, Eds. *The Metropolis Era; Volume 1: A World of Giant Cities*. Newbury Park, CA: Sage, 85–110.
12. Castro, E. and E. Swyngedouw. 2000. *Metropolitan Areas and Sustainable Use of Water: The Case of London*. Oxford: School of Geography and the Environment, University of Oxford.
13. Hassan J. 1998. *A History of Water in Modern England and Wales*. Manchester: University Press.
14. The centralization of power over London's water resources was intensified during World War II, when the War Emergency Water Committee was put in charge of coordinating water activities across the Thames watershed, thus further integrating the Greater London water supply system. The continuation of this *status quo* after the war was strongly opposed by local authorities and by most of the sixty-five water undertakers that shared the watershed. However, the 1945 Water Act and the 1948 Rivers Boards Act removed the responsibility for pollution control, water conservation, and river monitoring from the hands of local authorities and gave these tasks instead to 32 new River Boards, which were created in England and Wales, whereas central planning and water conservation were placed under the control of the Ministry of Health. The 1963 Water Resources Act increased the authority of the River Boards, which were renamed as River Authorities (RAs). In addition, the Water Resources Board (WRB) was created as the central water research agency. Centralization of power culminated with the 1973 Water Act, which created ten Regional Water Authorities (RWAs) in England and Wales. These replaced 29 River Authorities, 160 water supply undertakings managed by local authorities and joint boards, and about 1,300 sewage treatment and disposal units. The RWAs were made responsible for water resources and supply, sewerage and sewage disposal, pollution control and environmental protection. The largest amongst them, the Thames Water Authority (TWA), gulped up 10 water undertakings and 163 wastewater operators, and currently serves around 12.1 million people, almost 25 per-

cent of the total population of England and Wales. These changes produced one of the most radical transformations in the water sector: the total removal of local authorities from the process of water management. The centralization of power in water resource management complimented the amalgamation of local governance, which happened first in London, with the creation of the Greater London Council (1964/65), and later across England and Wales, with the Local Government Act (1972). See Okun, D. A. 1977. *Regionalization of Water Management. A Revolution in England and Wales.* London: Applied Science Publishers; Mukhopadhyay, A. K. 1975. The politics of London water. In: *The London Journal,* Vol 1, 2: 207–226; Castro and Swyngedouw, 2000.

15. Reed, E. C. 1977. *The Drought 1976.* London: Thames Water Authority; Freeman, L. The drought and all that. *Water* 1977;14:17–19.
16. Water Services Association (WSA). 1995. *Waterfacts 1995.* London: WSA.
17. Ibid.
18. Office of Water Services (OFWAT). 2001. *Leakage and the Efficient Use of Water.* Birmingham: OFWAT.
19. Castro, Kaika, and Swyngedouw, 2003.
20. Ibid.
21. Maloney, W. A. and J. Richardson. 1995. *Managing Policy Change in Britain: The Politics of Water.* Edinburgh: Edinburgh University Press; Castro, Kaika, and Swyngedouw, 2003.
22. Parker, D. J. and E. C. Penning-Rowsell. 1980. *Water Planning in Britain.* London: George Allen & Unwin.
23. Castro, E., M. Kaika, and E. Swyngedouw. Urban water: a political-ecology perspective. *Built Environment* 2002;28(2):124–137.
24. Gardiner, J. L. 1988. Environmentally sound river engineering: examples from the Thames catchment. In: *Regulated Rivers: Research & Management,* Vol. 2: 445–469.
25. Perera, M. C., M. A. F. Farley, and A. D. V. Farrow. The London water ring main—A new approach to London's water distribution strategy. *Aqua* 1985;6:304–310; Kean, M. A. and J. C. Kerslake. The London water ring main: an optimal water supply system. *Water and Environmental Management* 1988;2(3):253–267.
26. Maloney and Richardson, 1995.
27. Office of Water Services (OFWAT) Report, 2001.
28. See newspaper articles by Peachey, P. Long, hot summer leads to appeal on water use. *The Independent* (October 23, 2003); Sadler, R. and G. Lean. The threat posed by huge reservoir plan: outcry expected over confidential scheme for new reservoirs and desalination plants to meet soaring demand. *The Independent* (October 26, 2003).
29. BBC News, BBC Water Week. Profit for Thames Water was of the order of £1 billion in 1991. Available at: http://news.bbc.co.uk/hi/english/static/waterweek/region_thames.html [November 10, 2003]
30. 1998 figures, adjusted to inflation rates, compared to the period 1989/90. Even Thames Water's bills, which were the lowest in 1998 (9% less than the national average), were still 35 percent higher than those prior to privatization. BBC News, BBC Water Week. Rising prices. Available at: http://news.bbc.co.uk/hi/english/static/waterweek/issues04.html [November 10, 2003]
31. OFWAT, 1999. *Prospects for Prices. A Consultation Paper on Strategic Issues Affecting Future Water Bills.* Birmingham: OFWAT; OFWAT, 1999. *Report on Tariff Structure and Charges.* Birmingham: OFWAT; OFWAT, 1999. *The OFWAT Forward Programme 1999–2000 to 2001–2002.* Birmingham: OFWAT; OFWAT, 1999. *Draft Determinations. Future Water and Sewerage Charges 2000–2005.* Birmingham: OFWAT; OFWAT, 1999. *Approval of Companies Charges Schemes in 2000–2001.* Birmingham: OFWAT.
32. Bakker, K. Privatizing water: Producing scarcity: The Yorkshire drought of 1995. *Economic Geography* 2000;76(1).
33. Swyngedouw, Kaïka, and Castro, 2002.
34. BBC News, BBC Water Week. Availbe at: http://news.bbc.co.uk/hi/english/static/waterweek/issues08.html [November 10, 2003]
35. Department of the Environment, Transport and the Regions (DETR) and Welsh Office. 1999. *Taking Water Responsibly. Government Decisions Following Consultation on Changes to the Water Abstraction Licensing System in England and Wales.* London: DETR.
36. OFWAT. 2000. The current state of market competition. Birmingham: OFWAT.

37. See Willis, K. G., P. L. McMahon, G. D. Garrod, and N. A. Powe. Water companies' service performance and environmental trade-offs. *Journal of Environmental Planning and Management* 2002;45(3):363–379.

38. Maloney, W. A. Privatization and employment relations—the case of the water industry. Davidson, J, Ed. *Public Administration* 1994; 72(4):615–615.

39. Sabbidis, K. V., A. Ampakoumkin, S. Kotzampasakis, et al. 1988. *Workgroup Report on Mornos* (Εκθεση Ομάδας Εργασίας για το θέμα του Μόρνου). Athens: Technical Chamber of Greece.

40. Karavitis, C. A. Drought and urban water supplies: the case of metropolitan Athens. *Water Policy* 1998;(1):505–524. The Ministry of Agriculture estimated the amount at 400×106 m^3; the Ministry of Industry, Research and Technology at 221×106 m^3; while the Water Company of Athens gave an estimate of between 580×106 and 630×106 m^3.

41. Interview with executive member; ΕΥΔΑΠ, July 28, 1997.

42. Proceedings, the Greek Parliament ΟΘ Feb. 16, 1993: 4105; Kallis 2002; Konstantakos, 2002: 30.

43. Kallis and Coccossis, 2000.

44. Vasilakis, K. and D. Bourbouras. 1992. *The Diversion of Evinos River for the Water Supply of Attica: Consequences, Alternatives* (Εκτροπή του ποταμού Εύηνου για την υδροδότηση του λεκανοπεδίου Αττικής. Επιπτώσεις–εναλλακτικές λύσεις). Athens: Greek Ornithological Society.

45. Interview, Minister of Environment, Planning and Public Works. Newspaper *"Τα Νέα"* (May 5, 1990).

46. In the first round (June 1989) no single party achieved the necessary majority, and eventually a government was formed out of a coalition, unique in modern Greek political history, between the Conservatives and a Communist-led left alliance. A few months later, a second round of elections (November 1989) also failed to give majority to any of the main parties. This led to a second coalition between Conservatives, Socialists, and Communists (government of national unity). See Anastasakos, G., G. Boulgaris, I. Nikolakopoulos, and P. Kapsis. 1990. Elections 1989–1990 *Τα Νέα*; Chadjipadelis, T. and C. Zafiropoulos. Electoral changes in Greece during 1981–1990. *Political Geography* 1994;13(6):492–514; Zafiropoulos, C. and T. Chadjipandelis. The geography of elections 1985–1993. A principal of component analysis (Η γεωγραφία των εκλογών την περίοδο 1985–1993: μια ανάλυση κυρίων συνιστωσών). *TOPOS* 2001;16:91–110.

47. Ministry of Environment Planning and Public Works of Greece. 1990. *Preliminary Report for the Reinforcement of the Capacity of the Mornos Aqueduct System through the Evinos River Basin*. Athens: Division of Public Works, Ministry of Environment Planning and Public Works of Greece.

48. Vaiou, D., M. Mantouvalou, and M. Mavridou. Social inclusion and urban development in a United Europe. *Social Sciences Forum* (Το Βήμα των Κοινωνικών Επιστημών). 1995; 16:29–57.

49. Ministry of Environment Planning and Public Works of Greece. 1988. *Report and Five Year Plan for Water Resources Management*. Athens: Ministry of Environment, Planning and Public Works, 34; see also Delladetsimas, P. M. Sustainable development and spatial planning: the case of Greece. *TOPOS* 1997;12:31–54; Gerardi, K. 1998. *Strategy for a Sustainable Development of Greater Athens* (Η στρατηγική του σχεδιασμού για μία βιώσιμη ανάπτυξη της μητροπολιτικής περιοχής της Αθήνας). Athens: Department of Planning, National Technical University of Athens; Bithas, K., ed. 2001. *Sustainable Cities: Theory-Politic* (Βιώσιμες Πόλεις. Θεωρία–Πολιτική). Athens: Typothito.

50. To give an example: the average household of four members, who used to pay 885 dr. (€2.59) per month for their water bill (15.6 m^3 of water) would have to pay 2,187 dr. (€6.41) under the new rates. However, if the same family succeeded in saving 20% off its previous month's consumption, they would pay a "reduced" bill of 1,733 dr. (€5.08) per month instead (still higher than the original 885 dr.). Likewise, a family that consumed 60 m^3 would originally have paid 6,140 dr. (€18.01). With the new rates, the same family would pay 22,950 dr. (€67.35). However, if the same consumer achieved lower consumption (in comparison to that of the previous month) they would get a reduction of 500 dr. (€1.46) for every m^3 saved.

51. For example, a 30% saving in water consumption achieved by lower volume consumers of, say, 15 m³ per month, would save them around 132 dr. (€0.38) per m³. However, the same percentage (30%) in saving achieved by a higher volume consumer of say, 120 m³ per month, would save them 675 dr. (€1.98) per m³.

52. Newspaper *Εθνος* (Feb. 10, 1993).

53. Greek Centre for Planning and Economic Research (ΚΕΠΕ) 1996. *The Socioeconomic Identity of the Water Departments*. Athens: Ministry of Development, Centre for Planning and Economic Research.

54. I. Tsaklidis, MP. *Proceedings, IE*. Assembly of the Greek Parliament, Feb. 16, 1993: 4105, Archives of the Greek State; *Proceedings Assembly of the Greek Parliament*.

55. Newspaper *Τα Νέα* (May 11, 1990).

56. T. Zaharopoulos, interview in newspaper *Το Βήμα* (May 24, 1998); italics mine.

57. Ministry of Environment Planning and Public Works of Greece, 1990.

58. For case studies supporting a similar argument, see Kingdon, J. W. 1984. *Agendas, Alternatives, and Public Policies*. Boston: Little Brown; Nevarez, L. Just wait until there's a drought: mediating environmental crises for urban growth. *Antipode* 1996; 28(3):246–272.

59. Proceedings, IB Assembly of the Greek Parliament; May 11, 1990.

60. Interview, Ministry of Development, Division of Management of Water Resources; Sept. 11, 1996.

61. Emmanouil, D. 1985. Land use and housing policy in the case of urban expansion: a framework for analysis and planning for Athens. In: Kafkalas, G., Ed. *Planning: Theory, Institutions, Methodology (Πολεοδομικός Προγραμματισμός: Θεωρία Θεσμοί, Μεθοδολογία)*. Thessaloniki: Paratiritis; Panayiotatou, E. 1990. *Themes in Spatial Development (Θέματα Ανάπτυξης του χώρου)* Athens: Symmetria; Getimis, P. 1994. Urban development and politics (*Αστική ανάπτυξη και Πολιτική*). In: Getimis, P., et al., Eds. *Urban and Regional Development: Theory, Analysis and Politics (Αστική και Περιφερειακή Ανάπτυξη: Θεωρία, Ανάλυση και Πολιτική)*. Athens: Themelio, 307–333.

62. Topping, A. R. Ecological roulette—Damming the Yangtze. *Foreign Affairs* 1995; 74(5):132–146; Roy, A. 1999. *The Cost of Living*. London: Flamingo.

63. The promised wages were 700,000 dr. (€2,054) per month at the time when the minimum wages for Greece was of the order of 100,000 dr. (€293.47) per month. Newspaper (Sept. 26, 1993).

64. Baker, S., K. Milton, and S. Yearly, eds. 1994. *Protecting the Periphery: Environmental Policy in Peripheral Regions of the European Union*. Ilford: Frank Cass; Modinos, M. The excellent water. *Nea Oikologia* 1990; 69:6–19; Mantouvalou, M. and L. Martha. The economic 'wonder' and its traps. *Antipode* 1982; Kafkalas, G., N. Komninos, and A-P Lagopoulos, Eds. 1985. *Urban planning: Theory, Institutions, Methodology*. Thessaloniki: Paratiritis; Vaiou, D., M. Mantouvalou, and M. Mavridou. 2000. *Postwar Greek Planning between Theory and Chance*. Paper read at "Planning in Greece 1949–1974", 2nd conference of the Greek Society for Urban History and Planning. Giannakourou, G. 2000. The institutional framework of urban development in Greece: historical transformations and contemporary demands. In: Oikonomou, D. and G. Petrakos, Eds. *The Development of Greek Cities: Interdisciplinary Approaches for Urban Analysis and Politics*. Volos: University of Thessaly, 457–480.

65. President of St. Demetrios, one of the communities located in the Evinos River valley. Newspaper *Τα Νέα* (June 12, 1993).

66. Proceedings, ΟΘ' Assembly of the Greek Parliament, Feb. 16, 93: 4112.

67. Koutlas in *TEXNIKA*, issue 131, October 1997.

68. Proceedings, Assembly of the Greek Parliament, May 21, 1993.

69. The quantity of water to be transferred was set at 600,000 m³/day from Lake Trihonida and the Anavalos River, and 150,000–200,000 m³/day from the Aheloos River and Lake Paralimni. Proceedings, Assembly of the Greek Parliament, May 21, 1993: 7035–36.

70. Proceedings, ssembly of the Greek Parliament, May 21, 1993: 7035–36; see also Newspaper *Ελεύθερος Τύπος* (June 22, 1993).

71. The Technical Chamber's report found the suggested period of ten months insufficient for the realization of the project. Moreover, even if everything went according to schedule, the transportation of water would commence only six months before the scheduled full operation of the Evinos Dam project thus leaving only a very short period during which the transportation project would be of any use for alleviating Athens' water problems. News-

paper *Καθημερινή* (May 28, 199?) YEAR?. The fierce opposition from local communities often took the form of fierce localism bearing the motto "Athenians return to your villages and there you can drink as much water as you wish." Newspaper *Εθνος* (May 22, 1990).

72. Newspaper *Καθημερινή* (Sept. 9, 1993).
73. *Newspaper Το Βήμα* (Aug. 19, 1990).
74. Announcement of the Board of Scientific Staff of in *ΕΥΔΑΠ Οικονομικός* Review (July 29, 1993).
75. *Οικονομικός* Review (June 29, 1993).
76. Law 2124/96.
77. Newspaper *Το Βήμα* (Oct. 5, 1997).
78. Sanctioned by Law 2124/96; Interview, *ΕΥΔΑΠ* (Nov. 16, 1999).
79. Newspaper *Το Βήμα* (Aug. 22, 1999). The bill on the "Management and Operation of the Water and Sewerage Services Sector, and for the Regulation of the Athens' Water Supply and Sewerage Company (*ΕΥΔΑΠ*– A.E.)"
80. Newspaper *Το Βήμα* (Aug. 22, 1999); Interview, (Nov. 16, 1999).
81. Newspaper *Το Βήμα* (May 24, 1998).
82. For a critical theoretical approach on the social construction of nature see Gerber, J. Beyond dualism—-the social construction of 'nature' and the natural and social construction of human beings. *Progress in Human Geography* 1997; 21(1):1–17.
83. See Lefebvre, H. 1974/1994. *The production of space.* Oxford: Blackwell; Smith, N. 1984. *Uneven development: Nature, capital and the production of space.* Oxford; Blackwell; Harvey, D. and D. Harraway. Nature, politics, and possibilities: a debate and discussion with David Harvey and Donna Haraway. *Environment and Planning D: Society and Space* 1995;13:507–527.
84. Kaika M 2003 The Water Framework Directive: a new directive for a changing social, political and economic European framework *European Planning Studies* 11 (3) 303–320
85. Graham. S. and S. Marvin. 2001. *Splintering Urbanism.* London: Routledge.
86. Boyer C 1986 Dreaming the rational city: the myth of american city planning MIT Press, Cambridge, Massachussets
87. Heynen, H. 1999. *Architecture and Modernity: A Critique.* Cambridge, MA: MIT Press.
88. English translation, as quoted in Heynen, 1999: 12.

Epilogue

1. Aragon, L. 1994/1926. *Paris Peasant.* Boston: Exact Change.
2. In his brilliant book, *All that is solid melts into air: the experience of modernity* (London: Verso, 1983), Marwill Berman detects the archetypal modern hero in Goethe's *Faust*. In his capacity as the developer, Faust wishes to produce a better world, but his actions are marred by a deep and unavoidable tragedy: he cannot create a new world without destroying what used to be there before. And in order to make the "look and feel of the old world…disappear without a trace", to make space for the anticipated new social and spatial organization, Faust has to decoy the dedication of human labor. Not only nature, but people as well have to be allured into participating in modernity's creative destruction. To this end, Faust uses not only reason and his persuasive ability, but also crude power, where necessary. When an old couple stands in the way of his plans, Faust commits his first self-conscious evil act: he orders their displacement, which will eventually lead to their death. The desire to create a world where everyone is "free to act" produces the preconditions for social progress, but does so at an untold human cost.
3. Watts, J. 2003. After the flood. *The Guardian* (Oct. 30, 2003).
4. Vidler, A. 1992. *The Architectural Uncanny: Essay in the Modern Unhomely.* Cambridge, MA: MIT Press.

Index